1986

THE ONE-PARENT FAMILY IN THE 1980s

BENJAMIN SCHLESINGER

The One-Parent Family in the 1980s
Perspectives and Annotated Bibliography 1978-1984

University of Toronto Press

Toronto Buffalo London

© University of Toronto Press 1985
Toronto Buffalo London

ISBN 0-8020-6565-1

Canadian Cataloguing in Publication Data

Schlesinger, Benjamin, 1928-
    The one-parent family in the 1980s

    Rev. ed. of: The one-parent family.
    Includes bibliographies and index.
    ISBN 0-8020-6565-1

    1. Single-parent family. 2. Single-parent
    family - Bibliography. I. Title.
    II. Title: The one-parent family.

    A5118.F2S26 1984   306.8'56   C84-099716-7

PREFACE

The first edition of this book was published in 1969. At that time it was the first book of its kind, which compiled existing knowledge related to one-parent families in Canada and the United States. Fifteen years ago the annotated bibliography consisted of 280 entries.

This fifth edition is a completely new book, which does not contain any text of the previous editions. The five essays were written especially for this volume, and I am grateful to my colleagues who contributed their time and effort to this task. The essays are reviews of the literature dealing with varied aspects of one-parent families in Canada and the United States.

The four previous editions contained 750 items in the annotated bibliography which covered the 1930-1978 period. In this fifth edition I have included 490 entries which cover the period from January 1, 1978 to June 1, 1984.

The citations include published books, booklets, reports and articles written in English. The majority of entries are related to Canadian and American society. A small section relates to one-parent families in other countries. Since many one-parent families move into step-families, I have included a section on Remarriage. This was also done in previous editions. An author index can be found at the end of this book.

I would like to thank my Dean, Professor Ralph Garber, for his constant support, Felicity Coulter who typed the manuscript, and Helen Norman who compiled the author index. I am especially grateful to the Humanities and Social Sciences Committee of the University of Toronto, who gave me a grant to work on the annotated bibliography. My editor R.I.K. Davidson of the University of Toronto Press, guided me in this latest effort. My own immediate family consisting of my wife, Rachel, and children Avi, Leo, Esther and Michael gave me their usual support and love in producing this volume.

This book is dedicated to one-parent families around the world.

The Contributors

Anne-Marie Ambert, Ph.D. is in the Department of Sociology,
York University, Toronto, Canada.

Leo Davids, Ph.D. is at Atkinson College, York University,
Toronto, Canada.

Shirley M.H. Hanson, Ph.D. is the Chairperson of the
Department of Family Nursing, Oregon Health Sciences
University, Portland, Oregon, U.S.A.

Geoff Nelson, Ph.D. is in the Department of Psychology,
Wilfrid Laurier University, Waterloo, Ontario, Canada.

Benjamin Schlesinger, Ph.D. is with the Faculty of Social
Work, University of Toronto, Toronto, Canada.

CONTENTS

1. The Lone Parent Family in Canada: The   1
    Quantitative Background - Leo Davids

2. Custodial Parents: Review and a Longitudinal   13
    Study - Anne-Marie Ambert

3. The Single Teen-Age Canadian Mother in the   35
    1980's: A Review - Benjamin Schlesinger

4. Single Fathers with Custody: A Synthesis of   57
    the Literature - Shirley M.H. Hanson

5. Family Adaptation Following Marital Separation/   97
    Divorce: A Literature Review - Geoff Nelson

ANNOTATED BIBLIOGRAPHY

One-Parent Families: Overview   153
Children in One-Parent Families   164
Treatment and Services to One-Parent Families   169
Children and Divorce   171
Custody   180
Divorce and the Family System   185
Divorce Mediation   191
Joint Custody   193
Legal Aspects: Divorce   196
Parenting After Divorce   198
Process of Divorce   201
Statistics Related to Divorce   209
Treatment and Services: Divorce   211
Female-Headed One-Parent Families   218
Male-Headed One-Parent Families   221
Non-Married Parents   226
Children of Non-Married Parents   229
Fathers: Non-Married   229
Mothers: Non-Married   232

Services to Non-Married Parents   238

Separation and One-Parent Families   241

Widows and Widowers as One-Parent Families   250

Other Countries: One-Parent Families   252

Remarriage   258

Miscellaneous Items (found after completion)   269

AUTHOR INDEX   273

THE LONE-PARENT FAMILY IN CANADA:
THE QUANTITATIVE BACKGROUND*

Leo Davids

People in the Social Services are paying considerable attention to families headed by only one parent, and the literature has many assertions concerning the increase of such families and the resulting necessity to pay more attention to them, their needs, and how to best meet those needs. It is thus useful, no doubt, to look at the major basic facts regarding one-parent families in Canada as these are available in reports from the 1981 (and earlier) Census, so that we can get a firm grip on the factual situation. The importance and implications of the changes shown by these statistics is discussed by other authors in this book, but the story has to begin with the extent of the Lone Parent reality, which is our concern here.

It makes sense to begin with a few words about the sources of the information that we shall be reviewing in this essay. On one hand, we have numbers which are collected and issued every year under the heading Vital Statistics; these include information on Birth Rates, Marriage and Divorce, which give us a picture of the basic factors that constitute and shape the reality of family structure and behaviour in Canada and are, as well, the immediate causes of special family phenomena such as the Lone-Parent Family. The annual Vital Statistics reports are the source of information for our Table I, so that we can get a picture of the foundation on which the Lone Parent reality stands.

Our major information base in this essay, however, is the census of Canada. The census is carried out every five years, so we have information from 1971, 1976 and 1981. (Information that will be collected in 1986 will become available in the vicinity of 1988 or later, so that the most recent available material we have on Lone-Parent Families was gathered during the big census of 1981.) The bulk of the material herein comes from recent census reports, which are identified as the source of each table at the foot of the page. It is the census reports which

---

*The term "lone parent" is used by Statistics Canada for the one-parent family.

1

let us see the solid facts of the Lone-Parent Family numbers, size marital status or income, which are to a great extent the result of other variables that are reported on by other statistical materials, but since we cannot trace all of the causes in this essay we will have to look at just a few of them in Table I.

Knowing something, now, about data sources, let us begin to look at the information itself. The increase of Lone-Parent Families today (e.g., from 1971 to 1981) can only be properly assessed in the light of parallel developments in the frequency of Divorce and in Birth Rates, since the existence of Lone-Parent Families depends heavily (though not exclusively) both on marriage break-downs and on the existence of dependent children. Lone-Parent Families do occur in small numbers through out-of-wedlock births and through widowhood, but an increasingly sizeable part of all Lone-Parent Families in Canada come about through separation and divorce. Therefore, we would expect changes in the number of Lone-Parent Families to be strongly related to the Divorce Rate and the Birth Rate.

(SEE TABLE 1)

As can be seen in Table I, the crude Divorce Rate in Canada, (which counts the number of Divorces every year per one hundred thousand of the Canadian population) has continued to rise rapidly all during the 1970's. After the changes affecting divorce which became law in 1968, Canadian Divorce Rates had a spectacular increase. Specifically, the crude Divorce Rate more than doubled between 1971 and 1981, going from 137.6 (Divorces per hundred thousand in the population) in the earlier year to 278 (Divorces per hundred thousand) in 1981. As the table shows, this was an increase of 102 percent.

We also find in Table I that the Canadian Birth Rate has been declining during the 1970's, going from 16.8 births per thousand in the population to 15.3 births per thousand in this ten-year period, from 1971 to 1981. This decline in the Birth Rate is obviously not that spectacular, but over the long run will have a tendency to dampen down the number of Lone-Parent Families, because of the increasing number of situations in which divorcing couples have no dependent children, so the census will not find a Lone-Parent Family as a result.

Table I also shows the increase in the total number of Lone-Parent Families in Canada between 1971 and 1981. The rise from less than 480,000 in 1971 to about 714,000 in 1981 was an increase of 50 percent, which is obviously quite substantial. This may be contrasted with the rise in the total number of Canadian families during the same time period, which was 25 percent. (In 1971, total families in Canada were 5,053,170; this had risen by 25 percent in 1981 to a total of 6,325,315.)

2

One other thing to look at to make sure that we are not over-stating the increase in Lone-Parent Families out of context is to see how much the total population went up during the period from 1971 to 1981. In fact, population growth in Canada has slowed down during the 1971 to 1981 period as contrasted with the previous 10 years (1961 to 1971). In fact, total population in Canada rose 13 percent between 1971 to 1981, which shows the the rapid growth of Lone-Parent Families in the same time period is certainly not due to the general increase in the population but has appeared even though both population rise and the increase in the number of Canadian families has been much slower. So, the increase in Lone-Parent Families does not exactly parallel some of the other changes such as rising divorce rates, but certainly the movement is very much in the same direction. It is clear that the increase in Lone-Parent Families is responding to factors in the Family area itself, rather than being an aspect of growth in Canada's general population or family totals.

We now move on to examine the Lone-Parent Families of Canada as they were in 1981, to get a picture of some of their main characteristics as reflected in the census. Table II gives us a break-down of Lone Parents in Canada in 1981 by gender and marital status. Marital Status is of course an essential thing to know about family heads, so that we can answer questions such as: a) How many of Canada's Lone Parents had become that without ever being married -- reporting their marital status as "single or never married"? b) How many of the Lone Parent situations were created by the death of a spouse (so the Lone Parent would report his or her marital status as "widowed")? and c) How many of the Lone-Parent Families were created by Divorce? The answers to these questions are shown in our Table II.

(SEE TABLE II)

As Table II shows, there are far more female Lone Parents than male Lone Parents; the number of female Lone Parents was very close to 590,000 compared with 124,000 male Lone Parents, in 1981. Looking at marital status, we find that the largest single category of Lone Parents were widowed people, with almost two hundred thousand female Lone Parents having entered that situation due to the death of their husbands, while over 37 thousand men were Lone Parents in 1981 due to the death of their wives. Overall, just under 33 percent of all Canadian Lone Parents in 1981 were widowed.

The smallest category is that of Lone Parents who report themselves to have been "single, never married"; not quite one in ten Canadian Lone Parents fall into that category. The remainder of the Lone Parents are divided between Separated (31 percent) and Divorced (26 percent), with the trends of

3

today's urban life style suggesting that in future a higher percentage of Lone Parents will report that they are Divorced, while
a smaller proportion of them will become Lone Parents through
widowhood.

Moving on to other questions about the Lone Parents of
Canada, how large are Lone-Parent Families? In 1981, as we see
in Table III, the majority of all Lone Parents had only one child
in their care. In fact, all Canadian Families today tend to be
fairly small, and this is also the case for Lone-Parent Families.

(SEE TABLE III)

Table III shows us that among male Lone Parents, there
were a few thousand who had four or more children in their care,
but the total percentage of male parents involved with more than
one or two children is small. For female Lone Parents, the
absolute numbers are much larger, but the percentages are quite
in agreement with the situation for the Lone fathers. Clearly,
the majority of Lone-Parent Families in Canada is small; the
average number of children per Lone Parent is 1.70 for males
and 1.73 for females, as is shown in Table III. This puts some
of the Lone Parent problems in perspective, and represents a
possible trend of fewer dependent children without two parents
than was the case in earlier times when a large number of
orphans were involved in Lone Parent situations. On the other
hand, the continuing high Divorce Rates are likely, as we
suggested earlier, to increase the number of children who do
not live with both parents although they are not orphans.

Thus far, we have given a reasonably detailed account of
the total number of Lone-Parent Families in the context of certain Vital Statistics that play an important part in the
emergence of Lone-Parent Families; the gender and marital status
of Canadian Lone Parents in 1981; and the size of Canada's
Lone-Parent Families, indicating the extent of the parental
responsibilities that Lone Parents had to carry in 1981. We
also need information from the census, however, about some of
the economic characteristics of Canada's Lone-Parent Families
which will give some perception of the problems that they face
as a result of limited income and insufficient adult manpower
within the household.

We therefore proceed towards Table IV of this essay,
which presents information on their income as reported in 1981
and certain additional characteristics of those families
reflecting their economic well-being. In particular, we have
added a non-monetary measure of economic welfare by using
information on whether the home in which the Lone-Parent Family

resides is in need of major repairs. Our Table IV presents all
the information separately for male versus female Lone Parents,
enabling us to contrast the economic situation facing male with
those facing female Lone Parents.

(SEE TABLE IV)

Table IV shows that the total family income for male-
headed Lone-Parent Families in 1981 averaged over 23 thousand
dollars, whereas it was less than 14 thousand dollars for those
Lone-Parent Families headed by a female. The ratio was 59
percent (in the upper right hand corner of our Table IV),
showing that the income available to female Lone Parents, was,
on average, not quite three-fifths as large as the income of an
average male Lone Parent.

The age of the Lone Parent also makes a very substantial
difference. For those Lone Parents who were less than 35 years
of age, the income situation was very bad and the income ratio
of female to male Lone Parents (in this youngest age category)
was 47 percent. Where the Lone Parent is a little older, the
income situation is not so grim, since the children are in
school and the Lone Parent is likely to have more experience,
more assets, and a better job situation. As the table shows
us, the income of male Lone Parents aged 45-54 years was 26
and a half thousand dollars, whereas for female Lone Parents
of the same age bracket the average income was over 17
thousand dollars.

There are also differences shown in Table IV with
regard to income as related to the number of children. The
per-capita income in male-headed Lone-Parent Families
involving two children is shown as $8,640, but for female
Lone Parents (taking care of two children) the per-capita
income at that time came to about $4,725. The female to male
ratio also shows the tremendous difference in economic
problems facing female vs. male Lone Parents, because the
ratio of female to male per-capita income in situations involving one Lone Parent with two children was 55 percent; that means
that an average female Lone Parent with two children in her
care had just over half as much income available per person as
the male Lone Parent under the same circumstances.

Another way of looking at the problems facing Lone
Parents and of contrasting the male versus female situation is
to look at the number of cases in which the family dwelling
was reported as "in need of major repairs". This is hardly a
sign of affluence or comfort with regard to one's economic
situation -- it obviously occurs almost always because money
is so tight for food and other on-going necessities, that the
home is allowed to deteriorate until it is judged as requiring

5

major repairs. So, we have incorporated the relevant information into our Table IV.

What we find in regard to dwellings of Lone-Parent Families (concerning the need for repairs) agrees very closely with what we know about their income situation. Just as the Husband-Wife families have better incomes than male-headed Lone-Parent Families, with the female-headed Lone-Parent Families being the poorest, the situation about the percentage of dwellings which require major repairs in the three categories (Husband-Wife vs male Lone Parent vs female Lone Parent) descends in the same order.

While about 6 percent of dwellings inhabited by Husband-Wife families in Canada were reported to need major repairs, the percentage for male-headed Lone-Parent Families was a little over 9 (which is one and a half times as great). However, for the female-headed Lone-Parent Family we find just under 10 percent of the dwellings needed major repair, indicating that the money just wasn't there to maintain the home because all the income was required for food, clothing and similar basics. Again, this measure of economic well-being shows that the female-headed Lone-Parent Families are in somewhat worse condition than the male-headed ones, reflecting typical earning differences between male and female workers. Although one could go further in looking at statistics of this kind, Table IV certainly shows the relatively impoverished situation of Canada's Lone Parents, particularly when one contrasts women with men.

This essay cannot consider explanations for the various changes that we have reviewed here, but there is a literature (e.g., Ambert 1980; Davids 1980; or Statistics Canada 1983) which gives a picture of what is happening on the family scene which helps explain why these trends occur. In a recent study coming out of the 1971 census, the author writes:

> Apparently, an increasing number of people are beginning to question the previously taken-for-granted assumption that both a mother and a father were necessary for successful child rearing. This change may be facilitated by an increased tolerance for non-marital sexual relations...
> (Statistics Canada 1977: page 36)

It is also for other authors to explore the meaning and significance of Lone-Parent Families and the impact of the increases that we are seeing on welfare of the people involved

6

(Schlesinger 1978). What our review of the statistical facts
has tried to accomplish is to make it clear that the Lone-Parent
Family is a massive reality now and that it does have real problems. It follows that those involved in Family Policy and
Social Services have to reconsider their strategy for dealing
with all this. It is most unlikely that the problems suggested
by the data herein will "just go away" in the near future, so
the attention how being given to Lone-Parent Families and to how
their needs should be met is indeed justified by the facts.

Our review of income differences has shown how great
the financial problem is for female-headed Lone-Parent Families,
and so there is no doubt that those who are charged with pre-
paring appropriate strategies for coping must take these facts
into account in order to respond effectively to the lone-parent
challenges facing us all.

REFERENCES

Ambert, A.-M. Divorce in Canada. Don Mills (Ont.): Academic
    Press, 1980.

Davids, Leo. "Family Change in Canada, 1971-1976," J. of Marriage
    & Family, Vol. 42, No. 1 (Feb. 1980), pp.177-183.

Schlesinger, Benjamin. The One-Parent Family: Perspectives and
    Annotated Bibliography. Toronto: University of Toronto
    Press, 1978 (4th Ed).

Statistics Canada. The Family in Canada 1971 Census Study
    (Catalogue No. 99-725), 1977.

Statistics Canada. Divorce: Law & the Family in Canada
    (Catalogue No. 89-502), 1983.

Statistics Canada. Publications of the 1981 Population Census
    (as referred to individually in our Table sources).

TABLE 1:   CANADIAN DIVORCE & BIRTH RATES &
                  (Rounded) NUMBER OF LONE-PARENT FAMILIES, 1971 & 1981

	1971	1976	1981	Change, 1971-81
Crude Divorce Rate	137.6	235.8	278.0	Up 102%
Crude Birth Rate	16.8	15.7	15.3	Down 9%
Total Lone-Parent Families	477,500	559,300	714,000	Up 50%
Male Parent	100,350	95,000	124,400	Up 24%
Female Parent	377,150	464,300	589,450	Up 56%

Sources: Statistics Canada, Annual Vital Statistics,
           Vol. 1 & 11 (Catalogue No. 84-204 & 84-205)
           for the above years; 1976 Census of Canada,
           Report No. 93-822, Table 6; 1981 Census of
           Canada, Report No. 92-935, Table 1.

TABLE II: CANADIAN MALE & FEMALE LONE-PARENTS BY MARITAL STATUS, 1981

	Totals	Single (Never Married)	Separated	Divorced	Widowed
Male	124,380 100%	5,115 (4.1%)	49,775 (40.0%)	32,010 (25.7%)	37,480 (30.1%)
Female	589,435 100%	65,175 (11.0%)	172,845 (29.3%)	154,950 (26.3%)	196,465 (33.3%)
Both	713,815 100%	70,290 (9.8%)	222,620 (31.2%)	186,960 (26.2%)	233,945 (32.8%)

Source: Statistics Canada, 1981 Census Report No. 93-935, Table 15

TABLE III: CANADIAN MALE & FEMALE LONE-PARENTS
               BY NUMBER OF CHILDREN, 1981

	1 Child	2 Ch.	3 Ch.	4 Ch.	5 & More Children	Average No. of Children per Lone-Parent Family
Male	70,225 (56.46%)	33,750 (27.13%)	12,815 (10.30%)	4,730 (3.80%)	2,885 (2.30%)	1.70
Female	316,005 (53.61%)	172,945 (29.34%)	66,785 (11.32%)	22,090 (3.75%)	11,685 (1.98%)	1.73
Both	386,230 (54.1%)	206,695 (28.9%)	79,530 (11.2%)	26,820 (3.8%)	14,535 (2.0%)	

Source: Statistics Canada, 1981 Census Report No. 92-935, Table 18

TABLE IV: INCOME AVERAGES FOR CANADIAN LONE-PARENT FAMILIES
             BY CERTAIN CHARACTERISTICS, 1981

	Male Lone Parents	For Husband-Wife Families	Female Lone Parents	F/M Ratio
Total Family Income (All ages)	$23,243	$28,521	$13,790	59%
For those under age 35	$16,336	-	$ 7,652	47%
For those age 35-44	$22,610	-	$13,253	59%
For those age 45-54	$26,581	-	$17,161	65%
For those with 1 child	$22,900	$29,050	$13,800	60%
For those with 2 chn.	$25,900	$30,790	$14,170	55%
Per person, 1 parent & 2 children	$ 8,640	$ 7,700 (2 parents & 2 children)	$ 4,725	55%
Dwelling Needs Major Repairs	7,900 L-PF	303,475 H-WF	46,600 L-PF	
As Percent of all L-P Families, urban only, that Gender	9.2%	6.0%	9.9%	

Source: 1981 Census of Canada, Report No. 92-935, Tables 5 & 20

CUSTODIAL PARENTS: REVIEW AND A
LONGITUDINAL STUDY

Anne-Marie Ambert

In spite of the fact that the literature on the one-parent family has grown substantially in the past decade, there are still wide gaps in the state of our knowledge on the subject. The major emphasis of the literature has been on the consequences of parental separation on children, especially on the effect of father absence on children, especially boys (Biller, 1968, 1969; Hunt and Hunt, 1975, for example), while relatively few studies were carried out on girls (Biller and Weiss, 1970; Hetherington, 1972; Hunt and Hunt, 1977). Indeed, this literature indicates that boys tend to be more affected than girls by paternal absence as well as by familial strife. The effects of parental strife and of divorce on children have been studied (Anthony, 1974; Gardner, 1974; Hetherington et al., 1976, 1978; Kalter, 1977; Kelly and Wallerstein, 1976; Landis, 1960; Luepnitz, 1979; Morrison, 1974; Wallerstein and Kelly, 1975, 1980), and have included a comparison with legally intact families suffering from parental strife and unhappiness (Anthony, 1974; Berg and Kelly, 1979; Chombart de Lauwe, 1959; Despert, 1962; Landis, 1963; McCord et al., 1962; Nye, 1957). Other studies have compared children from legally intact families with those coming from separated/divorced families and widowed families (Ambert and Saucier, 1982, 1983; Saucier and Ambert, 1982, 1983). The results of these studies, although not uniform, indicate that children from separated/divorced families do less well on a variety of indicators than those from intact families, while children of widowhood score between these two categories.

Therefore, the research has been concerned mainly with the effect of parental behaviour and family structure on children. Recently, some researchers have turned their attention to the effect of children's personality and behaviour on parents (e.g., Hetherington and Parke, 1975; Lerner and Spanier, 1978). This approach, however, has yet to be applied to the one-parent family (for one exception, see Defrain and Eirick, 1981). In view of this lacuna, the research in this article was designed to explore and to suggest hypotheses concerning the interaction between children's behaviour and sociodemographic characteristics of their custodial parents, especially the parents' sex and socioeconomic status (SES).

13

A last gap in the literature on the single-parent family to
be mentioned here is the fact that the research is cross sectional
and, as a consequence of this methodological preference, we know
relatively little of the long-term dynamics in behaviour of parents
and of children of divorce. Two longitudinal studies are noteworthy.
Hetherington et al. (1978) and Wallerstein and Kelly (1980) found
that both parents and children generally stabilize over a period
of five years following divorce. (See also Kurdek et al., 1981,
and Goode, 1956). In addition, Hetherington et al. (1978, 1979)
reported that children exhibited more negative behaviour towards
mothers than fathers.

Our study is longitudinal and exploratory. In the first
phase (1978-1980), we followed the working hypothesis that there
might be a difference between children's behaviour toward their
custodial mothers as compared to their custodial fathers. Sex-
role theory (Ambert, 1976, 1980) and resource theories, especially
in terms of social support resources (Bigelow and Brodsky, 1979;
Chiriboga et al., 1978, 1979), led to the hypothesis that children's
behaviour toward custodial fathers may be less of a problem than
children's behaviour toward custodial mothers.

Then, in a second set of interviews two and a half years
later (1981), it was expected that children's behaviour toward
their custodial parents would improve and so would parental
satisfaction with the children. Second, it was anticipated that
children's behaviour and parental satisfaction would improve less
among families headed by lower-income women than by higher-income
women because of the cumulative effect of poverty on these
families (e.g., Bane, 1976; Ross and Sawhill, 1975).

METHODOLOGY

Twenty custodial mothers and seven custodial fathers were interviewed a first time in Toronto from October 1978 through September
1980. The interviews lasted two to four hours with an average of
nearly three hours. The focus of these interviews was on the
individuals' marital breakdown, as well as on their current
situation as formerly-married persons with children.

The referral method or convenience sampling was used and two
groups were created: one consisting of lower-SES persons and the
other consisting of middle-class or upper-clsss persons, herein
referred to as higher-SES persons. An equal number of individuals
in each category was sought but achieved only for custodial mothers.
Of the twenty custodial mothers, ten were of lower-SES; five were
on welfare, and the others held low-paying jobs (factory worker,
maid, clerk, waitresses). None earned above $12,000 a year. Ten
were upper class or upper-middle class (teacher, professionals,
executives, model, head nurse, researcher, wealthy student). Their

yearly income averaged $33,000. So as to achieve broader represen-
tation, only two of the ten lower-SES mothers were from the same
housing project or neighbourhood; all others interviewed were
scattered throughout the city. Moreover, respondents were asked
for names and addresses of people they knew of, rather than friends'
names or people they knew personally, so as to include a broader
spectrum of individuals than would have been otherwise possible.

It was not possible to obtain a large number of custodial
fathers nor was it possible to locate more than one father at
the lower end of the SES scale. (Other researchers have experienced difficulties in locating single fathers of all social
classes: Arnold et al., 1989; Defrain and Eirick, 1981; Orthner
et al., 1976: 432.) The seven custodial fathers held positions
such as banker, financier, commercial artist, skilled worker, and
three were professionals. If we except one father who was a
millionaire, the average, yearly income of the remaining six was
$50,000.

In addition to the indepth interview, this researcher saw
all the children in the families and kept a record of her observations on their overt behaviour and verbalizations. Observed interactions between children and the custodial parent were noted under
several categories such as: child displays affection; parent
displays affection; child talks back, argues, throws tantrums,
co-operates, obeys; parent scolds, threatens, punishes (type of
punishment noted). Interactions with the interviewer were
similarly recorded. Examples are: child shows interest in study;
child shows interest in interviewer's work, asks questions; child
disrupts the interview verbally. Each time any behaviour not
involving the interviewer was observed, it was entered during the
session; other behaviour was recorded when the interviewer returned
to her car. A personality profile and a description of each
child was written after the interview on the basis of the overall
observations. These recorded observations do not form the major
part of the current report because our focus is on parental
perceptions and feelings. In the current study, the profiles and
codings were used strictly for the purpose of validating parental
reports on their children. The parents were asked to describe
their children's behaviour and feelings toward them, including
the problems and the joys the children presented. In the analysis
of the data, interviewees' perceptions were checked against
researcher's coded observations.

The subjects were reinterviewed two and a half years later
in the spring and summer months of 1981 (Time 2). Then, the higher-
SES mothers were 38 years old on the average; the lower-SES mothers
were 35, and the custodial fathers were 40. The custodial fathers
had been separated four years and the custodial mothers for just

15

over five years. The ten individuals who had remarried or were living common-law were retained in this follow-up because re-marriage is one important type of adaptation to divorce and generally tends to be studied separately (Kitson and Raschke, 1981). There has been 72 children in these families, with the mothers averaging just under three children and the fathers 2.1 children. The children were 13.4 years old on the average at Time 2, with a range from 5 to 22 years. The children's age distribution was similar in the three categories of families studied.

The parents were asked how satisfied they were with their children's behaviour on a five-point scale and their replies at Time 2 were compared with those at Time 1. Again, as at Time 1, they were asked to talk about their children's behaviour both in general and toward them in particular. (For the importance of parental reports, see Fulton, 1979). Children's behaviour before, during, and after the interview period was again observed and entered on a check list in exactly the same manner as for the first intervew. Within each family, children's scores at Time 2 were aggregated and compared with those obtained at Time 1. Children living at home had to be present during both interviews, although in another room or part of the house. The researcher arrived just after or left just before a meal, thus gaining additional data bases, especially in terms of cooperative behaviour and help provided the parent. Observation periods before and after each interview consisted of small talk with the entire family and lasted on the average 15 minutes each.

RESULTS

We will begin by presenting the results of the first phase, or Time 1. This will be followed by an analysis of the results obtained at Time 2 and a comparison between the two times in terms of a longitudinal approach.

Children's Behaviour

The first difference between custodial mothers and custodial fathers appeared when the parents described their children's general behaviour, especially in terms of the problems it created for them. None of the seven fathers reported any major problems in their children (see, also Orthner at al., 1976: 433). In contrast ten of the twenty mothers reported major problems. Five other mothers described several problems of the minor type which, when totalled for each mother individually, amounted to quite a burden. Only five mothers were entirely positive about their children's behaviour in general and toward them in particular.

in order to explain this relationship between the sex of the custodial parent and reported behaviour of children, the age, sex,

16

and spacing of the children were examined serially. For instance, we wanted to know if the mothers who reported most problems were mothers of boys or of girls (as in Hetherington et al., 1978; Colletta, 1979a; Wallerstein and Kelly, 1980: 101), of younger or of older children; of children close in age or many years apart? However, none of these independent variables affected the results; and all were found equally among the problem-ridden mothers and the problem-free mothers and fathers. The one variable which might have provided an explanation was the number of children: Mothers who had four and five children reported more problems. (See also Marsden, 1969: 152). Unfortunately, because they all were of lower SES, one variable confounds the other or simply adds to the other.

The one variable that clearly affected the results was the socioeconomic situation of the mother (see also Colletta, 1979a,b; Hodges, 1979). Of the ten lower-SES mothers, only two were positive. The other eight lower-SES mothers reported mainly problems from their children and few joys. Indeed, seven of the ten lower-SES mothers had serious problems. The children's behaviour fell into a multiplicity of categories. First, the children were described as truant from school; disrespectful toward their teachers (one girl had assaulted a teacher); prematurely sexually involved (one girl was pregnant, and her brother had impregnated a young girl); engaged in shoplifting and vandalism; frequently absent from home late into the night; and failing in school. There had been three cases of convicted juvenile delinquency.

Behaviour toward the mother followed the same pattern: frequent disobedience, even in pre-schoolers; talking back; saying "no, I won't do it" and slamming the door behind them; throwing temper tantrums; not showing up for meals; refusing to do chores; messing up the house; yelling at the mother; laughing at her when other children were around; acting ashamed of her. Two of these mothers were regularly hit by their sons who were following the absent father's example. This researcher also observed less positive interaction between lower-SES mothers (and some higher-SES mothers) and their children--more arguments, more disobedience, some taunting, much more disrespectful behaviour--than between custodial fathers (and several higher-SES mothers) and their children. In two cases the mothers asked the interviewer to control their children's destructive behaviour. Moreover, we had to return to two lower-SES homes because children were not home when they were supposed to be, and had to await the late return of children after two other interviews had been completed-- in two cases the children were only between eight and ten years old. Children of custodial fathers were always home for the interviews, as were most of the children of higher-SES custodial mothers.

17

The seven lower-SES women who had serious problems with their children were members of multi-problem families. They combined low job skills; poverty; lack of general knowledge in certain domains of life (ability to budget, to do comparison shopping, to plan ahead, to know where to get help); desertion in some cases, alcholism in some former spouses; delinquency in some children; and children who generally did poorly in school. However, these women were not toally isolated socially: they had parents, siblings, other relatives, a couple of female friends, two steady male companions. In three cases the material environment also was tolerable. But the difficulties of their daily interation with their children was visible; these women looked tired, worn out, older than their age. Misery showed on the faces of the children, who were themselves victims of deprivation and social ostracism and who were captive in their delinquent milieu--the housing developments of the poor, or the neighbourhoods of the poor.

Of the ten women who had little positive to say about their children's behaviour, seven were of lower-SES. The three others who also had little positive to report belonged to the higher-SES group. Of the ten higher-SES mothers, only three reported severe problems; and their problems were a repetition of these described by lower-SES mothers, excluding assault, teenage pregnancy and convicted juvenile delinquency. Four others had a series of minor problems and quite a few complaints, but generally several reported positive elements as well. Three described their children's behaviour only in positive terms.

Children's Feelings

All seven custody fathers emphasized that their children appreciated them as fathers. In fact, the key words "appreciative", "appreciate," were spontaneously offered in all seven interviews. In contrast only two women out of 20 spontaneously said that their children were appreciative: one was an upper-middle-class woman and the other a woman on welfare who was returning to school. Later in the interviews, when asked how appreciative their children were, only one woman replied in a clear-cut affirmative: "Yes, they definitely appreciate the time I spend with them." The other responses, however, were very ambivalent: "You know how children are nowadays. They don't appreciate what we do for them. It is nothing personal, just the mentality." Another woman answered, "I suppose they do, but they sure don't show it." A third: "Not as appreciative as they are of their father's rare visits." And the fourth: "They could be...they could show it much more. I know they appreciate what I do for them, but they act as if they didn't."

The father's responses were quite different. "My children are well behaved, thoughtful, considerate, and all in all they have a lot of respect for me and a lot of love...(How does it show?)

They're affectionate, even for boys. They tell me how they have the best dad, that they really are proud of our family even though it's different. I can feel that they appreciate my keeping the family together." Another father reported: "No, they certainly are not the type to be disrespectful because they know that I wouldn't tolerate it. I have made it clear that if we are to survive as a family with only one adult to take care of four children, rules have to be followed; and I tell you, they follow them. I'll even tell you this: they appreciate them. And they appreciate their father, me! How many fathers do what I do? That's what they say." Therefore, for fathers, the themes are obedience, respect, good behaviour, expressed affection and above all, appreciative children--very much as observed.

As we have seen, the recurrent themes in mothers were much more ambivalent and reflected the negative elements discussed earlier, perhaps as well as the double standard that children may apply to custodial parents according to the gender of the parent. Six mothers explained how their children compared them (and their lives with them) unfavorably with their fathers. This was obviously very distressing to these mothers and this topic was brought up repeatedly during the interviews. The children's comparisons were generally triggered by gifts from the father while they were visiting him, gifts that the mothers had themselves been unable to buy because they could not afford them (see also Marsden, 1969: 149). Disciplinary actions on the part of these mothers often resulted in similar comparisons, including threats to go and live with the fathers. These women were bitter and felt handicapped in their ability to bring up their children properly. In contrast no custodial father had such a problem.

Follow-up Results

Parents' satisfaction with their children had generally increased between Times 1 and 2. Children's behaviour had also generally improved during the same period. As at Time 1, we did not find any difference between families with more male children (e.g., Bergman and Turk, 1981; Colletta, 1979) and those with more female children. In fact, custodial fathers had more male than female children: all father-headed families had at least one, or only one, male child. Yet, these families were the ones that were functioning the most smoothly. However, sons of lower-SES mothers were reacting more aggressively than sons in the other families, and than girls in lower-SES families. The girls also were often very aggressive and abusive towards their mothers, but were so verbally. Therefore, at home, both boys and girls in lower-SES mother-headed families tended to be aggressive, but the behavioural symptoms of this aggressiveness differed. Outside the homes, only lower-SES boys showed physical aggressiveness even to the extent of being arrested or evicted from school.

Contrary to what we had anticipated, lower-SES custodial mothers experienced the highest level of improvement both in terms of their satisfaction with their children and, in all but one category, in terms of their children's observed behaviour. They were followed by higher-SES custodial mothers who experienced a great deal more satisfaction with their children at Time 2 than at Time 1, and whose children also showed substantial behaviour improvement in several categories. Custodial fathers' satisfaction was stable while their children's behaviour improved in certain areas.

For children with custodial mothers, observed displays of anger and rudeness towards mothers had diminished substantially by Time 2 and were the two categories in which behaviour showed the greatest improvement. At Time 1, several mothers had reported that their children would threaten to move out. These threats had all but ceased by Time 2, a factor which contributed to the increase in the custodial mothers' level of parental satisfaction. Some mothers explained that, during the first two years of separation, noncustodial fathers had threatened openly to get custody of their children; children were aware of these threats and used them as a leverage against their mothers. As the fathers settled into a life of divorce or of impending remarriage, these threats ceased because custody of the children would have been dysfunctional to their new lives. Deprived of this leverage, the children ceased their threats. There were other children, especially at the lower-SES level, whose fathers had showered them with gifts at Time 1 during their rare visits. These children harbored a vision of a rich and generous father and the poor mother paled by comparison (see, also, Tooley, 1976). But, by Time 2, the fathers had disillusioned their children: five of these lower-SES fathers (50%) had completely disappeared from their children's lives. (These mothers' reports of paternal desertion were confirmed during the interviews with the non-custodial fathers: both ex-spouses were interviewed at Time 2.)

We then proceeded with a case by case examination of the families of lower-SES mothers. Five of the six cases of notice-able improvement in maternal satisfaction and children's behaviour were related to the fact that a problem child (and even children) had left or had been removed from the family unit. In one instance, a difficult twenty-year-old son was in jail and the troublesome teenage unwed-mother had moved out to marry. In two families, three teenagers had been moved to group homes. In a fourth case, a juvenile delinquent son was on probation and living on his own. In a fifth case, the oldest daughter, a problem child at Time 1, had married. In these five families, or half of the families of lower-SES mothers, seven children had left or had been removed from the home. All seven children had been judged to be very difficult by this researcher at Time 1. Two of the sons used to hit their mothers; by Time 2, both sons had been arrested, although for other offences. The five mothers expressed great relief that these difficult children were no longer home.

20

Their absence also meant that the remaining children were easier to handle because they were no longer subject to the detrimental example provided by the more difficult children and because the mothers were more relaxed.

There was no difference in behavioural change (or constancy) over time between families in which the custodial parent had re-married and families in which the parent was still un-remarried. Also, using the Time 1 data and the Time 2 data separately, we compared remarried and un-remarried families: no differences emerged for families of custodial fathers and higher-SES custodial mothers. However, lower-SES custodial mothers who had remarried by Time 2 had been more satisfied with their children at <u>both times</u> and their children had more positive behavioural scores at <u>both times</u>. Thus, whether or not the custodial parent remarried did not make a diff- erence over time in terms of children's behaviour; but, among lower-SES mothers, only those mothers who had less difficult children at Time 1 were remarried by Time 2. In other words, lower-SES mothers with very difficult children at Time 1 had not remarried by Time 2. These same women generally had 4 or 5 children which means that number of children and children's behav- iour are largely confounding variables for this category of mothers. Because children's behaviour was <u>not</u> related to family size in the other two types of families, it is possible that the confounding of variables exists only at the lower-SES level. This would constitute an important research question for large-scale studies.

The gap in satisfaction between custodial fathers (six of whom were of higher-SES) and higher-SES mothers had narrowed between Times 1 and 2. Lower-SES custodial mothers' scores of parental satisfaction had been extremely low at Time 1. Yet, in spite of the fact that their satisfaction with their children had more than doubled, and despite the departure of their most difficult children, lower-SES mothers' score remained the lowest of all three categories of custodial parents: 3.3 versus 4.2 for higher-SES mothers and 4.9 for fathers. The average scores of children's behaviour had improved in the lower- SES mother-headed families because there were fewer children left at home and because the most problematic children had been selected out. The remaining children were the less difficult ones; they had improved mildly when considered in familial aggregates, although individually, a few had deteriorated. Very little change had occurred among custodial fathers and their children.

CONCLUSIONS

In this exploratory research, we note that apart from the gender of
the custodial parent, socio-economic status is the key variable:
"net" longitudinal improvements of children's behaviour and of
parental satisfaction in these divorced family units occurred
strictly in families that enjoyed a decent standard of living.
The improvement in children's behaviour in mother-headed families
at the lower end of the economic scale was very substantial, but
this improvement cannot be considered to be a net gain because it
occurred mainly as a result of the departure of the more difficult
children rather than because of a general improvement in children's
behaviour. Thus, both phases of this study emphasize the difficulties inherent in child-rearing in a mother-headed family of
lower-socio-economic status. Second, the follow-up also confirms
that, holding SES constant, custodial mothers in our sample
experience more difficulties than fathers in the fourth and fifth
years after separation, although this female disadvantage
decreases during this time. In fact, if we examine only the
positive aspects of the children's behaviour (help, for instance),
we see that, by Time 2, children of higher-SES mothers were doing
slightly better than those of fathers.

As we analyzed our results concerning other but related
topics (Ambert, 1982b; 1983) we found SES to be a key variable in
understanding the life conditions of separated/divorced persons.
Such an observation, however limited the sample size, may suggest
that studies on divorce which present results based on one SES
group, or even without considering SES, may be seriously limited,
no matter how sophisticated their research design, sample size,
and analysis.

Equally important for future studies was the observation
of a possible link between a lower-SES mother's chance of remarrying
at Time 2 and her children's behaviour at Time 1. Behavioural
variables have been neglected in studies of a predictive nature,
especially variables concerning children's behaviour.

The fact that higher-SES custodial mothers in this sample
enjoy a more pleasant relationship with their children than lower-
SES mothers begs for an explanation. Is it because of the social
status of the mother, or more particularly, her better financial
position (see Marsden, 1969: 154)? Is it her access to important
resources and her ability to act as a source of resources,
including social resources? Other studies have concluded that two
of the important variables affecting children in one-parent
families are economic status and the adjustment of the custodial
parent (Colletta, 1977; Herzog and Sudia, 1973; Lowenstein and
Koopman, 1978; Wallerstein and Kelly, 1980). Indeed, our results
indicate a close relation between child behaviour, parental
adjustment, and economic status. The mothers who were educated,

had reasonable financial means, had a career and benefitted from a relatively high social status reported more pleasure with their children, were more in control of the situation (see also Bould, 1977), and in turn, their children seemed more pleased with themselves and their mother.

Society's behaviour toward both sets of mothers, as compared to fathers, may provide the core explanation. The lower-SES mother has little that is socially valuable to offer society and much that she needs or has to request from it (economic assistance, health care, legal assistance, and so on). Thus, in terms of exchange, she is indebted, dependent, and can contribute little to redress the imbalance (Blau, 1964; Thibaut and Kelley, 1959). Such mothers are under the control of welfare agencies and patronized by their children's schools and health practitioners; they do not even obtain respect at stores or in their neighbourhood (Kriesberg, 1970). As women without partners, their circumstances are even less favourable than that of their married counterparts at the same SES. These women have little control over their existence; they can only react to it. Their children inherit the low social status of the mother and often end up at the bottom of the totem pole in a school system that rewards material possessions (Marsden, 1969: 69). Children of lower-SES mothers have few material and social advantages, although many attempt to develop a suitable facade; and it is this facade which leads them to posit rejecting acts toward their mother, who becomes the scapegoat for their frustration. The mother is a "nobody," as one seven-year-old child declared. Another mother explained how her 14-year-old pregnant daughter kept telling her that she "didn't want to grow old to become like me, a woman men do not want." She compared her mother unfavourably with her father, who was living with another woman and contributing nothing to his children's existence.

Since most children are awarded to their mothers at separation, a mother-headed family is the situation in a majority of cases. Yet these same mothers, mainly those of lower SES, did less well than the fathers. The mothers were more subject to the vagaries imposed by restricted socioeconomic conditions in terms of their children's behaviour towards them, while the fathers seemed to benefit from their masculine status in the interaction with their children. Indeed, the sex of the custodial parent was the only variable that would explain the wide range of reported and observed differences between fathers and mothers. Both the fathers and the children view their situation as one in which children should be thankful to their fathers. Indeed, all seven men described in great detail how their co-workers and neighbours admire what they do, how their friends are supportive, how their children's teachers respect them. In other words, there is a "conspiracy" involved: the father is generally appreciated and the children hear about it or see it. In turn the father also hears it and believes it, perhaps eagerly so, because such belief certainly contributes to the bolstering of his ego. He in turn subtly passes on the message to the children, a communication which further reinforces the internalization process.

The fathers as males seemed to command authority and respect from their children quasi-automatically when they had their custody (not necessarily so otherwise). The mothers, by contrast, seemed to lack that benefit (Hetherington et al., 1976: 425). They had to prove themselves--which may explain the finding in other studies that separated mothers tend to be more restrictive and authoritarian in the first two years after separation (Hetherington et al., 1976). It was also obvious that children took it for granted that their mothers keep them and even tolerate unpleasant behaviour on the children's part: "It's your natural duty," a six-year-old girl candidly explained to her mother.

REFERENCES

Ambert, A.-M.

1976   Sex Structure (Second edition, revised and expanded). Toronto: Longman of Canada.

1980   Divorce in Canada. Toronto: Academic Press of Canada.

1982a   "Differences in children's behaviour toward custodial mothers and custodial fathers." Journal of Marriage and the Family 44: 73-86.

1982b   "Drug use in separated/divorced persons: gender, parental status, and socio-economic status," Social Science and Medicine 16, 971-976.

1983   "Physical health of separated women and men by socio-economic and parental status." Paper presented at the 1983 meetings of the Canadian Sociology and Anthropolgy Association, Vancouver.

1983   "Differences in remarriage behaviour between financially independent women and financially dependent women." Journal of Divorce 6 (Spring).

Ambert, A.-M. and J.F. Saucier

1983   "Adolescents' perception of their parents and parents' marital status." Journal of Social Psychology (in press).

Anthony, E.J.

1974   "Children at risk from divorce: a review." Pp.461-477 in E. Anthony and C. Koupenick (Eds.), The Child in His Family: Children at Psychiatric Risk (Volume 3). New York: John Wiley.

Arnold, R.

1980   Separation and After: A Research Report (Mimeographed). Ontario Ministry of Community and Social Services.

Baker, M.

1980   "Support systems and post-marital problems: The experiences of separated and divorced men and women." Paper presented at the Annual Meetings of the Canadian Sociology and Anthropology Association, Montreal.

Bane, M.J.

  1976   Here to Say: American Families in the Twentieth
              Century. New York: Basic Books, Inc.

Berg, B., and R. Kelly

  1979   "The measured self-esteem of children from broken,
              rejected, and accepted families." Journal of
              Divorce 2 (Summer): 363-369.

Berman, W.H. and D.C. Turk

  1981   "Adaptation to divorce: problems and coping
              strategies," Journal of Marriage and the Family
              43: 179-189.

Bigelow, D.A., and G. Brodsky

  1979   Quality of life theory of mental health. Oregon:
              Department of Human Resources, Mental Health
              Division.

Biller, H.B.

  1968   "A note on father absence and masculine development
              in lower-class negro and white boys." Child
              Development 9 (September): 1003-1006.

Biller, H.B.

  1969   "Father absence, maternal encouragement, and sex
              role development in kindergarten-age boys." Child
              Development 40 (June): 539-546.

Biller, H.B., and S.D. Weiss

  1970   "The father-daughter relationship and the
              personality development of the female." Journal
              of Genetic Psychology 116 (March): 79-93.

Blake, P.

  1972   The plight of One-Parent Families. London:
              Council for Children's Welfare.

Blau, P.M.

  1964   Exchange and Power in Social Life. New York:
              Wiley.

Bould, S.

    1977   "Female-headed families: personal fate control and
                the provider role." Journal of Marriage and the
                Family 39 (May): 339-349.

Bronfenbrenner, U.

    1976   "Who cares for America's children?" Pp. 3-32 in
                V.C. Vaughan and T.B. Brazelton (Eds.), The
                Family--Can It Be Saved? Chicago: Year Book
                Medical Publishers.

    1979   The Ecology of Human Development. Cambridge, Mass.:
                Harvard University Press.

Brown, C.R. Feldberg, E. Fox, and J. Kohen

    1976   "Divorce: chance of a new life-time." The Journal
                of Social Issues 32 (1): 119-134.

Canadian Council on Children and Youth

    1978   Admittance Restricted: The Child as Citizen in
                Canada. Ottawa: Canadian Council on Children
                and Youth.

Carter, H., and P.C. Glick

    1976   Marriage and Divorce: A Social and Economic Study
                (Revised Edition). Cambridge, Mass.: Harvard
                University Press.

Chester, R.

    1971   "Health and marriage breakdown: experience of a
                sample of divorced women." British Journal of
                Preventive and Social Medicine 25 (4): 231-244.

Chiriboga, D.A., J. Roberts, and J.A. Stein

    1978   "Psychological well-being during marital
                separation." Journal of Divorce 2 (Fall): 21-36.

Chiriboga, D.A., A. Coho, J.A. Stein, and J. Roberts

    1979   "Divorce, stress and social supports: a study of
                help-seeking behaviour." Journal of Divorce 3
                (2): 121-135.

Chombart de Lauwe, Y. M.-J.

 1959   Psycho-pathologie Sociale de l'Enfant Inadapte.
         Paris: Centre National de la Recherche
         Scientifique.

Colletta, N.D.

 1977   "Divorced Mothers at Two Income Levels: Stress,
         Support and Child-rearing Practices." Unpublished
         doctoral dissertation, Cornell University, Ithaca,
         New York.

Colletta, N.D.

 1979a   "The impact of divorce: father absence or poverty?"
         Journal of Divorce 3 (Fall): 27-35.

 1979b   "Support systems after divorce: Incidence and
         impact." Journal of Marriage and the Family 41
         (November): 837-846.

Corcoran, M.

 1976   "The economic consequences of marital dissolution
         for women in the middle years." Paper presented
         at the Conference on Women in Mid-life Crises,
         Cornell University, Ithaca, New York.

Defrain, J., and R. Eirick

 1981   "Coping as divorced single parents: a comparative
         study of fathers and mothers." Family Relations
         30 (April): 265-274.

Desimone-Luis, J., K. O'Mahoney, and D. Hunt

 1979   "Children of separation and divorce: factors
         influencing adjustment. Journal of Divorce 3
         (Fall): 37-42.

Despert, J.

 1962   Children of Divorce. Garden City. New York:
         Dolphin Books.

Ferri, E.

 1976   Growing up in a One-Parent Family: A Long-Term
         Study of Child Development. London: NFER
         Publishing Co.

Fulton, J.A.

1979   "Parental reports of children's post divorce
        adjustment." Journal of Social Issues 35: 126-
        139.

Garbarino, J.

1976   "A preliminary study of some ecological correlates
        of child abuse: the impact of socioeconomic stress
        on mothers." Child Development 47 (March): 178-
        185.

Gardner, R.A.

1974   "Psychological aspects of divorce." Pp. 496-512
        in S. Arieti (Ed.), American Handbook of Psychiatry
        (Vol. 1, 2nd ed.). New York: Basic Books.

George, V., and P. Wilding

1972   Motherless Families. London: Routledge and Kegan
        Paul.

Giovannoni, J., and A. Billingsley

1970   "Child neglect among the poor: a study of parental
        adequacy in families of three ethnic groups."
        Child Welfare 49 (April): 196-204.

Goode, W.J.

1956   Women in Divorce. New York: Free Press

Herzog, E., and C.E. Sudia

1973   "Children in fatherless families." Pp. 141-232 in
        B.M. Caldwell and H.N. Riciuti (Eds.), Review of
        Child Development Research (Vol. 3). Chicago:
        University of Chicago Press.

Hetherington, E.M.

1972   "Effects of father absence of personality develop-
        men in adolescent daughers." Developmental Psycho-
        logy 7 (3): 313-326.

Hetherington, E.M., and R.D. Parke

1975   Child Psychology, A Contemporary Viewpoint. New
        York: McGraw-Hill.

Hetherington, E.M., M. Cox, and R. Cox.

1976   "Divorced fathers." Family Coordinator 25 (October): 417-428.

Hetherington, E.M., M. Cox, and R. Cox.

1978   "The aftermath of divorce." Pp. 149-176 in J.H. Stevens and M. Mathews (Eds.), Mother-child, Father-child Relations. Washington, D.C.: National Association for the Education of Young Children.

1979   "The development of children in other-headed families." In D. Reiss and H. Hoffman (Eds.), The American Family, New York: Plenum Press.

Hodges, W.F., R. Wechsler, and C. Ballantine

1979   "Divorce and the preschool child: cumulative stress." Journal of Divorce 3 (Fall): 55-67.

Hong, K.M., R.D. Wirt, A.M. Yellin and J. Hopwood

1979   "Psychological attributes, patterns of life change, and illness susceptibility." Journal of Nervous and Mental Disease 167 (5): 275-281.

Hunt, J.G. and L.L. Hunt

1977   "Race, daughters and father-loss: does absence make the girl grow stronger?" Social Problems 25 (October): 90-102.

Hunt, L.L., and J.G. Hunt

1975   "Race and the father-son connection: the conditional relevance of father absence for the orientations and identifies of adolescent boys." Social Problems 23 (October): 35-52.

Jacobsen, D.S.

1978   "The impact of marital separation/divorce on children: II Interparent hostility and child adjustment." Journal of Divorce 2 (Fall): 3-19.

Kalter, N.

1977   "Children of divorce in an outpatient psychiatric population." American Journal of Orthopsychiatry 47 (January): 40-51.

Kelly, J.B., and J.S. Wallerstein

    1976   "The effects of parental divorce: experiences of the child in early latency." American Journal of Orthopsychiatry 46 (January): 20-32.

Kitson, G.C. and H.J. Raschke

    1981   "Divorce research: what we know; what we need to know." Journal of Divorce 4: 1-37.

Kriesberg, L.

    1970   Mothers in Poverty, A Study of Fatherless Families. Chicago: Aldine.

Kurdek, L.A., D. Blisk, and A.E. Sieskey Jr.

    1981   "Correlates of children's long-term adjustment to their parents' divorce." Developmental Psychology 17: 565-579.

Landis, J.T.

    1960   "The trauma of children when parents divorce." Marriage and Family Living 22 (1): 7-13.

    1962   "A comparison of children from divorced and non-divorced unhappy marriages." Family Co-ordinator 11 (July): 61-65.

    1963   "Dating maturation of children from happy and unhappy marriages." Marriage and Family Living 25 (August): 351-353.

Lerner, R.M., and G.B. Spanier

    1978   "A dynamic interactional view of child and family development." Pp. 1-23 in R.M. Lerner and G.B. Spanier (Eds.). Child Influences on Marital and Family Interaction. New York: Academic Press.

Lowenstein, J.S. and E.J. Koopman

    1978   "A comparison of the self-esteem between boys living with single-parent mothers and single-parent fathers." Journal of Divorce 2 (Winter): 195-208.

Luepnitz, D.A.

    1979   "Which aspects of divorce affect children?" Family Co-ordinator 28 (January): 79-85.

Marsden, D.

    1969   Mothers Alone: Poverty and the Fatherless Family. London: Penguin.

    1973   Mothers Alone: London: Allen Lane & Pelican Press.

McCord, J., W. McCord, and E. Thurber

    1962   "Some effects of paternal absence on male children." Journal of Abnormal and Social Psychology 64 (March): 361-369.

Mendes, H.A.

    1976   "Single fatherhood." Social Work 21 (July): 308-312.

Morrison, J.

    1974   "Parental divorce as a factor in childhood psychiatric illness." Comprehensive Psychiatry 15 (2): 95-102.

Nelson, G.

    1981   "Moderators of women's and children's adjustment following parental divorce." Journal of Divorce 4: 71-83.

Nye, F.I.

    1957   "Child adjustment in broken and in unhappy unbroken homes." Marriage and Family Living 19 (November): 356-361.

Orthner, D.K., T. Brown, and D. Ferguson

    1976   "Single-parent fatherhood: an emerging family life style." Family Coordinator 25 (October): 429-437.

Raschke, H.J.

    1977   "The role of social participation in post separation and post divorce adjustment." Journal of Divorce 1 (Winter): 129-140.

Riley, L., and C.E. Spreitzer

1974   "A model for the analysis of lifetime marriage patterns." Journal of Marriage and the Family 36 (February): 64-70.

Ross, H.L. and I.V. Sawhill

1975   Time of Transition: The Growth of Families Headed by Women. Washington, D.C.: The Urban Institute.

Sanctuary, G., and P. Whitehead

1970   Divorce--and After. London: Gollancz.

Santrock, J.W. and R.A. Warshak

1979   "Father custody and social development in boys and girls." Journal of Social Issues 35: 112-125.

Sewell, W.H., and A.O. Haller

1959   "Factors in the relationship between social status and the personality adjustment of the child." American Socilogical Review 24 (4): 511-520.

Spanier, G.B. and R.F. Castro

1979   "Adjustment to separation and divorce: An analysis of 50 case studies." Journal of Divorce 2 (Spring): 241-253.

Tcheng-Laroche, F., and R.H. Prince

1979   "Middle income, divorced female heads of families: their lifestyles, health and stress levels." Canadian Journal of Psychiatry 24 (1): 35-42.

Thibaut, J.W., and H.H. Kelley

1959   The Social Psychology of Groups. New York: John Wiley.

Tooley, K.

1976   "Anti-social behavior and social alienation post divorce: the 'man in the house' and his mother." American Journal of Orthopsychiatry 46: 33-42.

Wallerstein, J.S., and J.B. Kelly

    1975   "The effects of parental divorce: experiences of
            the child in later latency." American Journal of
            Orthopsychiatry 46 (April): 256-269.

Wallerstein, J.S., and J.B. Kelly

    1980   Surviving the Breakup: How Children and Parents
            Cope with Divorce. New York: Basic Books.

THE SINGLE TEEN-AGE CANADIAN MOTHER
IN THE 1980's: A REVIEW

Benjamin Schlesinger

We will examine the existing trends and research studies in Canada (1980-1984) related to single teen-age mothers. A previous article by Schlesinger (1979) reviewed the Canadian studies on this topic up to 1979.

TRENDS

Table 1, contains the 1981 trends related to teenagers in Canada.

(SEE TABLE I)

The estimates are that about 80-90% of all single teen-age mothers (STM) are keeping their children to form a growing one-parent family category. Thus in 1981, about 23,464 - 26,397 family units called the single teen-age mother and her child were formed.

If we project this over a five-year period we may expect 125,000 STM families. Even if the present decline of births to this age group continues the estimate would be about 112,000 families.

In examining Canadian national data related to decreasing numbers of teen pregnancies, Powell and Deber (1982) suggest three explanations for the decline: (a) fewer teenagers are having intercourse, (b) they are having intercourse less frequently and (c) they are using contraception more often.

The authors feel that the number of pregnancies among teenagers has not increased; indeed, it is declining. However, the number of live births is declining even more rapidly because the number of therapeutic abortions is increasing. Although almost two thirds of pregnant teenagers continue the pregnancy to term, abortion has become a common solution to an unwanted pregnancy. Those who do not choose an abortion tend to keep their babies.

35

They conclude their study by stating (Powell and Deber, 1982:495)

> Hence, solutions to the problems of pregnancy among teenagers must be addressed to these altered consequences rather than to misleading comments about "epidemics", with their suggestion of increased rates of pregnancy. Programs might well be directed at studying and providing contraception services geared to the needs of teenagers, at addressing the consequences of abortion among teenagers, and at supporting teenaged mothers and encouraging them, when appropriate, to consider adoption. Answers to the unsolved question of why fewer teenagers are becoming pregnant may improve the effectiveness of such program.

In a recent Toronto study Mitchell (1983), shows that the rate of teen pregnancy has gone up only by one percent in the past 20 years.

Information of repeat births (1960-1982) for women under 20 years of age residing in the City of Toronto indicates that the number of repeat births to women less than 20 years old decreased from 364 in 1960 to 86 in 1982. In 1960, 60 third, fourth or fifth children were born to teenagers; in 1982; six third children and no fourth or fifth children were born to women under 20 years of age.

Age specific repeat birth rates for the City of Toronto, 1960-1982 indicate there has been a decrease in the repeat birth rate for all adolescent women. The rate of repeat births has dropped from 18.6 in 1975, to 4.0 in 1982.

Information on repeat abortions among City of Toronto teenagers has only been recently available. The data in 1982 shows that 10.5% of the total number of repeat abortions were for 15-19 year olds compared with 20.5% performed in the 20-24 year age group. Expressed as a rate 7.16 women per 1000 aged 15-19 had repeat abortions in the City of Toronto (1982).

The author concludes her report by stating: (Mitchell, 1983:8)

> Women who have least choice to their lives are most likely to experience a repeat pregnancy. Furthermore, without choice in other aspects of their lives young women cannot be expected to be able to prevent a repeat pregnancy. From a review of the

literature and interviews with health professionals
and teens one can infer that in order for young
women to have control about child-bearing decisions,
it is vital that they have choice about their role
in society, their relationships, birth control,
resolving an unplanned pregnancy, and the conditions
within which they live.

It is vital that any programs designed to meet the
needs of teenagers experiencing a repeat pregnancy
address these issues.

Concerns to Reduce Adolescent Pregnancy

In their study of Ontario's Adolescent births, Orton and Rosenblatt (1981) point out some of the social problems associated
with teenage motherhood (pp. 13-15).

1.   Pregnancy, with or without premature parenthood, is
     often a tragedy for adolescent women. It involves
     high risks to the health of both mother and child.
     Children raised by adolescent mothers are often
     short-changed in their emotional and social develop-
     ment. Pregnancy and parenthood are a major barrier
     to young people, especially women, seeking to
     complete their education and develop work skills as
     a basis of self-support.

2.   In our industrialized society, adolescent pregnancy
     breeds poverty. All our young people (male and
     female) are vulnerable to the risk of accidental,
     unwanted pregnancy. Women and children bear the
     harsh brunt of the consequences. Men are becoming
     increasingly disconnected from their fatherhood--
     in responsibility for contraception and for
     parenting. These facts have serious personal and
     social implications. Adolescent pregnancy is con-
     tributing significantly to the rising numbers of
     single-parent families headed by women.

3.   All Canadians pay heavily for our failure to help
     young people avoid pregnancy before they are
     prepared to be parents. We pay financially to provide
     agency counselling services, therapeutic abortion
     services, adoption services, income support to
     adolescent single parents via General Welfare Assis-
     tance and Family Benefits, extra demands upon health
     care services, temporary child-care placements, etc.
     These are essential services and we shall always need
     them. We would greatly reduce the need for them by
     preventing accidental pregnancies.

37

a)   Community Surveys

In Manitoba, a Community Task Force (1981) investigated adolescent pregnancy. There were 1,312 births to single teenagers in 1980.

The great majority of sexually active adolescents did not want to become pregnant. For many, however, the lack of knowledge and difficult access combined with fear of discovery, fear of the contraceptive method and the peer pressure for increasing involvement, made this group very susceptible to pregnancies for which they were ill prepared.

Continuing school attendance was often a problem for pregnant adolescents. Presently, options include corres- pondence courses, the Winnipeg School Board special school for pregnant teenagers or maternity home schools. Few adolescents remained in the normal education stream during pregnancy.

O'Hanlon (1983) surveyed 89 single mothers in Red Deer, Alberta. The profile of the respondents included the following features.

The average age of the single mother was 20.1 years. At the time the questionnaire was completed, 30% were preg- nant and 70% had delivered the child. The average age of the child was less than 1 year. Thirty-nine percent of the respondents lived alone. Thirty percent lived with their parents and another nine percent lived with relatives for a total of thirty-nine percent. Only ten percent lived with their baby's father. Sixty percent of the respondents said they had lived at their current address for six months or less. Twenty-four percent had moved three times during the past three years and twenty-seven percent had moved four-six times in the past three years. Eighty percent of the respondents were not working. Sixty-five reported that they had two, three, or four jobs during the past two years.

The information contained in this report profiled a young 20-year-old unwed mother, generally living alone and parenting a baby less than a year old. This is usually her only child. She has a low educational back- ground; she generally has not completed high school. She has a history of changing jobs and she has made many moves during the past three years. She received little support from the father of the baby, either emotional or financial. Her family would appear to offer emotional support but not financial support for the girl.

Although she has received some sex education it would seem she does not use birth control effectively and would appear to be a good candidate for a subsequent pregnancy.

In Saskatchewan, Ferguson (1983) in a background paper reviewed single teenage pregnancy and motherhood in that province. In 1979, there were 1,423 births to single women 19 years and under, which constituted 8.4 percent of all births during that year. The author also pointed out that of all births to adolescents in 1979, 58% were to single teenagers.

b)   Research Studies

In a Montreal study, Lipper (1980) examined 55 women who had their babies during their adolescence. Of the 55 young women, 45 kept their babies and 10 relinquished their children for adoption. The investigator compared the "keepers" and the "adopters".

The "adopters" and the "keepers" profile was quite different and they chose different life styles after having their baby. As a group, the adopters were from two-parent families and they went through the pregnancy without the putative father (p.f.). It is suggested that a girl from an intact family who breaks with the p.f. before the baby is born is a good candidate to give up her baby for adoption as she would like her child to grow up in a two-parent family like herself. The "adopters" were less likely than the "keepers" to be married or to have a repeat pregnancy, and more likely to be in school or employed full time. Most of the "keepers" in the study were at home looking after their children. The majority formed long-term, stable relationships with a male partner, often the p.f., and many of them had a planned repeat pregnancy. This group chose motherhood as a career.

In a study of 246 single adolescent mothers in Ontario's maternity homes, Lightman and Schlesinger (1982) also developed a profile of the "adopters" and the "keepers".

The "adopter" was more likely to be in school, and was planning to return to school after the birth of the child. She would be living at home with her parents in a two-parent family unit. Her parents were paying some board to the maternity home, and her parents were involved in decisions concerning the baby. The adopter appeared to have little contact with the putative father, and was not planning any future contact. The putative father's family was not involved in the woman's decisions and plans related to the baby.

Her friends were not non-married mothers, nor did she report any serious illness, or handicap, or psychiatric treatment in her past. The adopter was not in contact with a social work agency, and was not planning to relate to a social agency after the birth of her child.

The Keepers: The single mother who planned to keep her child will have left school and will have done so at a slightly younger age than the adopter. It is less probable that she was living at home with her parents. She was residing permanently in public housing, an apartment, or some other situation that does not involve home ownership. Over three-quarters of this group reported they have other non-married mothers as friends. The woman who was planning to keep her child reported serious illness or handicaps and was three times as likely to have undergone psychiatric treatment in the past. The family structure at home was primarily a parent unit which involved divorce or separation. The "keeper" was more likely to be in contact with the putative father and his family and to have them involved in her own decision for the future. This woman was in contact with some social work agency in the past with much greater frequency, including the payment of board on her behalf to the home, and was planning to retain such contact with the agency in the future.

Hoppe (1983) examined 141 residents in 13 maternity homes in Ontario. The profile of a resident in the maternity home included the following characteristics:

- The majority were teenagers between 15 and 19 years of age.
- While the majority (60%) lived in a two-parent family, a substantial portion (40%) lived in a one-parent family.
- Almost two-thirds of the residents were students prior to entering the home.
- Slightly more than half of the residents had worked immediately prior to their pregnancy mostly in part-time service positions.
- Parents and friends were seen by the residents as being more accepting and supportive of the pregnancy than the putative fathers.
- The largest source of referrals was self, family and friends.
- More than one in four residents had been a ward of a children's aid society.
- A small proportion had been receiving counselling, mental health services or probation services.
- Slightly more residents were planning to release their babies for adoption rather than keep and raise their babies themselves.

40

- The residents' intention to keep and raise their
  babies or relinquish their babies for adoption
  did not vary with the following variables: age,
  education, marital status of persons with whom
  residents mainly lived and the residents' self-
  reported condition of health.
- Of the residents who intended to keep their babies,
  more planned to cope with child rearing by:
  receiving emotional support and assistance from
  their parents; other relatives and friends; living
  on their own or with parents; and receiving
  financial support mostly from the government or
  parents.
- The majority (87%) of the maternity home residents
  were at risk on at least one factor suggested by
  the literature and more than one-fifth had
  elements of risk in a number of different areas of
  their life.

A well-documented study was completed in Nova Scotia by
Macdonnell (1981). A sample of 353 single adolescent mothers
was compared to 332 married mothers. A larger proportion of
non-married mothers came from families that were not intact
either because of divorce, separation, death or illegitimacy.
By the time they were 16 years of age, one out of every three
non-married mothers no longer lived with both natural parents.
For the majority of their fist 16 years, approximately one-
quarter were not raised by both natural parents. They had
very limited schooling, with only 20 percent having completed
high school education or better, compared to 65 percent of
the married mothers. Eighty percent (compared to 35 percent of
the married mothers) were without any job training, and at the
time of conception, 34 percent were working, 38 percent were
in school and the remaining 28 percent were at home.

The child's father was also quite young and had only
limited education. The vast majority were single men and
slightly more than two-thirds of the mothers had known the
father over a year before they became pregnant. In all, 16.4
percent of the non-married mothers were known to have been
living with the baby's father prior to the birth.

The majority of the non-married mothers had neither
wanted nor planned their pregnancies. Mothers who were young,
who had been in school when they became pregnant, and who came
from homes where their parents were married and living together
were most likely not to have wanted the pregnancy.

All but one of the single mothers had some knowledge of
birth control but, of those who had not wanted to become
pregnant, 41 percent felt they had not known enough. Again,
the youngest mothers and those who had been in school when
they became pregnant were less likely to have had adequate
birth control information.

Nearly half of the mothers in the study had used a
method of birth control at some time prior to their pregnancy.
Most of the non-married mothers in the study said that finding
someone to help care for their children had not been a problem
during the eighteen months of the study. The fact that so many
lived with family probably accounted for this, as well as the
fact that relatively few had returned to school or taken jobs.
Those who did have problems finding babysitters reported that
doubts about reliability, scarcity of sitters, financial costs
and odd working hours made finding alternate child care a problem.

Approximately one out of every two single mothers received
financial aid at some time during the 18 months' study. Most
did not receive any financial assistance from the fathers of
their children.

The children of non-married mothers experienced many more
hospitalizations and emergency treatments compared to the
children of married mothers. The majority of the single mothers
said that they were happy and content with the way their life
had turned out, despite parenting problems.

Sacks et al (1982) completed a descriptive study which
examined the problems, needs, supports and outcomes of a sample
of 50 adolescent mothers and their children, who received
pediatric care at the Hospital for Sick Children's Adolescent
Medical Clinic in Toronto.

In addition to the interviews the level of the youngest
child's development was assessed using one of the two standardized psychometric tests--The Bayley Scales of Infant Development
and the Stanford-Binet Intelligence Scale. The psychometric
tests were performed and scored by one of two trained and
qualified psychometrists who were both graduates from the
Institute of Child Study in Toronto.

The mother's age at the time of the birth of their child
ranged from 15 to 22 years, with an average of 17.4 years.
Three quarters of the mothers gave birth when they were 16, 17
or 18 years old. The average age of the mothers at the time
they were interviewed was 19.2 years. Most mothers were not
married when their babies were born.

The living arrangements of the mothers also differed
greatly. Approximately one third lived alone with their child,
another third with members of their family, while the final third
had other living arrangements, typically with their boyfriends.

Two out of five mothers were active during the day, either
attending school full time (22%) or employed full time (18%).

Another 16% had part-time jobs, which helped to support themselves and their child. About one-third of the mothers (34%) were receiving welfare. Only 38% reported financial assistance from the child's father and 12% received unemployment benefits.

In terms of ethnic and religious backgrounds, most mothers were either Protestant (44%) or Catholic (36%). Just over half of them were born in Canada (56%), and the remainder in either the West Indies (28%) or Europe (16%).

Only 22% or 11 mothers were enrolled in high school on a full-time basis at the time of the interviews.

In general, while a minority of mothers were continuing their schooling, most (78%) were not. Of the 39 not in school, only 2 had completed Grade 12 and 33 Grade 10 or less. The future educational prospects of these mothers seemed bleak.

Much of the interview with the mothers concerned problems they might be experiencing generally or those specifically related to their parenting experience.

"Getting enough money to meet expenses" was by far the most common problem, and it was a concern of almost half of the mothers.

Interestingly, the next three problems dealt with areas of interpersonal problems which manifested themselves in the form of "arguments" with others. About one quarter of the mothers said that "arguments" regarding child rearing practice constituted a problem for them. This suggests that acceptance of their role as mother was not always forthcoming from others in their lives.

Next in order were "finding work", "getting enough free time for youself", and "loneliness". One can only surmise the degree to which they may be problems common to teenagers in general. The next two problems on the list were more practical in nature--"finding babysitters" (22%) and "inadequate housing" (20%).

The overwhelming majority of these young women enjoyed their maternal role and did not regret the decision to keep their child. Of the mothers, 80% agreed with the statement, "Compared to other mothers, I feel I have had an easier time bringing up my child than most." Nevertheless, many mothers indicated that the birth of their child had created personal and family problems. For example, 32% said that bringing up their child was harder than they had anticipated. About a third, said that their child often made them angry or frustrated and

43

10% said that the birth of their child had led to a deterioration
in their relationship with their family. Thus, while there was
almost universal agreement that the mother truly enjoyed her
new role as parent and would not have wanted it any other way,
their decision to keep their child had, for many, a negative
impact on their personal lives and family situation.

As a group, the children were much like other normal
healthy children. The maximum and minimum scores also show that
within the group of 50 children, some are in the "superior"
range in terms of cognitive development while others could be
characterized as "borderline".

MacKay and Austin (1983) completed a mailed questionnaire
investigation to study 87 young single mothers in four cities in
Ontario. All were mothers to a one-year-old child, were living
on social assistance, and were either living alone or with their
parents. Three-fifths of the mothers had completed Grade 10
or less. One in four said they lacked freedom, felt restricted,
and were socially inactive. Two-thirds of the fathers of the
children had not visited the child in the previous four weeks.
Three-fifths of the 87 single adolescent mothers provided 20-24
hour child care. A majority estimated they spent at least
eight hours per day relating to their child.

The great majority reported mental health needs, mainly
for emotional support and closeness with their families. One-
third reported "unmet" mental health needs over the first 18 months.

Many sought medical attention for themselves or for their
child, and this need increased sharply after six months. Only
one in seven felt their physical health needs were unmet or
poorly met.

Almost all reported child care needs by the 13-18 month
period. Informal care by family, friends and neighbours was
used by a large majority of mothers. A declining and small
minority of child care needs were unmet or poorly met.

Those with "met" social, housing, income and school-and
employment needs were white, daughters of married mothers in
higher level jobs, living with parents, not on welfare, who
were older at the birth of their first baby and more highly
educated.

Projects for Single Teenage Mothers

An educational project related to single teenage mothers
had been reported by Weizmann et al (1983).

44

The Montrose Infant Care Centre was set up to provide a program to serve two high-risk populations, teenaged mothers who are attending secondary school in the City of Toronto, and their young children. The daycare program, located to provide easy access to student mothers attending secondary schools, is in an inner-city area with a large population of low-income families and a large immigrant population.

The primary school in which the daycare program is located has a population of children for most of whom (83.97%) English is not the first language and many (42.76%) families whose incomes fall below the official poverty line.

The program objectives involve both the mothers and their babies. The overall goal of the project is to mitigate factors that prevent teenage mothers and their babies from thriving to their fullest capacity.

The primary intervention consists of provision of a high-quality care program for the infants. It is intended to meet the needs of the young mothers by providing a stable, contin-uous, caretaking situation for their babies so that they are able to attend school full time and to meet the babies' needs by providing an environment where they are able to develop to their optimum. The intervention includes other elements as well. One program assists the participants in their daily lives by, for example, opening the centre early so that they can attend a work placement, helping to straighten out a school-related problem or helping to find housing.

The investigators questioned 35 STM's, of whom 55% were of West Indian background. Their average age was 18 years, and they had their first and only child at about age 17. Abortion was not considered as an option to pregnancy. The West Indian single teenage mothers had also relationships with their mothers, and they gave low priority to marriage. The most frequently cited areas of difficulty by all the single mothers were money (the majority were on mother's allowance), followed by a restricted social life and conflicts within the family. The father of the child was on the average 21 years old, going to school, working or both. For the West Indian STM's the fathers gave considerable financial and social support. The families of the fathers also added their support to the single mothers. Most STM's stated that they would like another child sometime within the next three-year period. This study focused quite a bit on the ethnic (West Indian) aspects of single teenage motherhood.

In Calgary, the Louise Dean School (1982) handled 173 STM's in their adult day care centre during the 1981-82 school year. Their average age was 16.1 years. Of 110 students who

delivered their babies, 61% kept their babies while 39% opted for
adoption. (Alberta averages: 86% kept, 14% surrendered in 1981).
Of all the young women who became pregnant, 82% did not use birth
control before the pregnancy. After the delivery of the baby,
59% were financially supported by their parents, and 28% by
income security. Only 12% were supported by the putative father
or boyfriend.

The following list is representative of the scope and
complexity of the majority of problems with which the social
workers have been confronted in this setting; depression, anxiety,
family breakup, alcoholism, parenting problems, decisions
regarding surrendering a young child, custody issues, delinquency,
various legal problems, abuse by boyfriend, sexuality and birth
control, grief responses, individual identity crises, adaptation
to single parenthood, child welfare concerns (abuse, neglect)
incest, sexual problems, subsequent unplanned pregnancies,
behaviour problems, housing crises.

In the fall of 1982, group counselling was offered for
the first time as a "special project" for which the students
attending earned a high school credit. Several groups were run
over the school year. While these groups were voluntary in
membership, they were well subscribed to and met with positive
responses from involved students. Indications are that there
was growth of trust, self-esteem, and peer support with many
group members.

Several students identified material needs that they
had in common, and a "self-help" committee of students was
organized to help deal with these needs. With the counselling
co-ordinator acting as advisor, this committee organized a
large supply of young children's clothing for the use of the
students. Memos were sent to the entire student body sharing
information on this project and other common issues.

The committee gathered information regarding the setting
up and running of a toy library, which is being considered
for a future project.

In co-operation with the assistant principal and infant
care supervisor, a "buddy" system was set up whereby a new
student was paired up with an older student whose responsibility it was to familiarize the student with the school
setting and students. This process proved to be beneficial.

The Jessie's Centre for Teenagers in Toronto developed
a "Respite Care Program" under the leadership of Miriam Urback
(Globe and Mail, 1983).

Respite Care, which works in conjunction with Family Day Care Services, celebrated its first birthday in December 1983. It's designed to give teenage mothers, 18 and under, a breathing space from their children, to cope with a crisis, get over a cold, or simply to get some time to themselves.

The babies can be taken for a period of one to 21 days, and are placed into private homes screened by Family Day Care Services. The mother can visit her child at a convenient time for herself and the family, at the home, and can elect to have her baby back even before the agreed-upon date without any fuss or paperwork.

In this way the Respite Care program differs from Children's Aid Society services, where a mother might only be able to visit her child at the agency, or need the agency's permission to visit.

The program is Metro wide, and free to the mothers who use it. It's financed by the city and the province, which pays the fees of the families of "providers" who offer the temporary shelter. While most of the providers are notified of an incoming baby a few days in advance, they must always have a crib available, because there are times when a one-hour notice is all that is given.

For this, providers are paid $3.25 a day as a retainer fee, and $15.00 a day when a baby is there, which covers the cost of food and diapers. Jessie's provides such things as playpens, car seats and booster chairs. The providers range from young mothers to grandmothers, and must pass a careful check to become eligible. Not only must they meet provincial standards for day care, but the program looks for providers who have an empathy and understanding of teenage mothers.

Teen Mothers Resource Group

Two examples of a co-ordinating group dealing with single teenage mothers can be found in Calgary and Toronto. In Calgary (Expectations, 1983), issued a newsletter which gives the reader the resources in Calgary, related to this population. A few short articles describe some approaches in working with this group. In Toronto (Resources for Young Mothers Newsletter, 1983) points out the following objectives of the Resource group.

1. To provide support for the members of the group.

2. To share information in order to identify areas of need.

3. To improve the utilization of research:

 - sharing summary research from our agencies
   in a formalized, research-oriented manner in
   order to identify and priorize needs;

 - providing a resource to others doing research;

 - providing a forum for sharing others' research.

4. To provide a vehicle through which appropriate
   social action may be initiated.

5. To do advocacy within our own agencies and other
   community groups including Young Mother's Resource
   Group.

6. To act as a resource to each other and to the
   larger community.

Health Survey

Grindstaff (1983) examined 1659 cases of adolescents in
the London, Ontario region from two obstetrical units.

Infant outcomes, provided the most compelling results
from the analysis. The results for the inter-related variable
of prematurity (both by weight and gestational age) and perinatal mortality indicated that teenagers were especially at
risk of giving birth to highly compromised infants whose neo-
natal course was not without complication. Evidence also
suggested that these differences cannot be wholly attributed
to differences in birth-weight alone as infants born to teenage mothers were subject to importantly elevated rates of
respiratory distress, and feeding problems.

The most powerful and important outcome however, remained
that infants born to teenagers were subject to elevated rates
of perinatal mortality. That infants born to young teens died
twice as frequently than those born to controls was of substantive importance. Since infant survival is the entire
purpose of reproduction, the observation of important gradients
in death (as well as their antecedents) should alert us to the
need for much closer scrutiny of the circumstances surrounding
adolescent reproduction.

Commentary

In examining the Canadian studies and projects during the
1980-1984 period (up to January 1984) one comes to the conclusion that there are multi-issues involved in Single Teenage
Motherhood. Table 2, summarizes these issues:

(SEE TABLE II)

It is evident that the issues were interrelated, and do not
stand in isolation. We are aware that not all single mothers
face all the issues. We are also aware that many systems are
related to the teenage mother. Table 3 contains the major
ten systems.

(SEE TABLE III)

In working with teenagers we have to have in mind that these
systems play an important part in their lives.

In reviewing existing research studies one is struck
by the fact that little research has been done in the following
areas.

1. The father of the baby and his family.

2. The family life of the teenage single mother.

3. A five-year follow-up study of the lives
of these mothers.

4. Only a few provinces have examined the
trends related to this population.

5. We do not have any national studies on
this topic.

6. We do not know how many mothers relinquish
their children during the first five years
after birth.

7. We also need a financial picture of the cost
to Canadian society of this increasing one-
parent family (see as an example: Mecklenburg
Council of Adolescent Pregnancy, 1979).

8. We are only beginning in selected cities to
form co-ordinating teen-mothers' groups,
where all agencies who serve this population
meet to share their experiences. Valuable
research can be completed in these groups.

9. The Health and Welfare Department of the
Federal government could house a Resource Centre
where all available knowledge related to this
group would be gathered, stores, and disseminated
to interested groups.

Conclusions

We have attempted to review existing knowledge related
to single teenage mothers in Canada. We have made some
suggestions for further examination and research. As we
move towards the year 2000, we have to continue to monitor
the progress of thousands of Canadian single teenagers who
have decided to become mothers.

REFERENCES

Community Task Force on Maternal Health. Adolescent Pregnancy
in Manitoba: Current Status and Future Alternatives,
Winnipeg, December 1981.

Expectations. Calgary: Faculty of Continuing Education, 1983
(A Newsletter).

Ferguson, C.M. "Adolescent Pregnancy in Saskatchewan: A
Background Paper", (in) C.M. Ferguson ed. Proceedings
of the Prevention of Adolescent Pregnancy Symposium,
Saskatoon, Saskatchewan, 1983. XI-IIV.

Globe and Mail. "Giving Young Mothers a Breathing Space."
December 15, 1983.

Hoppe, B. Review of Maternity Homes in Ontario. Toronto:
Ministry of Community and Social Services, March, 1983.

Grindstaff, C.F. Teenage Pregnancy and Health Complications
in Canada. London: University of Western Ontario,
Department of Sociology, July 1983.

Lightman, E. and B. Schlesinger. "Pregnant Adolescents in
Maternity Homes: Some Professional Concerns", (in)
I.R. Stuart and C.F. Wells eds. Pregnancy in
Adolescence: Needs Problems and Management. New York:
Van Nostrand Reinhold, 1982, 363-385.

Lipper, I. Follow Up Study of a Clinic Population of
Adolescent Mothers. Montreal: Montreal Children's
Hospital, 1980 (unpublished).

Louise Dean School. Year End Report, Sept. 1981 - June 1982.
Calgary, 1982.

MacKay, H. and C. Austin. Single Adolescent Mothers in
Ontario. Ottawa: The Canadian Council on Social
Development, 1983.

Macdonnell, S. Vulnerable Mothers, Vulnerable Children.
Halifax: Nova Scotia, Department of Social Services,
1981.

Mecklenburg Council on Adolescent Pregnancy. Financial Report:
Adolescent Pregnancy in Charlotte Mecklenburg.
Charlotte, North Carolina, 1980 (P.O. Box 2835).

Mitchell, S. "Repeat Pregnancies Among Teens", Family Planning Bulletin. Toronto, Department of Public Health, No. 27, December 1983.

O'Hanlon, L.A. Unwed Mothers Study: Red Deer, Alberta. Red Deer, Alberta, January, 1983.

Orton, M.J. and E. Rosenblatt. Adolescent Birth Planning Needs: Ontario in the Eighties. Toronto: Planned Parenthood Ontario, 1980.

Powell, M. and Deber, R.A. "Why is the Number of Pregnancies among Teenagers Decreasing?" Canadian Medical Association Journal, 127 (September 1982), 492-495.

Resources for Young Mothers. Resources for Young Mothers Newsletter. Toronto: September 1983.

Sacks, D., Macdonald, J.G., Schlesinger, B. and C. Lambert. The Adolescent Mother and Her Child: A Research Study. Toronto: Faculty of Social Work, University of Toronto, 1982.

Schlesinger, B. "The Unmarried Mother Who Keeps Her Child", (in) B. Schlesinger (ed) One in Ten: The Single Parent in Canada, Toronto: Guidance Centre, Faculty of Education, University of Toronto, 1979, 77-86.

Weisman, R., Friendly, M. and G. Gonda. Evaluation of the Montrose Infant Care Centre. Toronto: Ministry of Community and Social Services, July 1983.

TEENAGE STATISTICS IN CANADA 1981
                PREGNANCIES, LIVE BIRTHS, AND ABORTIONS

<u>Total Number of Girls Aged 15-19 in Population: 1,132,870</u>

Number of pregnancies	47,740
Live births to teenagers (T.A.)	29,330
Abortions to teenagers (T.A.)	18,410
- precentage of T.A. who were pregnant	4.2%
- percentage of T.A. who gave birth	2.6%
- percentage of T.A. who had abortions	1.6%
- percentage of births to T.A. of total births to all Canadians	7.9%
- abortions to T.A. as percentage of all abortions in Canada	28.3%

TABLE 2:   SINGLE TEENAGE MOTHERS: SELECTED ISSUES

1)   Medical

      - poor nutrition
      - pre-natal care
      - inadequate diet
      - prematurity
      - toxemia

      Note: if good pre-natal care these may not occur

2)   Education

      - reduced education
      - do not complete education
      - do not catch up
      - drop out of school
      - income, occupation, fertility, unemployment all
        related to education

3)   Social

      - single parenthood
      - no father figure at home
      - limited social life
      - high cost of babysitters
      - type of support from putative father
      - own family support

4)   Fertility

      - possible repeat pregnancy
      - use of contraceptives/family planning

5)   Housing

      - if not living at home, cost of housing is high
      - mobility, moving frequently

6)   Economic

      - not working
      - on welfare - less prestigious jobs
                   - little job opportunity
      - living in poverty
      - social class factors

TABLE 2 (cont'd)

7) <u>Child Care</u>

- cost of day care if wants to go to work
- time spent with young baby

8) <u>The Putative Father</u>

- teenager himself
- paternity oath
- how much is he involved in parenting, decision making, financial help

9) <u>Adolescent Development</u>

- conflicts of adolescence and being a mother
- motherhood vs independence, parenting role

10) <u>Societal Supports</u>

- social/health agencies

11) <u>Long-Term Effects</u>

- growth of child
- future relationships
- future family plans (marriage, etc.)

TABLE 3:   SYSTEMS RELATED TO SINGLE
                             TEENAGE MOTHERS

1.   Family/Relatives

2.   Father of Baby and his family

3.   Friends/Peer Group

4.   Health System/Hospital/Outpatient Department

5.   Welfare System - Family Benefits

6.   Voluntary Social Services/Maternity Homes

7.   Educational Services - Schooling

8.   Vocational Services - Retraining

9.   Child Care Services - Day Care, etc.

10.   Employment - Work System

SINGLE FATHERS WITH CUSTODY:
A SYNTHESIS OF THE LITERATURE

Shirley M. H. Hanson

INTRODUCTION

Family structures in North America are undergoing a
metamorphosis. The increase in single parent families, in
particular, represents a large portion of these changes. At the
same time families are experiencing alterations in the way
that parents and children work and relate to each other.
Coinciding with the increase of marriage dissolutions and women
entering the job market, there is a movement of men, albeit small,
toward greater participation in household and child care
activities. Nowhere are these changes in the role of men and
fathers more evident than with the group of people called single
custodial fathers. Single custodial fathers are men who have
physical custody of their child(ren). They assume the primary
parental responsibility without the assistance of a co-parent
living in the family home. This includes fathers who are
separated, divorced, widowed or adoptive parents.

The purpose of this chapter is to define and describe
single custodial fathers and their children. The literature on
this special group of parents will be reviewed and data on common
themes and variables will be highlighted. Finally, implications
for social policy and further research will be made.

FATHERS AND CUSTODY

Fathers with custody are not a new phenomena. Throughout
history until the middle of the 19th century, custody of children
almost always went to the father. Men literally owned their
children as well as their wives (Orthner & Lewis, 1979) and
they were more able than women to provide financially for their
offspring. At the beginning of the industrial revolution about
the turn of the 20th century, courts started to award children
to their mothers. This preference for maternal custody continued

with fathers seldom receiving custody unless the mother died or was proven to be unfit. In the past ten years, many changes have taken place and now there are three ways by which fathers receive custody of minor children: death of spouse, adoption, and separation/divorce.

Historically, the primary cause for single father custody was maternal death resulting in widowhood. Before the advent of modern medicine, large numbers of women were lost through childbirth and men automatically received custody of their children. Most of the time, these children were reared by women in the man's extended family. Despite variations in the percentage, the actual number of widower families (106,000) in the United States has remained relatively constant in recent years affecting about 181,000 children (U.S. Bureau of the Census, 1982b, 1982c).

Single father adoption is the newest way by which men receive custody of children. Single parent adoption first became available in 1950 with the first reported case in 1965; the first formal single father adoption took place about 1980. The U.S. Bureau of the Census (1982b) indicates that there are 78,000 single-custodial fathers in this category of "never married" which includes the legal and informal adoption of about 112,000 children.

The largest number of men receive custody of children through separation and divorce. As the divorce rate has increased, so has the number of father custody families. Fathers can obtain custody by legal and nonlegal means. Non-legally, children can live with fathers while mothers retain legal custody; this is a common occurrence. Child snatching is another means of obtaining nonlegal custody. Legal or court ordered custody includes sole, split, divided or joint custody. Most single fathers have sole custody but the occurrence of joint custody is increasing. About 1.7 million children live with their 509,000 single custodial fathers due to separation or divorce (U.S. Bureau of the Census, 1982b).

In America, one-parent families account for 21 percent of the 31.6 million families with children in 1981, an increase of 3.4 million or 111 percent since 1970. (Bureau of the Census, 1982c, 1983). This means that one out of every five children live with single parents. Of the 12.6 million children in these homes, 90 percent live with their mothers and approximately 10 percent with their fathers. The number of children residing with fathers increased 101 percent between 1970 and 1982.

The actual number of children living with fathers is probably closer to 3.5 million due to the variety of informal arrangements made between parents who are divorced (Lewis, 1978).

REVIEW OF RESEARCH

There has been a paucity of research about fathers in general and single custodial fathers in particular. However, since 1976 an increasing amount of research has been published. The purpose of the following synopsis is to share a composite of the findings of the past eight years. Accompanying the synopsis is a table which summarizes eleven of the major published articles in the field according to common themes or variables of interest across studies. (1) The studies that were used in this synthesis of research include: Bartz and Witcher (1978), Chang & Deinard (1982), Defrain and Eirick (1981), Gasser and Taylor (1976), Gersick (1979), Grief (1982, 1983, 1984), Hanson (1980, 1981a, 1981b, 1982, 1983, 1984), Katz (1979), Lewis (1978), McKee and O'Brien (1982), Mendes (1976a, 1976b), Orthner, Brown and Ferguson (1976), Orthner and Lewis (1979), Rosenthal and Keshet (1981), Santrock and Warshak (1979), Schlesinger (1978)

See Table 1

Subjects and Methodology

The number of subjects in most of the studies is generally small; the majority of researchers reported N's of 30 to 40 people. Subjects were self-selected resulting in non-randomized samples. Studies have been conducted on subjects across the North American continent as well as England and Australia.

Larger samples are being tapped, however. DeFrain at the University of Nebraska is presently analyzing data from a large study of single parents (N = 738). An initial report of this work compared single mothers to single fathers, compared different kinds of custody arrangements (sole, joint, and split), and studied the adjustment of children to divorce (Fricke, 1982). Grief (1982, 1983, 1984) obtained a very large sample of 1,100 single fathers (both widowers and separated/divorced men) and published several articles in The Single Parent magazine.

Most investigations have been descriptive obtaining information through interviews and questionnaires. The majority focused on single fathers themselves and what they report about their parenting and children. Few studies collected data directly from the children (Hanson, 1980, 1981a, 1981b, 1982, 1983, 1984; Santrock and Warshak, 1979; Ambert, 1982).

59

Additionally, some studies went beyond description utilizing more standardized measurements and compared single father families to norms of more traditional family units (Gersick, 1979; Santrock and Warshak, 1979; Hanson & Trilling, 1983). Other investigators compared groups of single custodial fathers such as widowed versus separated/divorced (Grief, 1982, 1983, 1984; Katz, 1979), single fathers with different kinds of custody (Fricke, 1982; Hanson & Trilling, 1983), and custodial and noncustodial fathers to fathers in two-parent families (Gersick, 1979). The time has now come for higher level questions using both qualitative and quantitative designs if social scientists are going to be able to predict events or develop a conceptual/theoretical understanding about this group of parents.

Purpose of the Studies and Variables Identified

The purpose of and variables investigated in the studies presented in Table 1 have changed, and become more sophisticated since 1976 when the first researchers reported their work. Most of these early writers seemed to be interested in finding out, Who are single fathers? and How are they faring as primary caretakers of children? Did the role they assume conflict with that which they learned through socialization during their growing-up years? What were single fathers' problems and successes? Were they able to handle homemaking and child rearing? What was their reason for divorce and did a typology emerge that would expaoin why they assumed custody? As the understanding went from description to relationships, correlational questions were asked. For example, is there a relationship between the background characteristics of single custodial fathers and the interaction they develop with children?

Currently researchers are trying to discern if and why one family unit might be a "healthier place to live" than another. Since sole custody which favors one parent over the other is being set aside for joint custody, it is important to investigate how best to assess and determine how parents can meet the "best interests of the child" imperatives that prevail in family law. Examples of questions that are being asked include: What characteristics of mothers or fathers are most predictive of success with the sex, age and personality of children? How can courts of law best determine or assist parents in arriving at the most beneficial custody arrangement for children? Does divorce mediation help parents focus on meeting the needs of children" How can investigators use standardized instrumentation in measuring and predicting the various issues?

Demographics: Socio-economic Status (SES), Race, Religion, Age of Parent, Employment

Not all studies reported the demographics of their subjects. In the United States, fathers who have custody of their
children are generally better educated, occupy more prestigious
occupational roles, and receive higher income than fathers in
the average two-parent household. For the most part, it has
taken a man with special resources and motivation to obtain
custody through existing legal systems so this finding is not
too surprising. Higher socio-economic status does not seem to
be the rule of thumb in England, Australia and Canada where
single fathers include men in all social and economic strata.

The racial representation varies widely but the majority
of single custodial fathers appear to be Caucasian. This is
consistent with higher SES for white males since most minorities
have traditionally been excluded from higher education, income,
and occupation. This is different in the military, however,
where there is a high percentage of single custodial fathers
many of whom are not Caucasian.

Very little information on the religious practice of
single fathers is available. Hanson (1980) reported a cross-
section of religious preference with the percentage of Catholic,
Protestant, and Jewish fathers proportionate to that of the
general U.S. population. (2)

Single fathers range in age from 30 to 45 years. These
are the traditional child rearing years for most male parents
in this country. Researchers who have compared separated/
divorced versus widowed fathers have generally found the
widowers to be about 5 years older than their separated/divorced
counterparts.

Most fathers remain in the same jobs they had before
becoming single parents. Since many American single fathers
hold higher occupational status, they possess a certain amount
of flexibility in their jobs. Some fathers report changing
positions or changing the hours of their employment in order to
accommodate child care needs. Gasser and Taylor (1976) found
that single fathers reported some curtailment in job-related
travel or upward career mobility because of their more
restricted home circumstances, but this did not present a
psychological problem for most men. It should be noted that the
military has been concerned about the combat readiness of single
fathers in the service, i.e., their ability to leave children
at the spur of the moment for extended periods of time.

Most single fathers work for pay and do not take advantage of the income enhancement programs that are available and used by many single mothers in the same position. This is especially true in America where single custodial fathers do not report taking advantage of welfare, aid to dependent children, food stamps and other assistance programs. This may change as more and more men from lower SES status take on single fatherhood and more men declare their equal rights from government assisted programs. It appears that a higher proportion of Canadian and Australian single fathers do utilize these options.

Family of Origin

Some researchers asked single fathers questions about their upbringing in their families of origin. Several theorists (social learning theory, identification theory, and concepts of intergenerational continuity) have been used in an attempt to explain why these men were willing to take on the non-traditional role of primary parenting.

Mendes (1976a, 1976b) found that single fathers who actively sought custody seemed to identify with and emulate their mothers (and not their fathers) as role models. In a comparative study between fathers with and without custody, Gersick (1979) wrote that fathers with custody described more intense relationships with their mothers but felt distant from their fathers. Additionally, fathers with custody were more likely to have had mothers who were full-time homemakers and they would have chosen their mothers rather than their fathers to live with, if they had had to make such a choice when they were youngsters. Gersick also found that single custodial fathers were not more "feminine" on the Bem Sex Role Scale. Hanson (1980, 1981b) reported that single custodial fathers named their male parent (and not their mothers) as their primary parental model but most of the men felt they were much more emotionally involved with their own young children than their dads had been with them. In other words, they made a conscientious effort to be expressive and physically affectionate with their children. The question still remains. that is, where do single fathers acquire the attitude, knowledge and skills to assume the primary nurturing roles that children need, when men are not socialized for that role?

Homemaking

Although not all single fathers were active in household activities (house cleaning, cooking, laundry, etc.) before becoming single parents, there is evidence that most fathers experience little difficulty in taking on these additional duties (Gasser & Taylor, 1976; Mendes, 1976a, 1976b; Orthner, Brown &

Ferguson, 1976; Victor and Winkler, 1977). In fact, contrary to common assumption, single fathers do not hire out or coerce relatives into taking on these responsibilities for them. A 1982 study reported that single fathers perceived themselves as having more ability with homemaking and parenting skills that the "average" father in a two-parent family (Chang & Deinard, 1982). Most household chores are shared with children, and when problems arise it is in the area of time and energy for meal preparation and housecleaning. Weiss (1979) even states that the additional chores placed on children in single parent homes is positive and helps them to "grow up faster".

Support Networks

There is little doubt that strong social and kinship network systems provide important emotional sustenance to single parent families and promote their healthy adjustment following divorce (Burden, 1979; Metcalf, 1980; Santrock and Warshak, 1979). It is supposed that because of their sheer uniqueness, single fathers elicit more community sympathy and support. It is commonly thought that fathers are supposedly not as active as mothers in community organizations due to differences in ways that males and females are socialized. However, Santrock and Warshak (1979) found that single fathers utilized their professional and community resources as well as their extended families to a high degree. Gasser and Taylor (1976) and Hanson (1980) found that single fathers become especially involved with community agencies for the period of time they were in crisis (pre- and post-divorce), but they relinquished these associations over time. Single fathers appeared to know of other men in their circumstances, but they did not seem to seek their companionship or support. Instead, they turned to single mothers for help and friendship although many men complained of the lack of suitable social and sexual partners.

DeFrain and Eirick (1981) found that single fathers were less likely than single mothers to move from their home and community following divorce. This continuous stability in home environment probably enhances the adjustment of the single-father family. No doubt this phenomenon is due to the more stable job situation most men have following divorce in comparison to women in similar circumstances.

Motivation for custody

Single fathers seek and/or receive custody for a number of reasons, and many researchers discern between two distinct and different motivational origins. Gasser and Taylor (1976), Greene (1977), Hanson (1980), Mendes (1976a, 1976b), and Orthner,

Brown, and Ferguson (1976) utilized a typology differentiating fathers who obtained custody be seeking it (adjudication) and fathers who assented to custody (allocation). One end of the spectrum implies active aggressiveness and the other end implies passiveness and/or resistiveness. In the studies reported, fathers who actively seek custody adjust faster and better to their roles as single parents, perform more adequately as parents, and view themselves as more nurturing parents. However, even though seekers spend more time initially in the parenting role, there is evidence that men who assent to custody also learn or adjust to their roles.

There is good reason for believe that fathers who have been involved in child care since their children's early infancy are more likely to actively seek custody and are better equipped both physically and emotionally to assume the primary care of their children. In the research to date there was little indication that men who seek custody do so to spite their former wives or that men who have custody wish they did not. However, some custodial fathers thought their former spouses were equally fit to be custodial parents, and they, the fathers just happened to have custody at this time.

Chang and Deinard (1982) found that new single fathers sought custody because they considered themselves to be the better parent, because of their love for their children, or because their wives did not want custody. Very few of the subjects in this study reported their former wives to be unfit for parenthood.

Visitation and child support

There is a variety of visitation arrangements with the non-custodial mothers, providing they are available. Some single fathers reported a good relationship between themselves and their former spouses regarding visitation issues, but most fathers reported some of the same problems that single mothers report about the noncustodial parent. That is, she spends too much time with the children, she doesn't spend enough time, she doesn't show up when she is supposed to, the children return upset when they have been with her, I don't like her boyfriend (lifestyle, behavior), the children don't want to see her, or she doesn't contribute anything to their financial welfare. Actually, in one comparative study of single mothers and single fathers, DeFrain and Eirick (1981) reported that single fathers are more likely to say negative things to their children about the non-custodial mother, than single mothers say about the noncustodial father. However, children in father custody homes are in more frequent contact with noncustodial mothers than their counter-parts in mother custody homes (Santrock and Warshak, 1979).

64

There seems to be less of a battle between "you pay child support or you don't see the kids" in single father homes than in single mother homes. This may be primarily due to the fact that few mothers are paying child support. Burden (1979) found 34 percent of noncustodial fathers still paying child support four years after divorce, while Hanson (1980) reported only 10 percent of the noncustodial mothers paying child support. This difference may well be due to the overall discrepancy between men and women's education and salaries in our society. Child support will be an interesting issue to follow with most non-custodial mothers now working, and the recent enforceable child support laws and the pending ERA.

Sex and Age of Children

Reports show that 57 percent of father-only households had custody of boys, whereas 43 percent had girls. In contrast, the division between male and female children was equally with single custodial mothers (U.S. Bureau of the Census, 1980). The higher incidence of male children living with single fathers (Hanson, 1981; Chang and Deinard, 1982; Ambert, 1982) may be a factor in men's decisions to seek custody and in judges' decisions to grant custody. Although single fathers may have custody of both boys and girls of all ages, that arrangement is not typical. Characteristically, single mothers usually have custody of the younger children, both male and female. If fathers have custody it is more likely to be adolescent-aged children. Also, fathers are more prone to have teenage sons living with them since mothers more often retain custody of teenage daughters (Orthner and Lewis, 1979). However, about one-third of single custodial fathers are rearing daughters that range in age from infancy to young adulthood. Men do not appear to have anxiety over raising daughters without their mothers, but the issue of sex education, appropriate clothing, and hair styles become concerns for which fathers seek help (Lynn, 1979).

For years, scholars have been concerned about the effect of parental absence on the sexual and social development of children. Most of the work in this area investigated the effects of father absence on boys. In one of the few studies comparing children from single-mother, single-father and two-parent homes, Santrock and Warshak (1979) investigated the interaction between the sex of the child(ren), the sex of the parents, the type of custody, and the social development of the children. They reported that children of single parents living with the same sex parent were better socially adjusted than children living with opposite sex parents. (3) That is, boys seem to fare better with fathers and girls fare better with mothers. If these findings are substantiated through further research, it may affect custody decisions in the future.

65

Child Care

Single fathers tend to rely on child care resources in the
community. Despite their favorable economic position, these men
do not hire housekeepers. Neither do they rely or depend on
relatives or friends to provide babysitting. Fathers with pre-
school children utilize nursery and day care centres, fathers
with young school-age children paid neighbours to tend the
children after school, and older children (age 10 and above)
were usually left by themselves for short periods of time
following school until the fathers cam home (Lynn, 1979). Since
single custodial fathers are not in frequent communication with
each other, they are not likely to exchange babysitting services.
The lack of high-quality, low cost child care services was a
reported concern of fathers, more so in the United States than
in other English speaking countries.

Father-Child Relationships

The relationship between the father and child is deter-
mined by the quality and quantity of the earlier interactions.
That is, single fathers who interacted frequently and effectively
with children from very early infancy, adjusted more readily to
single parent roles (Orthner and Lewis, 1979; Gasser and Taylor,
1976), felt warmer and more comfortable with their custodial
children (Lynn, 1979), were more likely to have sought custody,
and they felt they were doing a good job (Mendes, 1976a, 1976b;
Greene, 1977; Hanson, 1980, 1981).

One of the common concerns expressed about men serving as
primary custodians to young children is their ability to provide
emotional support and understanding as well as physical and
psychological nurturance. Hanson (1980, 1981) studied the
relationship between single fathers and their children with a
focus on the nurturing quality of their interaction. On four
separate measures, she found that fathers viewed themselves as
affectionate nurturing parents, and children perceived their
fathers as loving and concerned parents. Furthermore, fathers
who sought custody viewed themselves more supportive and
nurturing than men who assented to custody. One of the
interesting findings of this study was that children of single
fathers reported their dads to be more nurturing than children
rating either parent from two-parent families.

Smith and Smith (1981) were concerned about the ability
of single fathers to meet the emotional requirements of children.
They found that single fathers do meet the emotional needs of
children, appropriate to their age and sex. They also discovered
that the problems that single fathers face, could be solved by
the following strategies: (1) earlier preparation of men for
parenthood, (2) more participation by men in household
activities while still married, (3) increased involvement in the

66

early discipline and limit setting of children, and (4) learning to provide more nurturing supportive interaction with women and children early in the family's history.

Finally, in relation to parent-child relationships, Ambert (1982) studied children's behaviour toward their custodial parents in one-parent families. When comparing children's behaviour toward custodial mothers versus custodial fathers, she found that: (1) custodial fathers reported better child behaviour toward them than did custodial mothers, and (2) the children of custodial fathers verbalized their appreciation for their fathers, but children of custodial mothers did so rarely. Hence, single custodial fathers reported more satisfaction with their roles and children appeared to be happier in these households than children in single mother households.

Child Rearing Problems

As reported earlier, single fathers feel successful in their child rearing practices. In one study discussed in a book published in England, The Father Figure (1982), Hipgrave found that single fathers questioned their competence as parents. Bartz and Whitcher (1978), Orthner, Brown and Ferguson (1976), and Hanson (1980) all report that fathers do not feel they have enough time and patience to do everything they would like to with their children. Grief (1982, 1983, 1984) in his national study, found that rarely did fathers report unhappiness about their children or unhappiness at having custody of the children. However, some fathers of teenagers discuss adolescent conflict especially if they have adolescent daughters. Men in Katz's study (1979) report behaviour problems with custodial children. There were so few reports of difficulties with child rearing, that one wonders if men do not have problems as sole parents, or if they prefer not to report them in order to give a positive impression. Data collected directly from children themselves might yield different findings.

Other Problems

In the research reported, fathers were more willing to share their own personal problems than their child rearing problems. The issues varied but some of the more commonly mentioned problems were: (1) role overload (not enough time to work, socialize, parent and keep house), (2) financial problems (having to buy services that were free while married), and (3) loneliness (making decisions by oneself and the lack of social life). Sixty-nine percent of a group of fathers in Katz's study (1979) had to seek help for "personal problems". In the study by Chang and Deinard (1982), fathers reported their difficulties as: restricted chances to date, inability to pursue employment opportunities when they arose, and a

dearth of time and energy. Half of the men from this study
also reported depression and loneliness as well as an increase
in drinking and smoking.

STRENGTHS OF SINGLE CUSTODIAL FATHERS

Throughout this chapter, there has been discussion of the
strengths of single father families. Rather than reiterate them
again, they can be summarized. Single fathers with custody of
children are doing well as primary caregivers. Those who are
doing the best have involved themselves in child care and household tasks before divorce, have actively sought additional
counselling and education prior to or following the divorce, and
have purposefully worked toward a more meaningful interaction
between themselves and their offspring. Many are willing and
able to use the resources that the community has to offer them
and their children and they are not afraid to become joiners and
admit their need to need others. Even if they did not know
how to do housework before divorce, they quickly learn these
skills and involve their children in these activities. For the
most part, these fathers work very hard to fulfill the emotional
and psychological requirements of their children, and from the
few reports available from the children themselves, these ends
are accomplished. Initially, single fathers hope to find a
female companion who will assume the role of surrogate mother
but as time passes they become more confident as well as capable
and the need for a surrogate mother disappears. The relationship
between fathers and children is reported to be tenacious; they
cling to each other. Most dads are happy with their decision to
have sought or agreed to custody and they feel that they were
clearly the better choice of parent. Children report happiness
with this arrangement and there does not appear to be much
yearning to live with the noncustodial parent.

IMPLICATIONS FOR SOCIAL POLICY

There is no organized family policy in the United States as
there is in other European countries (Aldous and Dumond, 1980;
Dempsey, 1981). In fact, there is no clear cut definition that
distinguished between family policy, social policy and public
policy. Zimmerman (1979) wrote that family policy is synonymous
with social policy whereas family policy is everything that the
government does to and for families. Kamerman and Kahn (1978)
differentiated between explicit and implicit family policy.
Explicit family policy are specific programs designed to achieve
specified goals and/or policies which deliberately do things to
and for the family such as day care, child welfare, income
maintenance, etc. Implicit family policy are governmental actions
not specifically or primarily addressed to the family but which
have indirect consequences (e.g., decisions about road-building

68

sites, immigration policy, industrial locations). This author is not debating whether the United States or Canada should have an organized family policy but instead, will attempt to enumerate the various areas in which social policies can or do affect single-custodial fathers.

Custody law and issues

Of all the issues that have ramifications for social policy pertaining to single fathers, marriage and custody laws have been the most debated in recent years. No-fault divorce laws were instigated in the early 1970's with individual states also amending their statues governing the judicial award of child custody (Pearson, Munson and Theonnes, 1981). In 1973, the American Bar Association drafted a proposed Uniform Marriage and Divorce Act whereby the repeal of mother preference for custody began. Instead of the proscribed standards of maternal preference or fault, sex neutral standards, commonly called the "best interests of the child doctrine", were instigated. By 1979, only three states were automatically awarding children to mothers by law (Burden, 1982).

Since it has become easier for men to obtain custody of minor children, more fathers are seeking custody despite the discouragement they are getting from lawyers (Bartz and Witcher, 1978). As stated earlier, in 90 percent of the cases custody is awarded to the mother, 10 percent go to fathers. Eighty percent of all custody decisions are undisputed. Of the 20 percent that are disputed, one-half are won by the father (Burden, 1982). With more fathers petitioning for divorce, custody disputes are also on the increase (Pearson, Munson and Theonnes, 1982).

In 1968, the Uniform Child Custody Jurisdiction Act was enacted to curb child snatching. Prior to this, frustrated fathers deprived of contact with their children, were kidnapping their own offspring at an estimated rate of 25,000 per year. These newer custody laws have curtailed parents from snatching in one state and gaining legal custody in another state, but they have not provided the entire solution to the problem.

The most recently hotly disputed issue pertaining to custody is that of joint custody. In 1980, California enacted a law by which joint legal custody was seen to be in the best interest of the child. Recently an activisit group, the Joint Custody Association, is advocating that joint custody to be of first preference distinct and apart from sole custody. This new law would mandate joint physical as well as joint legal custody to both parents except where a given parent does not want this arrangement or this arrangement is not in the best interest of the child.

69

Professionals from a variety of disciplines support the joint custody movement which is taking place right now. Studies indicate that children who are least adversely affected by divorce are those whose fathers continue to be actively involved (Burden, 1982), and fathers with joint custody continue their involvement with children (Grief, 1978). Joint custody should reverse the menacing recourse by excluded parents to "child steal" and should reduce the incidence of abandonment and loss of financial support which is thought to be due to the lack of meaningful, frequent contact with children (Cook, 1980). These reasons for joint custody don't even address the larger issue of parents equal rights and access to their own children.

The American Bar Association, when writing the Uniform Marriage and Divorce Act, also called for protection of children's rights. Should there be a separate attorney or guardian ad litem appointed to represent the child's best interests when parents are in turmoil and both parents might be equally qualified to parent? How can children be protected in family conflicts when their parents are antagonists? Should the courts listen to input from children of all ages concerning their preference for the parent with which to live?

There are multiple questions and problems pertaining to child custody. Suffice it to say that it appears that mandatory joint custody is likely to become the most common form of custodial arrangement. This will in turn force social and legal agencies into taking action on many other issues that effect single fathers which are discussed below.

Child Support

Child support and visitation are two of the most volatile issues for divorcing couples. Few fathers in the studies reported received child support payments from their former wives. This may be due to the discrepancy between men and women's salaries. Hanson (1980) reported 10 percent of noncustodial mothers paying child support. Burden (1979) reported 34 percent of noncustodial fathers paying child support after four years, while another investigator found that 47 percent of divorced female heads received alimony and child support (Jenkins, 1978). The 1974 Amendments to the Social Security Act created a federal/state child-support enforcement program designed to locate fugitive fathers and assure children of their right to parental support (Jenkins, 1978). Should such a program also be used to seek child support from fugitive but noncustodial working mothers? Should child support be mandated and vigorously enforced for parents of both sexes? If the ERA passes, what are its implications for child support, spousal support (alimony) and adherence to communal property settlement after divorce?

70

Income Support Program

Although single fathers enjoy higher socioeconomic circumstances than single custodial mothers (Burden, 1982; Payton, 1982),
the large majority of single custodial fathers remain on the job
as before divorce with little choice as to whether or not they
want to continue to work outside of the home.   In our society,
it is more acceptable for women with dependent children to make
the choice between child care or outside employment.   Most high
SES men continue with present employment when they obtain custody,
but how many men from the spectrum of social-economic status would
choose to be custodial parents if they had the option of staying
home with the children and drawing on public assistance?   There
is a strong stigma attached to able-bodied men tending house and
caring for children.

There are no income support programs for families in the
U.S. beyond aid to dependent children, welfare and unemployment.
Moreover, today's welfare society has turned child-rearing into
paid employment largely for women and has transformed children
into sole providers for the family.   Not only does there need to be
a major welfare reform with an income maintenance program and
incentives to increase earning through lower taxes for all
people, but this program should apply equally to men and women,
single mothers and single fathers.

Child Care

The problems that single fathers report concerning child
care are not much different than problems that all single and two-
working parent families have in obtaining quality economical care
for their children.   The research to date indicates that single
fathers are not hiring live-in babysitters (as per myth) but
are using the same resources that are available to all parents in
the community.   And these resources in the community have been
under attack for years for their quantity, quality, cost and
evailability.   In contrast to many other governments, the United
States does not see the provision of child care within the
jurisdiction of governmental policy.   In the United States,
efforts have been made since 1971 to pass comprehensive child
care legislation but it has been consistently vetoed or voted
down.   According to Kamerman and Kahn (1981), the United States
has a "do nothing approach".   They advocate that funds for child
care be allocated to parents with financial needs and that low-
cost loans be given to daycare centres for construction and
renovation.   Day care facilities need to be available for
children after school and they need to extend their hours in
order to accommodate working single custodial fathers who have
job requirements into the evening or weekend hours.   Some countries

71

even provide transportation between the school, the day care centre and the child's home. Men may also need some assistance in the establishment of babysitting cooperatives. Actually, economical and quality child care is not just a single father issue; it is the nation's issue.

Family counseling, mediation and conciliation services

The problems that single fathers encounter during the separation and divorce process are not much different from single mothers. Divorce is a time that parental stress has an extremely negative effect on children. The U.S. could benefit by shoring up services provided by family courts early in the divorce process to assist with issues such as custody, visitation, and child support. Mediation and counseling services could help parents separate out their personal struggles from what is in the best interest of the child. Mediation could help avoid custody battles in the courtroom by determining divorce/custody compromises outside the courtroom. Family caseworkers need assistance in what constitutes a systematic evaluation when they are assessing families and making decisions in disputed custody cases. Behavioural scientists need to serve as advisors to the courts as well as conducting clinics for pre- and post-divorce assistance.

If there were one consistent theme reported about single fathers, it was their fierce independence that they can do everything by themselves and they did not need assistance from anyone. This stance coincides with the fact that single fathers were not inclined to seek help or services that might be available. However, single fathers who are granted custody do need support and follow-up for such issues as parenting, personal adjustment and role changes.

Community Program Development

There are a number of community programs that would be of interest and assistance to single custodial fathers. Single parent support groups have become popular with women's groups but there are few such groups for custodial or noncustodial fathers. Father-only as well as mixed single mothers and fathers in self-help groups could be sponsored and funded by local agencies. Special classes could be offered to men who want to learn more about parenting, children's growth and development, and children's emotional lives (Tedder, Libbee, & Scherman, 1981). Single fathers have expressed interest in understanding and helping their pre-teen and teenage daughters in their sexual-social development (Hanson, 1981). Although many men reported social isolation, few were actively seeking each other out.

Classes for information and support would put single fathers in touch with each other and would provide social networks. Single fathers need to be informed of the ongoing programs in the community and this may require active recruitment on the part of professionals working in these areas.

Business and Industry

What is the responsibility of business and industry to single fathers or fathers in general? What are the rules, regulations and policies of businesses and how can they be helpful? Sweden adpted a paternal leave policy for the purpose of encouraging early bonding and participation of men in child care. Should industries in North America do something similar? Hanson's research (1980) showed that single fathers who were doing well as single parents, reported early involvement in the lives of their children, so this appears to be an important issue.

Many kinds of businesses and organizations could incorporate flexitime into their work schedules so that single custodial fathers could adjust their hours according to their families' needs. Dempsey (1981) suggested a written "Family Responsibility Statement" by organizations so that prospective employees could decide if the organization requirements were compatible with their desired family style. It seems as though a family sick leave policy where a parent can stay home with sick children and not use their own sick leave time is also a viable notion. Some companies even provide on-site day care and this needs to be further encouraged.

The banking and housing industry could make some adjustments. There are a number of single fathers who would like to buy homes together and share in the cost benefits and satisfaction that such arrangemens provide. Thus far, under our present loan and ownership policies, this kind of arrangement has been most difficult. There is also recent interest in multiple family dwellings built specifically for single parent families, where families can share common core facilities but maintain their privacy.

As a working parent, have you ever tried to bank or take care of a problem with your utilities in the evening. Many businesses in smaller towns aren't even open on the weekends. Society is still geared to the traditional nuclear family where the nonworking mother can take care of family business during the day. Undoubtedly, businesses need to review their policies to make sure that they are not discriminatory in preference for men or women and that equal opportunities exist for people of both sexes as well as all marital statuses.

73

School System

In recent study it was found that children in single-parent families do poorly in school and despite the fact that the study design and interpretation were scewed, this article received a considerable notoriety (NAESP, 1980; Nuta, 1981). Both the public and private schools need to be continually vigilant about the negative image they project toward children in single-parent families. Teachers need to make sure that these children are not singled out as "trouble children" perpetuating and reinforcing the old stereotypes.

Parenting classes should be required of all children graduating from high school. Although the majority of people become parents, there is little or no education provided to assist people in this endeavour. This is especially true for men. With ten percent of all men becoming the primary parents in single-custodial homes, and with the likelihood of this number increasing, eduction for parenthood will become even more important.

Health Care System

Although only one study was found on the health or health seeking behaviours of single fathers (Hanson & Trilling, 1983), their problems are probably no different than other families with similar socioeconomic resources. Single custodial fathers like all other citizens could benefit by a quality health care system that is available to all people despite their financial means. Additionally, health care services are not readily available for working parents, unless they take time out during the work day. Not only does this require a half-day's time for a simple doctor's appointment, but this is very costly. Free or inexpensive clinics could be established and opened during hours when single parents with children could get there and this is usually in the evenings or on the weekends. Additionally, a focus on preventive health care should be encouraged by our insurance industry. Many people take their children into costly emergency rooms because their insurance policies won't pay for ordinary doctors' office visits.

The critical point in relationship to health and single fatherhood, is the need for a large scale federal or state health program for families of all means, which would give fathers and their children equal access to their right to health care.

Cultural Message

Society needs to reexamine the way it socializes males. There needs to be more study and discussion by people of both sexes and all ages about changing roles of men. Professionals could help men change the macho image and help people strive for alternative images and expectations. This is easier said than done, of course, but men could support each other in this endeavour and lend assistance to men who are pursuing nurturing roles (e.g., fathering nursing, teachers of children). Quite frankly, women do not always allow men room for change and often reinforce and want the traditional behaviours to continue. Times are changing as Robert Lewis' book, Changing Roles for Men (1981) indicates, but the movement is slow.

DIRECTIONS FOR RESEARCH

Most of the research on single custodial fathers has been carried out in the past ten years. Even though there is fairly good empirical data about common themes, not surprisingly the research has raised more questions than it has answered.

In regards to methodology, there is a need to move beyond descriptive study toward more sophisticated research designs such as comparative, correlational, quasi-experimental and experimental studies or a combination of these methods. Future studies should incorporate conceptual and theoretical frameworks which lead to theory testing and theory building. Collaborative research endeavours between researchers of different disciplines should be encouraged. Longitudinal studies of fathers and children during the process of divorce adjustment would be of inestimable value.

There are multiple issues that could be explored, but some suggestions include the following (also see Hanson & Bozett, 1984).

1. Only successful single fathers appear in studies. Who are the "unsuccessful" single fathers and why did they fail?

2. What are the long-term effects of joint custody on children and on mothers and fathers alike?

3. Does an early attachment and bonding of fathers and children result in an increase in the quality of fathering or single fathering (custodial or noncustodial) during later years?

4.   What are the effects of mother-absence on children living with single fathers?

5.   What about the children who live with single fathers? More data needs to be collected from children directly instead of from the father.

6.   Do the different kinds of father-only homes differ from one another? For example, are there differences between widowed, separated/divorced and adoptive fathers?

CONCLUSIONS

The purpose of this chapter has been to synthesize current empirical knowledge about single custodial fathers and their children. Although it is admittedly risky, speculations can be made about the future.

Demographers prophesy that by 1990 approximately one out of every two American children will live in a single parent home before they are 18 years of age (Glick, 1979; Masnick and Bane, 1980). With the increasing divorce rates, the continuing trend of women working outside the home (60% in the United States in 1984), the increased acceptance of men in nurturing roles, and the demonstrated viability of single parent homes, there will be many more single fathers with custody in the future. Current trends indicate there will be an increase in male-only headed households resulting from separation/divorce, female mortality, male adoption and custody by never-married biological fathers.

Additionally, more fathers will not only continue to receive sole custody, but joint custody options will allow more men to remain active in child rearing post divorce. The courts have started to award split custody, allocating siblings to parents according to need and desire - a decision that was previously unthinkable. In the past, single custodial fathers were priviledged in education, income and occupation but increasingly lower and middle class fathers are starting to join the ranks of this variety of family structure.

Hopefully, single custodial fathers will not have to struggle so hard in the future to achieve custody. More judges, lawyers and former spouses will probably be willing to consider men as the primary nurturing parent with whom the children live the majority of the time. Too, working mothers, as they earn more money, will help provide more child support.

Times are changing and so are families. The families who have a single custodial father are here to stay and represent an acceptable and viable option for family life today.

FOOTNOTES

[1] The manuscripts include the major American work as well as one Australian and English study. See the bibliography for other significant works.

[2] According to the U.S. Bureau of the Census (1982a) Protestants make up 54 percent of the American population, Roman Catholic 37 percent and 4 percent of the population is Jewish.

[3] It should be noted that the type of parenting style and the amount of contact with additional adult caretakers was also associated with the positive social behaviours shown by these children.

BIBLIOGRAPHY

Abarbanel, A. Shared parenting after separation and divorce.
    American Journal of Orthopsychiatry, 1979, 49, 320-329.

Albin, R. New looks at single parenting: Focus on fathers.
    American Psychological Association Monitor, 1977, 8, 7-8.

Aldous, J. and Dumond, W. The Politics and Programs of Family
    Policy. Notre Dame, Indiana: University of Notre Dame
    Press, 1980.

Ambert, Anne-Marie. Differences in children's behaviour
    toward custodial mothers and custodial fathers. Journal
    of Marriage and the Family, 1982, 44, 73-86.

Appleton, William S. Fathers and daughters. Garden City, New
    York: Doubleday and Company, Inc., 1981.

Atkin, E. and Rubin, E. Part-time father: A guide for the
    divorced father. New York: The Vanguard Press, Inc., 1976.

Bain, C. Lone fathers: An unnoticed group. Australian Social
    Welfare, 1973, 3, 14-17.

Bane, M.J. Marital disruption and the lives of children.
    Journal of Social Issues, 1976, 32, 103-117.

Bartz, K.W. and Witcher, W.C. When father gets custody.
    Children Today, 1978, 7, 2-6.

Benson, Leonard. Fatherhood: A sociological perspective. New
    York: Random House, 1968.

Biller, H.B. Paternal Deprivation: Family, School, Sexuality
    and Society. Lexington, MA: D.C. Heath and Company, 1974.

Bird, R. Life with father. Parents Without Partners. 1975,
    18, (Jan-Feb), 18-20.

Bittman, Sam and Rosenberg, Sue. Expectant Fathers. New York:
    Ballantine Books, 1978.

Blechman, E. Are children with one parent at psychological risk?
    A methodological review. Journal of Marriage and the
    Family, 1982, 44, 179-195.

Boss, Pauline G. (Ed.) The father's role in family systems:
An annotated bibliography. Madison, WI: University of
Wisconsin, June 1979.

Bradley, Robert A. Husband-coached childbirth. New York:
Harper and Row Publishers, 1981.

Brandwein, R.A., Brown, C.A., and Fox, E.M. Women and
children last: The social situation of divorced mothers
and their families. Journal of Marriage and the
Family, 1974, 36, 498-514.

Burden, D. Parental custody after divorce. Unpublished
manuscript, 1982, (The Florence Heller Graduate School
for Advanced Studies in Social Welfare, Brandeis
University, Waltham, Mass.).

Burden, D. The single parent family: Social policy issues.
Paper presented at the annual meeting of the American
Sociological Association, Boston, August 27-31, 1979.

Burgess-Kohn, J. The fathers adjustment as a single parent.
Unpublished manuscript, 1976 (Department of Sociology,
University of Wisconsin, Waukesha, Wisconsin).

Cath, S.H., Gurwitt, A.R., and Ross, J.M. (Eds.), Father
and child: Developmental and clinical perspectives.
Boston: Little, Brown and Company, 1982.

Chang, P. and Deinard, A. Single father caretakers:
Demographic characteristics and adjustment process.
American Journal of Orthopsychiatry, 1982, 52, 236-243.

Colman, Arthur and Colman, Libby. Earth father, sky father.
Englewood Cliffs, NJ: Prentice-Hall, 1981.

Cook, J.A. Joint custody, sole custody: A new statute
reflects a new perspective. Conciliation Courts Review,
1980, 18, 1-14.

Daley, Eliot. Father feelings. New York: Pocket Books, 1977.

Defrain, J. and Eirick, R. Coping as divorced parents; A
comparative study of fathers and mothers. Family
Relations, 1981, 30, 265-274.

Dempsey, J.J. The Family and Public Policy. Baltimore, MD:
Paul H. Brookes Publishing Co., 1981.

Dodson, Fitzhugh. How to father. New York: Signet Books,
1975.

Douville, S. Children's rights - what children? What rights?
     Single Parent, 14, 15-19.

Espenshade, T.J. The economic cons quences of divorce. The
     Journal of Marriage and the Family, 1979, 41, 615-627.

Field, T. Interaction behaviors of primary versus secondary
     caretaker fathers. Developmental Psychology, 1978, 14,
     183-184.

Fricke, J.M. Coping as divorced fathers and mothers: A
     nationwide study of sole, joint, and split custody.
     Unpublished masters thesis, University of Nebraska,
     1982.

Gasser, R.D., and Taylor, C.M. Role adjustment of single
     fathers with dependent children. The Family Coordinator,
     1976, 25, 397-401.

Gatley, R.H., and Koulack, D. Single father's handbook: A
     guide for separated and divorced fathers. Garden City,
     New York: Anchor Books, 1979.

George, V. and Wilding, P. Motherless families. London:
     Routledge and Kegan Paul, 1972.

Gersick, K.E. Fathers by choice: Divorced men who receive
     custody of their children. In George Levinger and
     Oliver Noles (Eds.), Separation and Divorce. New York:
     Basic Books, Inc., 1979.

Glick, P. A demographer looks at American families. Journal
     of Marriage and the Family, 1975, 37, 15-26.

Glick, Paul C. The new nuclear family. Paper presented at the
     1978 Groves Conferences on Marriage and the Family.
     Washington, D.C., April 27-30, 1978.

Glick, P. Children of divorced parents in demographic perspec-
     tive. Journal of Social Issues, 1979, 35, 170-182.

Goldstein, J., Freud, A., and Solnit, Albert J. Beyond the best
     interests of the child. New York: The Free Press, 1973.

Goldstein, J., Freud, A., and Solnit, Albert J. Before the best
     interests of the child. New York: The Free Press, 1979.

Grad, Rae and others. The father book: Pregnancy and beyond.
     Washington, D.C.: Acropolis Books, Ltd., 1981.

Grady, Kathleen E., Brannon, Robert, & Pleck, Joseph H. The male sex role: A selected and annotated bibliography. Washington, D.C.: U.S. Department of Health, Education, and Welfare, 1979. (Superindendent of Documents, DHEW No. 79-790).

Green, Maureen. Fathering. St. Louis: McGraw-Hill, 1977.

Greene, R.S. Atypical parenting: Custodial single fathers. Unpublished doctoral dissertation, University of Maryland, 1977.

Gresh, Sean. Becoming a father. New York: Butterick Publishing, 1980.

Grief, Geoffrey L. Dads raising kids. Single Parent, 1982, 25, 19-23.

Grief, Geoffrey L. Widowers. Single Parent, 1983, 16 (7), 29-32.

Grief, Geoffrey L. Custodial dads and their ex-wives. The Single Parent. 1984, 17 (1), 17-20.

Grief, J.B. Fathers, children and joint custody. American Journal of Orthopsychiatry, 1979, 49, 311-319.

Halverson, L. The joint custody alternative. Washington State Bar News, 1982, March, 12-17.

Hamilton, Marshall L. Father's influence on children. Chicago: Nelson-Hall, 1977.

Hanson, S.M.H. Characteristics of single custodial fathers and the parent-child relationship. (Doctoral dissertation, University of Washington, 1979). Dissertation Abstracts Index, 1980, 40, 6438-A.

Hanson, S.M.H. Single custodial fathers. Paper presented at the annual meeting of the National Council on Family Relations, Milwaukee, WI, October, 1981.

Hanson, S.M.H. Single custodial fathers and the parent-child relationship. Nursing Research, 1981, 30, 202-204.

Hanson, S.M.H. Variations of fathering: Implications for social policy. Paper presented at the annual meeting of the National Council on Family Relations, Washington, D.C., October 1982.

Hanson, Shirley M.H. and Trilling, Jo. A Proposed Study of the Characteristics of the healthy single parent family. Family Perspectives, Spring, 1983. 17 (2), 79-88.

Hanson, Shirley. Father-Child relationships: Beyond Kramer Vs. Kramer. Marriage and Family Review. For special issue on "Men's changing roles in the family. In process.

Hanson, Shirley and Bozett, Frederick. Dimensions of Fathering. Boston: Auburn House (Book in Process).

Hanson, Shirley M.H. Parent-Child relationships in single father families. In Robert Lewis & Bob Salt's Men in Families. Beverly Hills: Sage Publications, in process.

Herzog, E. and Sudia, C.E. Boys in Fatherless families. Washington, D.C.: U.S. Government Printing Office, 1971.

Hetherington, E.M., Cox, M., and Cox, R. The aftermath of divorce. In J.H. Stevens, Jr. and Marilyn Matthews (Eds.), Mother-Child, Father-Child Relations. Washingtin, D.C.: NAEYC, 1977.

Hetherington, E.M., Cox, M. and Cox, R. Divorced fathers. The Family Coordinator, 1976, 25, 417-428.

Hetherington, E.M., Cox, M., and Cox, R. Divorced fathers. Psychology Today, April 1977, 42, 45-46.

Hetherington, E.M. The effects of father absence on child development. Young Children, 1971, 27, 233-248.

Hipgrave, Tony. (1982). Lone fatherhood: A problematic status. In McKee and O'Brien The Father Figure. London: Tavistock Publications.

Jenkins, S. Children of Divorce. Children Today, 1978, 7 (2), 16-21.

Kahan, Stuart. The expectant father's survival kit. New York: Monarch, 1978.

Kamerman, S., and Kahn, A. (Eds.) Child care, family benefits, and working parents. New York: Columbia University Press, 1981.

Kamerman, S., and Kahn, A. (Eds.) Family policy: Government and families in fourteen countries. New York: Columbia University Press, 1978.

Katz, A.J. Lone fathers: Perspectives and implications for family policy. The Family Coordinator, 1979, 28, 521-527.

Kelly, J. and Wallerstein, J. The effects of parental divorce: Experiences of the child in early latency. American Journal of Orthopsychiatry, 1976, 46, 20-32.

Kelly, J. Myths and realities for children of divorce. Educational Horizons, 1980, 59, 34-39.

Keshet, H.F. and Rosenthal, K.M. Single-parent fathers: A new study. Children Today, 1978, 7, 13-17.

Keshet, H.F. and Rosenthal, K.M. Fathering after marital separation. Social Work, 1978, 23, 11-18.

Kohn, J.B. and Kohn, W.K. The widower. Boston: Beacon Press, 1978.

Lamb, M.E. (Ed.) The role of the father in child development. New York: John Wiley and Sons, Inc., 1981.

Lamb, M.E. (Ed.) Nontraditional families: Parenting and child development. Hillsdale, NJ: Lawrence Eribaum Associates, Publishers, 1982.

Lamb, M. and Bronson, S.K. Fathers in the context of family influences: Past, present and future. School Psychology Review, 1980, 9, 336-353.

Lamb, M.E. and Sagi, Ahraham. (Eds.) Fatherhood and family policy. Hillsdale, NJ: Lawrence Eribaum Associates, Publishers, 1983.

Levine, J.A. Who Will Raise the Children? New York: Bantam Books, Inc., 1976.

Lewis, K. Single-father families: Who they are and how they fare. Child Welfare, 1978, 57, 643-651.

Lewis, K. Single father families. Ubpublished paper, New Haven, CT: Single Fathers Research Project, P.O. Box 3300, 1978.

Lewis, R.A. Men in difficult times. Englewood Cliffs, New Jersey: Prentice Hall, 1981.

Lockerbie, D. Bruce. Fatherlove. Garden City, NY: Doubleday and Company, 1981.

Loge, B.J. Role adjustments to single parenthood: A study of divorced and widowed men and women. Unpublished doctoral dissertation, University of Washington, 1976.

Lynn, D.B. Daughters and parents: Past, present, and future. Monterey, CA: Brooks/Cole Publishing Company, 1979.

McDonald, G. and Nye, F.I. Family policy. Minneapolis: National Council of Family Relations, 1979.

McFadden, M. Bachelor fatherhood: How to raise and enjoy your children as a single parent. New York: Charter Communications, 1974.

McKee, Lorna & O'Brien, Margaret. The father figure. London: Tavistock Publications, 1982.

Marriage and Divorce Today Editorial. Majority of absent fathers don't pay support. Marriage and Divorce Today, 1983, 8 (47), 1.

Masnick, G. and Bane, M.J. The nation's families: 1960-1990. Boston, MA: Auburn House, 1980.

Mendes, H.A. Parental experiences of single fathers. Unpublished doctoral dissertation, University of California (LA), 1975.

Mendes, H.A. Single fathers. The Family Coordinator, 1976, 25, 439-444.

Metcalf, A. Social networks in families headed by a single working mother. Unpublished manuscript, 1980, (School of Social Work, University of Washington, Seattle, Washington).

Mitchell, M., Redican, W.K., Gomber, J. Males can raise babies. Psychology Today, 1974, 8, 63-68.

National Association of Elementary School Principles (NAESP). One parent families and their children: The school's most significant minority. Principal, 1980, 60, 31-42.

Nuta, V.R. Single parent children in school - What can you expect? Single Parent, 1981, 14, 21-25.

Orthner, D., Brown, T. and Ferguson, D. Single-parent fatherhood: An emerging family life style. The Family Coordinator, 1976, 25, 429-437.

Orthner, D. and Lewis, K. Evidence of single father competence in child rearing. Family Law Quarterly, 1979, 8, 27-48.

Parke, Ross D. Fathers. Cambridge, MA: Harvard University Press, 1981.

Payton, Isabelle S. Single-parent households: An alternative approach. Family Economics Review. 1982, Winter.

Pearson, J., Munson, P., and Thoennes, N. Legal Change and
child custody awards. Journal of Family Issues, 1982, 3,
5-24.

Pedersen, Frank A. The father-infant relationship. New York:
Praeger Publishers, 1980.

Phillips, Celeste R. and Anzalone, Joseph T. Fathering:
Participation in labor and birth. St. Louis: The
C.V. Mosby Company, 1982.

Ploscowe, M. Who gets the children. In Ruth Cavan (Ed.),
Marriage and family in the modern world. New York:
Thomas Crowell Company, 1961.

Pruzan, M. A study of single-parent fathers. Unpublished
masters thesis, University of Washington, 1973.

Ricci, I. Mom's house, dad's house: Making shared custody
work. New York: Macmillan Publishing Company, 1980.

Richmond-Abbott, M. Sex roles in single-parent families.
Unpublished manuscript, 1980, (Eastern Michigan
University, Ypsilanti, Michigan).

Roman, M. and Haddad, W. The disposable parent: The case for
joint custody. New York: Holt, Rinehard and Winston,
1978.

Rosenthal, K.M. and Keshet, H.F. Fathers without partners:
A study of fathers and the family after marital
separation. Totowa, NJ: Rowman and Littlefield, 1981.

Rosenthal, K. and Keshet, H. The impact of childcare
responsibilities on part-time or single fathers.
Alternative Lifestyles, 1978, 1, 465-491.

Rypma, C. Biological bases of the paternal response. The
Family Coordinator, 1976, 25, 335 339.

Santrock, J.W. and Warshak, R. Father custody and social
development in boys and girls. The Journal of Social
Issues, 1979, 35, 112-125.

Santrock, J.W., Warshak, R.A., and Elliot, G.L. Social
development and parent-child interaction in father-
custody and stepmother families. In Michael E. Lamb (Ed.),
Nontraditional families: Parenting and child development.
Hillsdale, NJ: Lwarence Eribaum Associates, Publishers,
1982.

Schlesinger, B. One-parent families in Canada. Toronto:
University of Toronto, 1974.

Schlesinger, B. One parent families in Great Britain. The
Family Coordinator, 1977, 26, 139-141.

Schlesinger, B. The one-parent family: Perspectives and annotated
bibliography. Toronto, Canada: University of Toronto
Press, 1978.

Schlesinger, B. Single parent: A research review. Children Today,
May-June, 1978, 7, 12-19, 37 39.

Schlesinger, B. and Todres, R. Motherless families: An increasing
societal pattern. Child Welfare, 1976, 55, 553-558.

Schorr, A. and Moen, P. The single parent and public policy. In
Arlene Skolnick and Jerome Skolnick's, Family in transition.
Boston: Little, Brown and Company, 1980.

Schorr, A. and Moen, P. The single parent and public policy.
Social Policy, 1979, 9, 15-21.

Seagull, A.A., and Seagull, E.A.W. The non-custodial father's
relationship to his child: Conflicts and solutions.
Journal of Clinical Child Psychology, 1977, 1, 11-15.

Shepard, M.A. and Goldman, G. Divorced dads. New York: Berkley
Books, 1979.

Sifford, Darrell. Father and son. Philadelphia: Bridgebooks, 1982.

Silver, G.A. and Silver, M. Weekend fathers. Los Angeles: Strat-
ford Press, 1981.

Smith, M.J. The social consequences of single parenthood: A
longitudinal perspective. Family Relations, 1980, 29,
75-81.

Smith, R.M. Single-parent fathers: An application of role
transition theory. Paper presented at the annual meeting
of the National Council on Family Relations, Philadelphia,
October 1978.

Smith, R.M. and Smith, C.W. Child rearing and single-parent
fathers. Family Relations, 1981, 30, 411-417.

Steinberg, Davis, Father journal. Albion, CA: Times Change
Press, 1977.

Stevens, Joseph H. and Mathews, Marilyn (Eds.) Mother/child father/child relationships. Washington, D.C.: The National Association for the Education of Young Children, 1978.

Sullivan, S. Adams. The father's almanac. Garden City, NY: Doubleday and Company, 1980.

Tedder, S.S., Libbee, K.M., & Scherman, A. A community support group single custodial fathers. Personal and Guidance Journal. October, 1981, 60 (2), 115-119.

Thompson, Edward H. and Gongla, Patricia A. Single-parent families: in the mainstream of American society. In Eleanor D. Macklin and Roger H. Rubin's Contemporary Families and Alternative Lifestyles. Beverly Hills, CA: Sage Publications, 1983.

Thornton, Jeannye. When fathers raise children alone. U.S. News & World Report. April 12, 1982, 61-62.

Todres, R. Runaway wives: An increasing North-American phenomenon. The Family Coordinator, 1978, 27, 17-21.

U.S. Bureau of the Census, Current Population Reports, Series P-20, No. 365. Marital status and living arrangements: March 1980, U.S. Government Printing Office, Washington, D.C., 1980.

U.S. Bureau of the Census. Current Population Reports, P-23, No. 106. Child support and alimony: 1978. Washington, D.C.: U.S. Government Printing Office, 1980.

U.S. Bureau of the Census. Statistical Abstract of the United States: 1982-3. (103rd ed.) Washington, D.C.: U.S. Government Printing Office, 1982.

U.S. Bureau of the Census, Current Population Reports, Series P-20, No. 371, Household and family characteristics: March, 1981. Washington, D.C.: U.S. Government Printing Office, 1982.

U.S. Bureau of the Census, Current Population Reports, Series P-20, No. 372, Marital Status and Living Arrangements: March 1981. Washington, D.C.: U.S. Government Printing Office, 1982.

U.S. Bureau of the Census, Current Population Reports, Series P-20, No. 382. Households, families marital status and living arrangements: March, 1983. Washington, D.C.: U.S. Government Printing Office, July 1983.

Victor, I., & Winkler, W.A. Fathers and custody. New York: Hawthorn Books, Inc., 1977.

Wallerstein, J. and Kelly, J. California's children of divorce. Psychology Today, 1980, 13 (8), 57-65.

Wallerstein, J. and Kelly, J. Divorce and children. In J.D. Noshpitz (Ed.), Basic handbook of child psychiatry, New York: Basic Books, 1979.

Wallerstein, J. and Kelly, J. The effects of parental divorce: Experiences of the child in later latency. American Journal of Orthopsychiatry, 1976, 46, 256-269.

Wallerstein, J. and Kelly, J. The effects of parental divorce: Experiences of the preschool child. Journal of American Academy of Child Psychiatry, 1975, 14, 600-616.

Wallerstein, J. and Kelly, J. Surviving the Breakup. New York: Basic Books, 1980.

Washington Chapter of U.S. Divorce Reform. What you always wanted to know about divorce but were afraid to ask: A guide to divorce for the man (or woman) seeking child custody in a divorce or who wishes to have a joint custody arrangement. P.O. Box 11, Auburn, Washington, 1978.

Weiss, Robert S. (1979). Growing up a little faster: The experience of growing up in a single parent household. Journal of Social Sciences, 35 (4), 97-111.

Woody, R.H. (1978). Fathers with child custody. Counseling Psychologists, 7, 60-63.

Yablonsky, Lewis. (1982). Fathers and sons. New York: Simon and Schuster.

Zimmerman, S.L. (1979). Policy, social policy, and family policy: Concepts, concerns and analytic tools. Journal of Marriage and the Family, 41, 487-497.

TABLE 1. STUDIES ON SINGLE PARENT FATHERS, 1976 - PRESENT

Author(s), Year	Gasser & Taylor, 1976	Mendes, 1976	Orthner, Brown & Ferguson, 1976	Bartz & Witcher, 1978
Subjects	40 divorced, widowed, Columbus, Ohio	32 separated, divorced & widowed, Los Angeles, California	20 divorced, widowed, never married, Greensboro, North Carolina	34 divorced, Kansas City, Iowa
Methodology	Questionnaire	Interview	Interview	Interview
Variables/Purpose	Role conflict, role adjustment, household activities, society attitude toward single fathers	Nature of psychological social adjustment; child supervision, home-making, child emotional needs, rearing girls	Fathers lifestyle, problems successes	Learn about single families' adjustment, problems, pleasures
SES		43% - Middle 15-46% - Working	60% - Professional 25% - Blue collar 80% - Post high school ed. Mean = $18,000	82% higher SES
Race		43% - Black 46% - White		
Religion				
Age		Age - most 30 to 44 yrs.	Mean = 37 years	Younger than late 30's
Employment	50% pursuing job possibilities & problems	Job and family synchronization		↑ occupational adjustments; ↑ flexible jobs
Family of Origin	Involved in child care before divorce			66% - more involved in child care than pre-divorce
Homemaking Skills	Involved prior to divorce	87% - home management by self		No problem, share cooking, cleaning, shopping, dishes with kids

	Gasser & Taylor, 1976	Mendes, 1976	Orthner, Brown & Ferguson, 1976	Bartz & Witcher, 1978
Motivation for Custody			Wives didn't want or couldn't care for kids	Custody < 3 yrs. Majority via spousal allocation
Visitation/Child Support			Rare child support	5% - child support from mother
Support Networks	Divorced men: New friends, singles groups Widowed men: Old friends	Lack of help from kin for children	33% - public assistance 50% - singles groups 66% - family support	Friends & neighbors helpful; sought single friends; not cohabitating
Age & Sex of Children		Majority 6-9 years; Range 3-17 yrs. 62% - rearing girls	50% - preschool 50% - school age Mean < 2.0 children	Mean - 2 children 50% - male, 50% - female Range 18 m - 17 yrs. 44% - under 6 years
Child Care	Father himself	School age - unsupervised; Preschool - daycare	Day care, nursery schools	Preschool-daycare; private; neighbors; cost a problem
Father/Child Relationships	Share household activities	↑ affect with preadolescent children	Good parent/child relationship; demand more child independence	Father report: ↑ father/child increase in affection, changed parental style
Childrearing Problems		Some conflict with teens; female sexuality; ↓ female role model	Sex education for adolescent girls; time and patience; gone from home too much	↓ time and patience; emotional adjustment; school unsure of single parent family
Problems	50% - dating	Coordinate house tasks, job and child care; emotional needs of kids;	Making decisions alone; expect children too independent; two parents better than one	Time for everything; children's initial adjustment; financial adjustment
Strengths	70% - more active in organizations, homemaking skills		Active social life; happy with being single more child oriented; pride in coping.	80% - active sex life; child responsible; single father's a hero; children - good adjustment

Author(s), Year	Gasser & Taylor, 1976	Mendes, 1976	Orthner, Brown & Ferguson, 1976	Bartz & Witcher, 1978
Future Study				Adjustment of children; fathers who do not suceed; objective evaluation of father
Implications	Divorced better adjusted than widowed	Family life curriculum on on single parent teach homemaking, budgeting, marketing, child development, support group for fathers only	Day care hours; babysitting coops; classes on parenting; Big Sisters	Better child care
Future	Fathers' role adjustment better in future; more models to emulate	↑ single parent fathers custodial and non-custodial men in child care	New social policy	If roles more shared, less adjustment required

Author(s), Year	Gersick, 1979	Katz, 1979	Hanson, 1980, 1981, 1982, 1983, 1984	Keshet & Rosenthal, 1981
Subjects	40 - divorced, 20 with custody and 20 without custody Massachusetts	409 divorced & widowed, Australia	37 divorced Seattle, Washington	128 separated, divorced Boston, Massachusetts Divorced, custodial & non-custodial
Methodology	Interview	Questionnaire Interview subset	Interview, questionnaire Standardized instruments	Interview, questionnaire
Variables/Purpose	Factors related to custody: demographic, family of origin, child rearing, sex role orientation; marriage dissolution	Define problems of single families and suggest social policy	Characteristics of single fathers & parent/child relationships: SES, history, custody, nurturance/support	Relationship between father & child; effect of relationship on lifestyle and growth of personal men and children
SES	Above normal family	24% = trademen 15% = laborers 13% = professional Mean = $6,356 Mean education = 10 yrs.	Ed. mean = 15 years; 75% = professional or business Mean income = $23,500	College educated, professional or semi-professional; ↑ income
Race	Caucasian		92% = Caucasian	Caucasian
Religion	48% = Catholic		38% = Protestant 16% = Catholic 43% = Other	
Age	Median age - 38 years Custodial fathers older & better established than non-custodial	62% = 30-49 years	Mean = 42 years Range = 31-54 years	
Employment		89% - employed 51% - work less hours since divorce	95% - employed restraints on job prospects	
Family of Origin	Single fathers middle or last born child; 22% - parents divorced, closer relationships with mother		Prior parent relationships not significant; 22% parents divorced	
Homemaking Skills		75% - no problem	No problem	90% - performed household task with no problems

Author(s), Year	Gersick, 1979	Katz, 1979	Hanson, 1980, 1981, 1982, 1983, 1984	Keshet & Rosenthal, 1981
Motivation for Custody	Cause of divorce: Incompatibility, incapacitated wife, provisional marriage, wife unfaithful	Multiple causes for divorce & custody	53% - seeking 46% - asserters 65% - sole custody 11% - joint custody	
Visitation/Child Support			10% receive child support; problems with visitation	
Support Networks		New male & female friends, decreased old friends; 70% help from multiple sources	Single mothers, friends, family	Single mothers
Age & Sex of Children		Mean - 2.8 children 71% children 7-18 yrs. 54% male	Mean = 15 years; Mean - 2 children 66% male	
Child Care		36% - not in school 22% need help	After school care	Day care, babysitter
Father/Child Relationships	Participation in child care pre-divorce varied	80% - more time with children since divorce	Fathers & children rated nurturing and support increased past-divorce	Enjoy recreation with children
Child rearing Problems		37% - difficulty with children	Time/energy	Guidance, nurturance of children; meet emotional needs
Problems	Money; childcare; visitation; social life	26% - financial help; 46% - household help; 42% - role overload, lonely; 37% - not coping well; 47% - school doesn't understand	Custody & visitation issues; support from other single fathers	Time constraints; role strain; social opportunity
Strengths	None regretted new role; normal male sex role orientation	70% - sought help	Feel good about self	Positive self-esteem; grow emotionally; 75% closer to children now

Author(s), Year	Gersick, 1979	Katz, 1979	Hanson, 1980, 1981, 1982, 1983, 1984	Keshet & Rosenthal, 1981
Future study		Larger samples; study problems and successes	Study younger children; compare male/female children; compare single females to single males; compare divorced to widowed; study healthy single parent families	
Implications	Better legal system	Income support beyond unemployment for single families; intervention with children; policy initiatives and interventions to support single fathers	Group support for fathers; cooperative parenting pursued; teach parenting to males; encourage joint custody	Information re counseing
Future		Increase in single fathers	Increased number of single parents; increased number of joint custody	

	Chang & Deinard, 1982	Grief, 1982, 1983, 1984)	McKee & O'Brien, 1982
Author(s), Year	Chang & Deinard, 1982	Grief, 1982, 1983, 1984)	McKee & O'Brien, 1982
Subjects	80 divorced Minneapolis, Minnesota	1,100 Across U.S. and Canada	59 separated & divorced London, England
Methodology	Questionnaire	Questionnaire	Interview
Variables/Purpose	Reason for divorce; past & present roles; problems; assistance needed	Who are single fathers; how managing; suggestions to other single fathers	Men's entry into lone fatherhood
SES	67% - post high school education 46% - $20,000 52% - professional	Mean = $30,000	44% - middle class 56% - working class
Race	90% - White 1% - Black 9% - Other		
Religion			
Age	Mean = 35 years	Mean = 40 years	75% - 30-44 years
Employment	91% employed; decrease in employment flexibility post divorce	All areas	
Family of Origin	↑ domesticity & parenting before divorce		
Homemaking Skills	"Better than average father"	Little prior experience; no problem now	
Motivation for Custody	80% uncontested custody; Cause of divorce: incompatibility, wife change lifestyle. Sought custody: better parent, love for kids	Custody for 4 years; custody decision mutual agreement with wife; 16% custody battle; custody arrangement per child/father wishes	Majority of wives wanted divorce; Routes into single fatherhood: conciliatory negotiations, hostile seekers; passive acceptors
Visitation/Child Support		24% - mothers visit once/week; 22% - visit every other week; 14% - once a month	

Author(s), Year	Chang & Deinard, 1982	Grief, 1982, 1983, 1984	McKee & O'Brien, 1982
Support Networks			
Age and Sex of Children	More boys (p < .005)		35% one child; 40% two children
Child Care			
Father-Child Relationships		Satisfaction with father/child relationship; fathers rated themselves high	
Childrearing Problems		Minority didn't want custody	Parental competence
Problems	Adjustment: time for children & social life; lack of employment flexibility; child care; initial with job; daycare; daughers; interfere depression, anxiety, loneliness	Adjust to single life; reestablish social life; care of adolescent girls	Adjustment to singlehood & parenthood; time; financial problems; emotional difficulties
Strengths	Better than average father in household; child care, adaptation	Admired by friends and relatives	
Future study			
Implications		Counseling before divorce; concrete assistance: support group; child care costs; income support beyond unemployment	
Future	20% contested custody cases father wins		

FAMILY ADAPTATION FOLLOWING MARITAL SEPARATION/ DIVORCE: A LITERATURE REVIEW

Geoffrey Nelson

Ever increasing numbers of families are undergoing the experience of marital separation/divorce. For example, Bane (1979) has estimated that two-fifths of children born in the U.S. in the next decade will experience disruption of their parents' marriages. In the majority of cases, mothers are the custodial parent in the family. These trends reflect a growing social concern since research has shown that marital separation/divorce presents special problems and life changes for separated and divorced men and women (Bloom, Asher, & White, 1978), their children (Hetherington, 1979), and the entire family system (Ahrons, 1980). Over the last several years, there has been an enormous growth in the amount of research devoted to how families cope with the stress of marital separation/divorce.

In view of the rising social concern of the impact of marital separation/divorce on the family and the burgeoning of research on this topic, a thorough review of the literature is needed to clarify what we have learned to date. Therefore, the purpose of this paper is to review research on the impact of marital separation/divorce on the family. I begin by outlining theoretical developments which provide a useful conceptual frame-work to organize the rapidly accumulating findings on the topic and to provide a needed direction for more systematic inquiry. Next, I consider several important methodological issues per- taining to field research on marital separation/divorce. Having set this ground work, I then review the research on the impact of marital separation/divorce on adults, children, and the family system. The following section deals with advances in preventive intervention to promote growth and to prevent adverse effect of separation/divorce on family members. I conclude by highlighting some of the major issues and findings and by discussing areas in which further research is needed.

CONCEPTUAL FRAMEWORK

The Family Stress and Coping Paradigm

To date much of the research on the impact of marital separation/divorce has proceeded in an atheoretical fashion. However, several researchers have recently noted the absence of theory development on the topic and have adapted various theoretical viewpoints to the study of how families cope with the impact of marital separation/divorce (Ahrons, 1980; Beal, 1979; Pais & White, 1979; White & Mika, 1983). The most popular and appealing theoretical framework that has been applied to the study of the impact of marital separation/divorce is that of family stress and coping theory. The roots of this theory date back to Hill's (1949) conceptualization of how families cope with war-induced separation. According to Hill's ABCX model, a family crisis (X) is a function of one or more life stressors and related life strains (A) which interact with the family's stress meeting resources (B) and the perception, meaning, or definition that the family makes of the event (C). While there have been various modifications of Hill's (1949) initial formulation (Burr, 1973; Hansen & Johnson, 1979), the ABCX model has remained the dominant paradigm for investigating family stress and coping (McCubbin, Joy, Cauble, Comeau, Patterson & Needle, 1980).

Conceptualizing the impact of marital separation/divorce on families in terms of the ABCX model, one can view the stressful aspects of separation/divorce (the A factor) in terms of two major categories: acute life events (i.e., the separation) and chronic life strains ("daily hassles") that continue to occur on a day-to-day basis (Kanner, Coyne, Schaefer, & Lazarus, 1981). Separation/divorce is a life event which can create strain in several areas of life (e.g., financial problems, changes in parent-children relations, etc.). Family members' perceptions of the separation/divorce (the B factor) constitute the cognitive appraisal of the stressor (Lazarus, 1966). Stress meeting resources (the C factor) include personal resources, coping behaviour, social support, etc., which the family can use to deal with the stressful aspects of separation/divorce. Finally, the degree of crisis which occurs in the family (the X factor) refers to the positive and/or negative adaptation of family members.

Social Context

While Hill's (1949) formulation of the ABCX model provides a useful framework for research on the impact of marital separation/divorce, there are three other factors which need to be emphasized in the model. The first point is that the event of marital separation and family adaptation following marital separation/divorce takes place in a social context. Reading the voluminous literature on life stress, I am constantly surprised at how little attention is paid to the social context of life stress in current research. A few researchers have begun to integrate the systems-ecological perspective with that of the family stress and coping perspective to provide a more comprehensive model of how coping and adaptation to the stress of marital separation/divorce takes place in the context of family systems and larger social systems (Ahrons, 1980; Beal, 1979; Kurdeck, 1981). In Figure 1, I have attempted to depict a social systems model of family stress and coping (c.f., Lumsden, 1980).

<u>See Figure 1</u>

Along the left-hand side of the figure, the social context of life stressors is outlined, ranging from personal systems to larger scale social systems and systems which mediate between the person and the larger social system (cf. Kurdeck, 1981). Stressful life events, such as separation/divorce, do not occur randomly. Rather there are patterns to their occurrence which are pre-dictable from the social context in which they occur. One can examine the social context of the event of separation/divorce from several levels of analysis: personal interpersonal, organizational, and institutional. Moreover, the systems-ecological perspective contends that these levels of analysis are interdependent. Thus, for example, it is often found that poverty is related to family functioning which in turn is related to how well the individual functions.

The social system variables outlined on the left-hand side of the figure are often referred to as the antecedents or "causes" of marital separation/divorce. Since the focus of this review is on the consequences or "effects" of marital separation/divorce, I will discuss social systems variables as they relate to adaptation to separation/divorce, not as precursors to the event of separation/divorce. The interested reader is referred to two excellent recent reviews by Ambert (1980) and Kitson and Raschke (1981) for in-depth information on the antecedents of marital separation/divorce.

Proceeding from left to right across Figure 1, once the event of separation/divorce occurs, family members perceive and appraise the significance of the event. This perception is related to both the degree of strain or vulnerability family members feel in various spheres of life and the resources they mobilize to deal with those life strains. An important but often neglected or understated point is that mobilization of resources to deal with life strains takes place in a social context. The amount of change in the context from prior to separation/ divorce to following separation/divorce is an important factor in the family's ultimate adaptation. Again, the systems-eco-logical perspective emphasizes that coping with stress involves

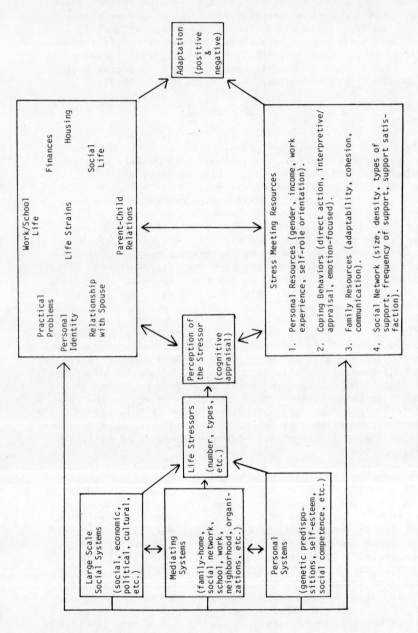

Figure 1. A social systems model of family stress and coping with the impact of marital separation/divorce.

transactions between the person and the social environment.

Process

A second important factor to add to the model is that of a
time perspective. Family adaption to marital separation/divorce
is not a "thing", but a process which changes with time. McCubbin
and Patterson (1982) have modified Hill's (1949) model to incorporate the time factor with the result being a double ABCX model.
This is a two-stage model which focuses first on how families
cope with a life stressor and secondly on how they cope with the
changes that have occurred as a result of coping with the initial
stressor. This model can be applied to the study of the impact of
marital separation/divorce. There have been recent attempts to
conceptualize the different stages and developmental tasks with
which families must cope during the process of adaptation to
separation/divorce (Ahrons, 1980; Price-Bonham & Balswick, 1980;
Spanier & Casto, 1979). The first stage has been described as a
reactive one involving adaptation to dissolution of the marriage,
including dealing with the strains of legal issues, practical
day-to-day routines and household management, housing, child
custody and visitation, explaining the separation to family and
friends, and the emotional problems of dealing with attachment
and disengaging from the relationship with the ex-spouse. The
second stage has been described as a proactive one of deciding
"What do I do now?" This stage of setting up a new lifestyle
includes economic changes, changes in work/school life, changes in
parent-child relationships, making new friends, dating, and
changes in identity. Peters (1983) has called these two
different stages "disengaging" and "re-engaging." The double
ABCX model is probably a somewhat oversimplified way of looking
at the change process, but it does draw attention to the dynamic
nature of coping with change.

Stress and Growth

The final factor that needs to be underscored in the stress
and coping process is the dimension of adaption. Much of the
research on the impact of marital separation/divorce focuses on
the negative aspects of adaptation and has a resounding "Ain't it
awful?" feeling to it. This research has ignored the point of
crisis theorists such as Caplan (1974) who have long argued that
successful mastery of major life crises can have growth producing
effects. To be sure, most of the time marital separation/divorce
is initially followed by considerable pain, turmoil, and
disorganization for family members (Kraus, 1979).

However, initial feelings of trauma can be overcome and
converted into feelings of self-confidence, when new coping skills

tencies are learned (Finkel, 1975). Thus, it is
to consider both positive and negative aspects of
in a long-term time perspective.

METHODOLOGICAL ISSUES

There are many methodological problems in this type of
naturalistic field research that make it difficult to render
definitive conclusions about family adaptation following marital
separation/divorce (Blechman, 1982; White & Mika, 1983). Thus,
before reviewing the literature on this topic, I will discuss some
of the important methodological issues involved in this area of
research.

Definition of One-Parent Families

As Shinn (1978) has pointed out, one of the most pervasive
problems in research on one-parent families is the definition
of terms. Many of the studies in this area have compared women
and/or children from "father absent" or "broken homes" and those
from "intact homes" on various measures of psychosocial adaptation.
Such gross comparisons gloss over many important aspects of the
separation experience, such as: first separation/divorce versus
subsequent separation/divorce, single versus multiple separations,
separation from mother versus separation from father, the length
of the separation, the age of the mother and children at the onset
of the separation, availability of father and mother following
the separation, and the availability of relationships with other
adults (step-parents, grandparents, etc.) following the separation.
Each of these factors may have profound consequences on the outcome
of studies on the impact of marital separation/divorce. For
example, in a study of poor black families in Chicago, Kellam,
Ensminger, and Turner (1977) identified 10 major family types
based on the number of adults living in the home, and the different
family types were associated with varying degrees of child maladaptation. Working from a systems perspective, Ahrons (1980)
has eschewed the use of terms such as "one-parent family" and
has offered the concept of the binuclear system. Thus, precise
definitions of the independent variable, the separated family,
are needed to clarify the exact nature of potentially widely
differing separation experiences.

Sampling

Another major methodological issue is that of representative
sampling. Several sampling strategies have been used. The first
involves sampling subjects from the records of guidance clinics
or psychiatric services. The results of studies using this type
of sampling procedure cannot be generalized to the normal
population of those experiencing marital separation/divorce.
While women and children from one-parent families may be over-

represented in guidance clinics or psychiatric services, one cannot conclude from such findings that marital separation/divorce is associated with psychopathology in the general population.

Another method involves "convenience samples" (White & Mika, 1982). That is, members of groups like Parents Without Partners or self-help groups for the separated or divorced are asked to participate in the research. Once again, this method is problematic since it involves unrepresentative samples. A somewhat better method is to advertise through the media, post notices in shopping centres, etc. (Bloom, Hodges, and Caldwell, 1983). Sample representativeness is less of an issue with this method and one can potentially identify families who have recently undergone marital separation. Probably the best method of identifying the population of those who have recently separated is to use separation and divorce petitions from county court records. This procedure is also not without its problems, however. Studies using this procedure often have response rates from subjects of less than 50%. This introduces the possibility of bias resulting from the use of volunteer subjects. Whenever possible, it is desirable to obtain any information on refusers, such as demographic data, to determine the representativeness of the study sample compared to the entire population. In summarizing research on the volunteer subject, Rosenthal and Rosnow (1969) point out that volunteers are better educated, less authoritarian, more sociable, higher in self-disclosure, and better adjusted socially and emotionally than non-volunteers. Thus, studies of volunteer subjects from separated families may underestimate psychosocial adaptation problems of the total population. However, one can also argue that following separation/divorce, subjects who are emotionally troubled may volunteer to participate in a study simply for the opportunity to talk to someone. Whatever the case may be, the problem of bias resulting from the selection of volunteer subjects can be reduced if similar sampling procedures are used to select subjects from separated families and comparison subjects from intact families.

Research Design

Investigations of the impact of separation/divorce are weak in terms of the criteria of internal validity (Campbell & Stanley, 1966) because of the natural selection of subjects into groups (i.e., groups are non-equivalent because subjects cannot be randomly assigned to groups) and because pre-test measures on the dependent variables, obtained prior to separation/divorce, are lacking. Thus, causal interpretation of the "effects" of the independent variable, marital separation/divorce, on the dependent variable, psychosocial adaptation, is very limited in such research. However, as Farrant (1977) has argued, the plausibility of rival alternative hypotheses in such studies can be reduced by controlling for potentially important extraneous variables through matching of "experimental" and "comparison" groups on those variables.

In studies of the impact of marital separation/divorce, it is necessary to control for several aspects of the separation experiences that were previously mentioned. First, one must document the amount of parent availability in separated and intact families. Blanchard and Biller (1971) have argued that father availability should be considered a continuum rather than a dichotomy. In some cases, fathers in separated families may have more contact with their children than fathers in intact families. Once the particular independent variable of interest has been decided on (e.g., mother as custodial parent versus father as custodial parent), other aspects of the separation (e.g., length of the separation) must be controlled for by matching.

Another important nuisance variable that needs to be controlled in studies of the impact of marital separation/divorce is socioeconomic status (SES). SES covaries with both the status of being a one-parent family and measure of psychosocial adaptation for both adults (Dohrenwend & Dohrenwend, 1969) and children (Hollingshead & Redlich, 1958). Thus, effects on psychosocial adaption due to SES might otherwise be attributed to marital separation/divorce if SES were not controlled for. Few studies have adequately matched separated families and intact families with respect to SES (Herzog & Sudia, 1973; Blechman, 1982), and those which tend to find that low income, father than family type, is related to maladaptation (Colletta, 1979). There are several potential measure of SES, including: the mother's occupation, working status, education, income, and housing. It is difficult to decide which of these measures to choose for purposes of matching. Thus, it is desirable to match mothers from both separated families and intact families on several of these variables.

It is difficult to match separated families and intact families in terms of income in view of the superior earning power of intact, two-parent families resulting from higher salaries paid to men and the potential of incomes from both the husband and wife. One alternative strategy is to match families on per capita income. Another strategy is to compare separated families with intact families who are experiencing economic problems (e.g., unemployment). Also, drops in SES following separation/divorce can be obtained by inquiring about both present and past (i.e., prior to separation/divorce) SES variables. Downward shifts in SES accompanying separation/divorce may be associated with psychosocial adaptation. In this type of quasi-experimental research, when the "experiemental" group is atypically low on a factor, such as income in the case of separated families, with respect to the "comparison" group, Campbell and Stanley (1966) recommend using covariance analysis rather than matching to control for that factor. Thus, income and other SES variables can be controlled for statistically by using them as covariates in analysing the differences between separated and intact families on a given measure.

104

There are limitations to the matching approach in attempting to equate "experimental" and "comparison" groups on relevant nuisance variables. The first problem is that matching is subject to differential statistical regression effects. Thus, when reducing the population of intact families to select those that can be matched on SES, for example, with separated families, one is selecting an extremely deviant sample with respect to SES compared to the general population. Thus, the "experimental" and "comparison" groups may have different regressions slopes to their respective population means on the dependent variables that are examined. Since SES is correlated in the same direction with both family status and psychosocial adaptation, the deviant "comparison" group will regress to a higher population mean than the more representative "experimental" group. The unfortunate consequence of this matching-regression problem is that it will lead to erroneous conclusions regarding differences between groups on the "experimental" variable. As was previously mentioned, when such is the case, Campbell and Stanley (1966) recommend using covariance analysis to statistically control for differences between the "experimental" and "comparison" groups on the nuisance variable. However, other discussions of statistical analysis of data from non-equivalent control groups designs (e.g., Cook & Reichardt, 1976) have challenged this assertion and have argued for the use of several different types of analysis in attempts to rule out different threats to internal validity. Finally, Farrant (1977) has argued that differential regression effects may not present a problem when the "experimental" and "comparison" groups are initially representative of their respective populations.

One final problem with the matching strategy is that one cannot match groups on all potentially relevant variables. Farrant (1977) has argued that while it is incumbent upon the researcher to control for empirically established confounding factors, it is not necessary to control for conjectural factors that have not been shown to have a confounding effect. In summary, while matching is not without its problems, equation of "experimental" and "comparison" groups through matching on demonstrated nuisance variables, along with other techniques of statistical analysis, can be used to strengthen experimental control in studies of the impact of marital separation/divorce. The benefits of enhanced internal validity, however, may be gained only at the expense of decreased generalizability of findings, when matching reduces the universe of potential subjects who can be studied.

Another important methodological consideration is the use of cross-sectional versus longitudinal designs. While useful information can be gained from cross-sectional studies, prospective, longitudinal designs are preferable in this area of research. Prospective studies are preferable because they permit examination of changes in the process of psychosocial adaptation over time following separation, whereas cross-sectional designs provide only a "snapshot" of how the individual is coping at one particular point in time. Thus, both short-term and long-term adaptation to marital separation/divorce can be discerned from research using longitudinal designs. It is also important to study families as close to the point of separation as possible, since this is a particularly stressful period. Even one year post separation, the family may have undergone considerable change and adaptation which can only be reported retrospectively. Prospective studies in the early stages of separation permit subjects to describe their experience as it is happening.

Measurement

Another major methodological issue is how to assess the key variables under consideration. Several methods have been used to study family adaptation following marital separation/divorce. Case studies using in-depth interviews have generated rich qualitative data of considerable heuristic value (Wallerstein & Kelly, 1980). In this cycle of the research process, meaningful questions and hypotheses can be formulated and subsequently tested using other methods. One must interpret such qualitative data with caution, however, since it is more prone to the biases of the researcher than may other methods.

By far the most frequently used methods in this area of research are structured interviews and questionnaires. In developing scales to measure the key variables previously outlined in the model of family stress and coping, it is important that such measures be tested for their reliability and validity. There are well established measures of life stressors for both adults (Holmes & Rahe, 1967; Sarason, Johnson, & Siegel, 1978) and children (Sandler & Ramsay, 1980). Also, more recent research has asked subjects to rate their perceptions of life stressors along several dimensions, such as desirable versus undesirable, controllable versus uncontrollable, predictable versus unpredictable, etc. (Dohrenwend & Marten, 1979; Vinokur & Selzer, 1975).

The realization that there are persistent stressful life conditions, as well as acute life events, has led to the development of scales that measure "daily hassles" (Kanner et al., 1981) and chronic life strains (Pearlin & Schooler, 1978). In the case of separation/divorce, Berman and Turk (1981) have developed a measure of "Problems and Concerns" that face separated or divorced adults. In the area of stress meeting resources, there have been recent advances in the measurement of coping (Berman & Turk, 1981; Billings & Moos, 1981; Folkman & Lazarus, 1980; Menaghan, 1983; Pearlin & Schooler, 1978), family strengths (Moos, Insel, & Humphrey, 1974; Olson, Russell, & Sprenkle, 1983) and social support (Barrera, 1981; Barrera & Ainlay, 1983;

Turner, Frankel, & Levine, 1983).

Measures of individual adaptation generally fall into two categores: emotional adaptation, focusing on self-reported feelings such as self-concept, quality of life, symptoms, etc., and social adaptation, focusing on the degree to which the individual meets social expectations in various areas of role functioning. Most of the developed measures for both adults and children focus on the negative aspects of psychosocial adaptation. Measures of the positive, as well as the negative, aspects of psychosocial adaptation are needed to assess growth promoting effects and to avoid the frequently unstated assumption that the status of being from a one-parent family is pathological.

To adequately assess a theoretical construct, such as those outlined in the model of family stress and coping, it is important to use multiple measurement methods since any single method is fallible and provides only a partial understanding of the construct. As I have noted, most of the research on the impact of marital separation/divorce uses questionnaires to tape the perceptions of those who are going through the separation experience. While this type of phenomenological data is useful, it provides only one side of the story. There is a need to augment this data source with information from other data sources such as key informant reports about the individual's behaviour (e.g., parent ratings of their children's behaviour) and direct observation of the individual's behaviour by external observers as in Hetherington, Cox, and Cox's (1978) study of parent-child interactions in divorced and two-parent families.

Another conceptual limitation of the questionnaire method is that it tends to treat theoretical constructs, such as coping or social support, as traits. The trait viewpoint generally ignores social context factors. Coping and social support are construed as "things" that one does or has in all situations, rather than variables which reflect dynamic interaction between the person and the environment. Direct observation, structured interviews, and daily diaries are methods which may be useful in examining the sequence of events in the stress and coping process.

In summary, there has been considerable progress in recent years in the development of methods to measure key variables outlined by the family stress and coping model. However, these methods tend to treat key variables as if they are traits, rather than transactions between the person and the environment; they tend to treat the experience as if it is static, rather than dynamic; and they emphasize negative adaptation and neglect growth. Thus there is a need for a change in methods to correspond to the changes in theory I outlined earlier.

THE IMPACT OF MARITAL SEPARATION/DIVORCE

Having provided the reader with a brief overview of theory
and method on the topic of family adaptation following marital
separation/divorce, I will now review the literature on this
topic. I will first consider the impact of marital separation/
divorce on adults (parents) and then the impact of this event
on children and the family system.

Adults

Beginning with separation/divorce as a stressful life event,
Holmes and Rahe (1967) have developed a scaling procedure for the
43 events covered in their instrument to quantify the amount of
change or readjustment necessitated by the experience of a
particular event. Scaling studies have consistently found that
marital separation and divorce rank second behind death of a
family member in requiring the most change or readjustment
(Cochrane & Robertson, 1973; Grant, Gerst, & Yager, 1976; Holmes
& Masuda, 1974; Holmes & Rahe, 1967; Masuda & Holmes, 1967; Paykel,
Prusoff, & Uhlenhuth, 1971; Paykel & Uhlenhuth, 1972). Since
separation/divorce is often accompanied by or triggers a number
of other stressful life events (e.g., loss of finances, moving, etc
etc.), the amount of "cumulative stress" (Hodges, Wechsler, &
Ballantine, 1979) or the "pile-up" of life events (McCubbin &
Patterson, 1982) is important to consider. The more stressful
life events one experiences, the greater likelihood of physical
or psychosocial maladaptation (Dohrenwend & Dohrenwend, 1978, 1981).

In the case of separation/divorce, the perception of the
event(s) is also an important variable. Research on other stressful life events had indicated that events that are perceived as
undesirable, unpredictable, and uncontrollable are more likely
to be associated with stress reactions than those that are
perceived as desirable, predictable, and controllable (Dohrenwend
& Martin, 1979; Vinokur & Selzer, 1975). In this regard, it is
important to consider which of the marital partners initiated
the separation or divorce. Several studies have found greater
feelings of attachment to spouse when the spouse initiated the
divorce or when the divorce was recently suggested (Brown,
Felton, Whiteman, & Manela, 1980; Kitson, 1982; Spanier & Casto,
1979; Zeiss, Zeiss & Johnson, 1980). This may be due to a
perception of the divorce as being undesirable, unpredictable,
and uncontrollable. Such perceptions may be related to gender,
since women initiate separation or divorce almost twice as often
as do men (Ambert, 1980; Peters, 1983). Clearly further research
is needed on the perceptions adults have about the events of
separation and divorce.

The events of separation and divorce often lead to life changes that produce considerable strain. Thus, it is important to consider the post separation/divorce context to which adults and their children must adapt. First of all, when there are children, mothers have custody in about 85 percent of the cases (Bane, 1979; Brandevein, Brown, & Fox, 1974). Secondly, in the past decade, the divorce rate has doubled in both the U.S. (Norton & Glick, 1979) and Canada (Peters, 1979), although the divorce rate in the U.S. (480 per 100,000) was double that of Canada (222 per 100,000) in 1975.

In view of these trends, an important concern is the economic situation of mother-headed one-parent families. Bane (1979) has reported that in the U.S. in 1975, the median income of two parent families with children was $15,534., while that of mother-headed one-parent families was $5,501. More than 50 percent of female-headed one-parent families fall below the poverty line in both the U.S. (Band, 1979) and Canada (McConville, 1978). Moreover, several studies have found dramatic drops in income for women following separation/divorce (Albrecht, 1983; Bloom & Hodges, 1981; Espenshade, 1979; Gongla, 1982; McLanahan, 1983; Nelson, 1982; Zeiss, Zeiss, & Johnson, 1980). To add to these financial problems, it has been estimated that less than one third of ex-husbands contribute to the support of their children (Hetherington, 1979). Thus, separated and divorced women with children suffer a huge financial burden. Ehrenerich and Stallard (1982) have noted the increasing feminization of poverty and have termed mother-headed families the "nouveau poor".

With diminished income following marital separation/divorce, many women who are primarily responsible for managing the children and the household must now also seek paid employment. Bane (1979) reported that 77.1 percent of divorced women with children in the U.S. in 1977 were employed. These women tend to work at low-paying jobs, face discrimination in male-dominated workplaces, and experience problems at work (Bane, 1979; Bloom, Hodges, & Caldwell, 1983; Gongla, 1982). Thus, many separated and divorced women experience the role strain of having to be both sole provider and sole parent to their children (Colletta, 1983; Ilgenfritz, 1969).

Being poor and stretched in so many directions can lead to additional problems, including: disruption of daily routines and practical problems of household management (Herherington et al., 1978), restricted opportunities for social interaction and self-development (Raschke, 1977; Smith, 1980; Spanier & Casto, 1979), having less time for one's children so that the children may be experiencing a "double loss" (Hetherington, 1979), changing residences (Asher & Bloom, 1983), etc. On top of all these problems, separated and divorced women must deal with the mixed feelings of pain, anger, guilt, love, etc., that result from disengaging from the relationship with the spouse. There is ample evidence that attachment to one's spouse continues to be strong for some time (Hetherington et al., 1978; Kitson, 1982; Weiss, 1975). Continued conflict with the spouse over issues of visitation, childrearing, property settlement, financial support, etc. is another facet of this life strain (Hetherington et al., 1976, 1978; Nelson, 1981).

Other social bonds may also be altered following marital separation/divorce. Ties to some married friends may decrease with time following the separation or divorce (Hetherington et al., 1977; Spanier & Casto, 1979; Weiss, 1975), after a brief initial increase in contact. Same sexed married friends may feel threatened by the newly separated persons; some friends may take sides in the separation and condemn one of the partners; the newly separated person may feel like "a third wheel" who does not fit in the world of married couples, etc.

Separated adults, particularly women, often seek help, increase contact with, and receive support from their family of origin, while they tend to decrease contact with the family of their former spouse (Anspach, 1976; Colletta, 1979; Spicer & Hampe, 1975). From the limited literature on the social networks of the newly separated and divorced, there is little information about changes in the quality of the relationships and social interaction following separation and divorce (Gongla, 1982; Saunders, 1983). Clearly more research is needed on this topic to determine when and how help is provided by family and friends, when it is withheld (Kitson, Moir, & Mason, 1982), and when family and friends are actively harmful and upsetting to the newly separated and divorced.

While the number of mother-headed families is increasing, separated and divorced women experience social stigmatization and challenges to their authority as head of the family from both their children and society (Brandwein et al., 1974). With all of these changes and life strains, it is little wonder that many women experience decreased self-esteem and confusion in personal identity. The post separation/divorce context to which they must adapt can be very stressful. Moreover, many of the areas of strain may be lengthy (e.g., conflict with spouse, loss of income, etc.) rather than transitory "events". In a large scale study, McLanahan (1983) found that chronic life strains and acute life events did not diminish in frequency until two years after the separation.

Given the high level of stress and strain of the post-separation/divorce environment, the next question is how do adults adapt to these changes? The first major study of divorce adaptation was done by Waller (1967) in 1930. Waller interviewed 33 persons who had been divorced for varying lengths of time, focusing on changes in friendships and sexual, economic, and

personality adaptation. Based on his interview data, Waller concluded that divorce is a crisis situation that has traumatic
consequences for divorced adults.

Some 25 years later, Goode (1956) studied 425 divorced
women between the ages of 20 and 38 from Detroit. He found
increased emotional adaptation problems in a substantial proportion of the sample during the separation process: 62%
experienced difficulty sleeping; 67% reported increased loneliness and poor health; 43% reported reduced work efficiency; and
many also reported increased drinking, smoking, and memory
problems. Women reported the greatest stress, in terms of
these emotional adaptation problems, at the time of separation,
with their emotional adaptation improving with the passage of time.

Hunt (1966) interviewed over 200 separated or divorced
persons and did a questionnaire survey of another 169 divorced
persons in another major study of divorce adaptation. Hunt
reported that a small minority of his sample felt that divorce
was either a totally negative or a totally positive experience.
However, the majority of the sample reported ambivalent feelings,
vacillating from depression to jubilant relief. Many of the
divorced reported problems with sleep and diet and an increase
in the use of alcohol, tobacco, drugs and professional help-
seeking following separation. Loneliness was the most common
negative feeling mentioned by the divorced. On the other hand,
many of the divorced reported positive feelings of relief, new
found freedom, and personal growth following separation.

Over the past few years, the number of studies of divorce
adaptation has substantially increased. Weiss (1975) provided
a clinical description of approximately 150 separated or divorced
men and women participating in seminars for the recently separated.
Following separation, Weiss found a number of common problems
that he termed "separation distress". These emotional adaptation
problems included: continuing preoccupation with the image of
the ex-spouse with accompanying feelings vacillating from bitter-
ness and a sense of betrayal to a desire for reunion, loss of
self-esteem and feelings of failure, anxiety, difficulty sleeping,
loss of appetite, memory problems, increases smoking and drinking,
and feelings of loneliness. On the other hand, Weiss also found
that many of the separated and divorced experienced feelings of
euphoria and relief following the separation.

Chiriboga and Cutler (1977) interviewed 96 men and 106
women who had been separated for an average of six months. The
divorced were asked to recall various aspects of emotional trauma and
relief that they had experienced at various points in the separation
process. There were clear-cut sex differences on these measures.
Separated women reported that the most stressful points were prior
to the decision to divorce and at the time of the final separation.

111

while the post-separation period was associated with the highest degree of feelings of relief. Separated men, on the other hand, reported experiencing the greatest amount of stress following separation rather than prior to or during separation.

In a questionnaire study of 126 separated or divorced individuals, Gray (1978) found the majority of her sample were preoccupied with feelings of guilt, resentment, and fear of the future. Furthermore, significant changes in alcohol consumption, weight, and job effectiveness were reported following separation. In a six month follow-up of 34 members of the original sample, there was a significant improvement regarding feelings of self-esteem.

Spanier and Casto (1979) interviewed 28 women and 22 men who had been separated for an average of 21 months. They identified two major stages of divorce adaptation: adaptation to the dissolution of the marital relationship and adaptation to establishing a new lifestyle and identity. Major problem areas in adapting to the dissolution of the marital relationship were the adversarial nature of the legal process of separation/divorce, issues regarding custody of the children, and continued feelings of attachment to the ex-spouse. Having supportive friends and family was the most positive factor during this period. In setting up a new lifestyle, women reported economic problems, job discrimination, the strain of having to be both parent and provider, and restricted opportunities for social involvement. Men, on the other hand, reported missing their children and being dissatisfied with the non-custodial relationship with their children.

Dasteel (1982) studied 161 adults who had been separated from one day to three years. This group described separation as a very stressful experience: 91 percent reported feeling an unusual degree of stress, and 67 percent reported feeling unhappy or worried about the future much of the time.

Baker (1983) studied 150 adults who had been separated or divorced for varying lengths of time. Practical problems were most common during the first year of separation. After the separation, emotional problems were frequently reported. Fewer emotional problems were reported by those in the second year of separation, but such problems were reported at a high level again for those in the second year of separation. Women tended to report more problems than men. Consistent with the findings of Raschke (1977), men reported more social and sexual activity following the separation than women, while women reported more practical problems to solve (e.g., child care, finances, employment, etc.). Baker (1983) interpreted these differences in adaptation in terms of the different post-separation/divorce networks of men and women. Men tend to have more loose-knit

112

social networks with new friends and opposite sex relationships, while women tend to have more close-knit networks with contact with family members to help with the many practical problems they face.

Bloom and his colleagues in Colorado have an active program of research on the impact of separation and divorce on adults. In one study, White and Bloom (1981) examined the adaptation of 40 men separated within the past six months. Three months after the initial interview, these men reported less loneliness and guilt and better sexual reintegration.

In another longitudinal study, Bloom and his colleagues have compared the post-separation adaptation of 100 adults participating in an intervention program with 50 adults assigned to a no treatment control condition (Bloom & Hodges, 1981; Bloom, Hodges, & Caldwell, 1982, 1983; Bloom, Hodges, Kern, & McFaddin, 1984). These adults were first intervewed within two months of separation. At this point, adults reported significant difficulties in adaptation in the areas of loneliness, lowered self-esteem, physical health problems, relationship with spouse, financial problems, changes in employment, practical day-to-day living problems, work-related problems, difficulties with children, etc. There was also a high level of help seeking for both men and women at that time (Bloom & Hodges, 1981). Women initially reported more psychological symptoms, more financial problems, more health problems, more relief from conflict, greater happiness, and less sexual dissatisfaction and loneliness than men.

At the first follow-up six months later, there were no changes from the initial assessment on any of the dimensions of a psychological symptom checklist for the 50 adults in the no treatment control group (Bloom, Hodges, & Caldwell, 1983). Moreoever, there continued to be a high level of help-seeking and significantly more problems were reported in the areas of child rearing, career planning, and parental relationships.

Additional follow-up assessments were completed at 18 months, 30 months, and four years later (Bloom et al., 1982, 1983; Bloom et al., 1984). Once again, the adults in the control group showed little improvement with the passage of time on dimensions of the symptom checklist. However, there was improvement with the passage of time in the specific problem areas of loneliness, guilt and self-blame, psychological problems, sexual dissatis- faction (for men), legal difficulties (for women), and trouble concentrating at work. Women also reported greater personal growth as time passed, while both men and women reported being happier at each of the follow-up periods after the initial separation.

113

Several recent studies of divorce adaptation have appeared that have included comparison groups. Blumenthal (1967) interviewed 50 divorced persons and 280 non-divorced persons and compared them on a variety of indices of psychosocial maladaptation including: drinking problems, depression and suicidal behaviour, treatment for psychiatric problems, and perceived "nervous breakdowns." Controlling SES through covariance analysis, Blumenthal found significantly more psychosocial adaptation problems for the divorced than the non-divorced. He argued that psychiatric problems precipitated divorce by citing the fact that 65% of the reasons for the divorce were suggestive of "psychiatric problems." These reasons were primarily adultery, incompatibility, and drinking problems, which could just as easily be interpreted as problems in living stemming from unhappy marriages.

Woodruff, Guze, and Clayton (1972) compared 121 divorced and 251 married psychiatric outpatients, who were well matched on several variables, with respect to several aspects of adaptation. Compared to the married group, the divorced group had significantly more problems pertaining to drug and alcohol abuse. Briscoe, Smith, Robins, Marten, and Gaskin (1973) compared 139 divorced persons one to two years after divorce with 61 married controls from the community. Structured interviews were used to elicit information pertinent to the diagnosis of psychiatric disorder. They judged that 75% of the divorced women compared to 20% of the married women had some type of psychiatric disorder. Of the divorced women, 40% were judged as having psychiatric depression and 11% were diagnosed as anti-social personality. Furthermore, divorced women were more likely to have sought psychiatric outpatient treatment than married women. From these data, the authors concluded that psychiatric disorder is a significant cause of marital breakdown. However, this conclusion is unwarranted because they presented no evidence to suggest that psychiatric disorder was present prior to marriage or divorce.

In a further study, Briscoe and Smith (1974) compared 40 divorced couples with 28 married couples from the original sample with respect to diagnosis of psychiatric disorder. They found that 92% of one or both partners in the divorced group compared to 43% of one or both partners in the married group had a psychiatric disorder. They also found that those in the married group who considered marital separation were judged as having a psychiatric disorder significantly more frequently than those who had not considered marital separation. The absurd conclusion of this study is that if you are married, you at least have the chance of the flip of a coin to determine if you are sane, but if you are divorced, you are automatically crazy. There are two major methodological problems that cast serious doubt on the validity of the findings in these studies. First, the authors who made the psychiatric diagnoses were blind to neither the research hypotheses nor the marital status of the subjects.

Secondly, the authors presented no evidence as to the reliability of their psychiatric diagnoses. Given the notorious unreliability of psychiatric diagnosis (Spitzer & Fleiss, 1974), their findings may provide more of an indication of the authors' pathology bias than of the psychosocial adaptation problems of divorced people.

In another study, Morrison (1974) compared the divorced and married parents of children seen at a psychiatric clinic with respect to psychiatric diagnoses. He found that divorced men, but not divorced women, were significantly more likely to be judged as psychiatrically disturbed than married men and women. Twice as many divorced women than married women were diagnosed as having an affective disorder or an "undiagnosed" disorder, but these differences were not statistically significant.

McKenry, White and Price-Bonham (1978) compared 20 married dyads and 20 divorced dyads on a variety of measures of adaptation. Those in the sample were white, middle class, with no children, and the divorced group had been separated for no longer than six months. The divorced reported significantly poorer emotional adaptation than the married.

Spivey and Scherman (1980) compared the psychological adaptation of women who had filed for divorce at various time intervals (0-6 months ago, 1-1½ years ago, 3½-4½ years ago, and 6½ years ago or more) with a group of newly married women and women who had been married for longer periods of time. They found that those women who had filed for divorce 1-1½ years ago reported significantly more psychological distress than those women who had filed for divorce longer ago and for both married groups. Thus, as was found in the Bloom study, it appears that while there are problems in adaptation in the first year and a half following separation, these problems diminish with the passage of time to the point that adaptation for the separated and divorced is no different from that of married women.

Nelson (1982) compared the adaptation of women who had been separated or widowed within the past two years with a group of married women. All of the women had at least one child in elementary school and the groups were matched on several variables with the exception of income. The separated women and widowed women reported significantly more positive and negative life changes and higher levels of help-seeking within the past two years than the married women. However, there were no differences in social and emotional adaptation between the groups with one exception: separated women reported significantly more friction and resentment in their relationships with others than did widowed or married women.

By far the most methodologically sophisticated and informative investigation of divorce adaptation is the study by

herington, Cox, and Cox (1976, 1978). The authors compared
divorced, mother-headed families with first and second-born
children with a matched control group of intact families. The
final sample consisted of 24 families with boys and 24 families
with girls in each of the divorced and intact groups for a total
of 96 families. Divorced and intact families were well matched
with respect to number and ages of the children, parents' age,
education, and length of marriage. Divorced families with step-
parents were excluded. The sample was predominantly young, white,
and upper middle class with respect to SES. The groups were
studied prospectively with evaluations conducted at two months,
one year, and two years following the divorce, not the separation.
Several measures were used to assess the psychosocial adaptation
of all family members, including: interviews, structured diary
records for the parents, personality scales for the parents,
parent and teacher ratings of children's behaviour, and
observations of parent-child interactions in the home and in the
laboratory.

For now, I will discuss only the results on the divorce
adaptation of the adults. In terms of practical problems, they
found that the households of divorced men and women were initially
more disorganized than those of intact families, but this
improved significantly after two years. Divorced adults also
reported more economic stress with the burden of having to maintain two households, but this was unrelated to psychosocial
adaptation problems.

The relationship between the divorced partners was a
significant problem at two months, but improved with time.
Roughly two-thirds of the contacts between divorced partners at
two months involved conflict. Common sources of conflict
concerned finances, child management and visitation issues, and
other opposite sex relationships. In spite of bitter feelings,
attachments to the ex-spouse remained strong initially. Even
after one year, divorced partners experienced feelings of
ambivalence and regret over the dissolution of the relationship,
but these feelings had significantly abated after two years.

Divorcees reported significantly more emotional adaptation
problems than married persons. The divorced reported feelings
of depression, anxiety, anger, rejection, and incompetence, and
these problems were more sustained for women than for men.
Social adaptation problems were prevalent for the divorced during
the two-year time period, especially for divorced women. Contact
with old married friends declined over time for both divorced
men and women. While divorced men were involved in many social
activities at one year, the social life of divorced women was
very restricted at one year, with many women complaining that
they felt "walled in" and "trapped" with their children.

116

To summarize the research on adult adaptation to marital separation/divorce, it appears that men and women experience stress reactions during the separation process. Retrospectively, they report increases in a variety of health and psychological problem areas during and immediately following the separation. Furthermore, research comparing the recently separated or divorced with married people tends to find more adaptation problems experienced by the separated or divorced. However, much of this comparative research is poorly controlled, especially regarding the important factor of SES.

There is also evidence that adaptation problems improve with the passage of time and that many adults experience growth and relief from stress following the marital separation. Because of inherent methodological limitations in this area of research, it is impossible to conclude that marital separation/divorce "causes" negative "effects" in adaptation for adults. An equally plausible alternative explanation to this social causation hypothesis is the social selection hypothesis which holds that people with problems in psychosocial adaptation are predisposed to and can contribute to marital breakdown (Dohrenwend & Dohrenwend, 1981). Research which has attempted to retrospectively determine if significant problems were present prior to the marital breakdown, as well as following the separation, has found support for both of these hypotheses (Bloom, Asher, & White, 1978; Bowen & Gerritsen, 1978; Smith, 1971).

The final set of variables to consider in examining the impact of marital separation/divorce is the stress meeting resources that can help individuals to better adapt to this stressful life event. These variables can moderate the relationship between life stress and adaptation, as well as being directly associated with adaptation. Understanding the role of these variables in the adaptation process is important not only for theoretical reasons, but for practical reasons as well. While some moderating variables are unmodifiable (e.g., age, gender, etc.), others are potentially modifiable (e.g., income, social support, coping skills) so that research on the stress-buffering effects of these variables could be useful in the design of intervention programs to smooth the transition from two-parent to binuclear family status (Kitson & Raschke, 1981).

There has been a considerable amount of research on the social and psychological resources that adults have to deal with stress, but almost no research on the coping styles and responses that separated or divorced adults do in response to stress. Beginning with age and length of marriage, several studies have found that the longer the marriage and the older the person, the more problems in adaptation (Chiriboga et al., 1978; Goode, 1956; Hetherington et al., 1978) and the less positive affect (Nelson, 1981). Research on gender differences had found that women initially experience both significantly more distress (Albrecht, 1980; Baker, 1983; Bloom, et al., 1983; Chiriboga & Cutler, 1977;

Spanier & Thompson, 1983; Zeiss, Zeiss, & Johnson, 1980) and significantly more happiness and relief (Bloom et al., 1983; Chirigoga et al., 1978; Spanier & Thompson, 1983) than men. It is important to note that gender is associated with several other moderator variables, such as who suggested the divorce, economic problems, child custody, etc. Given these other factors, it could be that many women have both more to gain, in terms of relief from stress, and more to lose, at least economically, than men. However, men also have a lot to lose and they tend to report different feelings of post-separation stress, such as loneliness and missing their children (Bloom et al., 1983; Spanier & Casto, 1979). Having economic problems (Goode, 1956; Pearlin & Johnson, 1977; Pett, 1982; Spanier & Casto, 1979) and having children (Goode, 1956; Hetherington et al., 1977; Pearlin & Johnson, 1977), both of which are much more likely to be experienced by women following separation or divorce, have been found to be associated with adaptation problems. One other personal resource which has consistently been found to relate to post-separation adaptation for women is sex-role orientation. Women with a non-traditional sex-role orientation have fewer problems than those with a more traditional sex-role orientation (Bloom & Clement, in press; Brown & Manela, 1978; Brown, Perry, & Harburg, 1977; Felton, Brown, Lehman, & Liberatos, 1980; Granvold, Pedler, & Schellie, 1979).

A growing body of research is examining the influence of social support networks on post-separation adaptation. In the early stages of the separation, Hetherington et al. (1978) and Nelson (1981) have found the quality of the current relationship with the ex-spouse to be the most potent moderator of adaptation. Having an active social life (Raschke, 1977) and new relationships with the opposite sex (Hetherington et al., 1977; Spanier & Casto, 1979) are also related to post-separation adaptation. Hetherington et al. (1978) found that intimacy in a relationship was crucial for positive adaptation, while Spanier and Casto (1979) reported that dating several people was as helpful as having one close, steady relationship.

Other studies have found that the amount of social support provided by one's network and the quality or satisfaction with that support is related to one's adaptation (Pett, 1982; White & Bloom, 1981) and one's quality of parenting (Colletta, 1979). Also, it has been found that the less dense or loose-knit one's social network, the better the adult's adaptation (McLanahan, Wedemeyer, & Adelberg, 1981; Wilcox, 1981). Only one study of which I am aware has examined the stress-buffering properties of social support for the recently separated or divorced. The stress-buffering hypothesis holds that there is an interaction between life stress and social support such that under conditions of high stress, the presence of social support reduces adaptation problems (Mitchell, Billings, & Moos, 1982). Caldwell and Bloom (1982) found evidence for this hypothesis at eight months following separation.

A final important moderator of adaptation to separation/ divorce, but one which has been neglected to date, is that of coping. The only study which specifically focuses on coping with separation/divorce is that of Berman and Turk (1981). They found the following coping styles to be associated with positive adaptation, as assessed by self-reported mood state and life satisfaction: involvement in social activities, expressing feelings, and developing autonomy. Clearly, more research is needed on coping styles.

In summary, several stress-meeting resources have been identified as potential moderators of the stress of separation/ divorce. Further research on this important aspect of the adaptation process will be useful for designing programs to smooth the transition from being married to being separated or divorced.

Children and the Family System

The number of studies on how children and the entire family system adapt to marital separation/divorce is increasing at a rapid rate (for other reviews, see Hetherington, 1979; Kurdeck, 1981; Lamb, 1977; Longfellow, 1979; Magrab, 1978; Felner, Farber, & Primavera, 1980). As is the case with adults, separation and divorce of one's parents is viewed as one of the most potent stressful life events for children (Coddington, 1972; Gersten, Langner, Eisenberg, & Orzek, 1974). Also, as is the case with adults, the more cumulative stress or pile-up of life events and life strains coinciding with the separation or divorce, the more children experience problems in adaptation (Hodges, Wechsler, & Ballantine, 1979; Hodges, Tierney, & Buchsbaum, in press; Stolberg & Anker, in press).

While separation/divorce is a stressor for both parents and children, in many cases it may be perceived very differently by parents and children. Women may tend to perceive the separation/ divorce as predictable, controllable, and desirable, since they most often suggest or initiate separation and divorce; while in some cases, their children's perceptions may be just the opposite. Wallerstein and Kelly (1980) have found that children's perceptions of divorce often include fear of abandonment, blaming one parent, both parents, or one's self for the separation/divorce, negative evaluation of one parent, both parents, or one's self, confusion about the meaning of separation/divorce, denial of the finality of divorce, a strong desire for parental reunion, etc.

Kurdeck and his colleagues have conducted several studies of children's perceptions of their parents' separation/divorce. Kurdeck and Siesky (1980a) found that children with an internal locus of control and a high level of interpersonal knowledge, both of which are positively correlated with age, are more likely than children who are low on these variables to have a healthy, mature understanding of their parents' divorce (i.e., define

119

divorce in terms of emotional separation, perceive the divorce as final, have realistic perceptions of parents' strengths and weaknesses, etc.). Moreoever, children whose reactions and adaptation to the divorce are fairly favourable, according to both parents and teachers, tend to have a healthy, mature understanding of the divorce (Kurdeck & Berg, 1983; Kurdeck & Siesky, 1980b) and a high level of internal control and interpersonal knowledge (Kurdeck, Blish, & Siesky, 1981).

Young (1983) has found that children report more anxiety and adaptation problems when they blame themselves or their mother for the divorce and fewer problems when they blame their fathers or do not blame anyone. Clearly, the little research that has been done on children's perceptions of their parents' separation/ divorce has shown that appraisal of the stressor is an important aspect of the adaptation process. Further research on the discrepancy between the perceptions of children and their parents should be useful in understanding part of the strain that families must deal with following separation/divorce.

Turning to the context to which children and families must adapt, much has been written about the changes and strains placed on children and families following separation/divorce (Anthony, 1974; Despert, 1962; Roberts & Roberts, 1974; Sugar, 1970). Some of the sources of strain on children and the family system are: loss of income, inter-parental conflict and disagreement on child rearing, visitation, etc. (Cline & Westman, 1971; Westman, 1971; Westman, Cline, Swift, & Kramer, 1970), missing the non-custodial parent (Wallerstein & Kelly, 1980), experiencing "double loss" if the custodial parent must immediately begin working (Hetherington, 1979), changed relationships with each parent, particularly in the areas of communication, discipline, and authority (Hetherington et al., 1978; Santrock & Warshak, 1979), moving and changing schools, practical problems in household management and daily routines, the reaction of friends and peers to the separation/divorce, parents' dating and remarriage, etc. All of these factors can place a strain on the family system and require changes in adaptation.

The question of how children adapt to their parents' separation/divorce has been the subject of many studies during the past ten years. Wallerstein and Kelly (1974, 1975, 1976, 1977, 1980; Kelly & Wallerstein, 1975, 1976, 1977) have presented the results of a longitudinal study on the effects of parental divorce on children. Sixty families with 131 children between the ages of two and 18 years from Marin County, California participated. All children were drawn from a normal population, excluding children who were emotionally or intellectually deviant prior to divorce. The sample was predominantly young, white, amd middle-to upper-class. Data covering a number of areas of psychosocial functioning were collected in clinical interviews.

The majority of children of all age groups were reported
as having significant psychosocial adaptation problems immediately
following parental divorce. After one year, more than 50% of
the children had improved, but the remainder of the children
experienced sustained adaptation problems. Pre-school children
did not appear to understand the divorce and many blamed themselves for their parents' separation. Pre-school girls had
more problems at follow-up than pre-school boys, with many
appearing to be anxious and dependent.

School-aged children experienced mixed feelings of sadness,
anxiety, and anger. Many of these children had conflicts of
divided loyalty, wished for their parents to reconcile, and
openly expressed anger towards their parents. Academic performance and peer relationships deteriorated for many of these
children. Boys, in particular, missed their fathers and
rebelled against their mothers for what they perceived to be
mother driving father away. Increased irritability and
aggressiveness and alignment with one parent against the other
characterized the adaptation patterns of many of the school-
aged children.

McDermott (1968) studied 16 nursery school children, whose
parents were recently divorced. He found that 10 of the
children (62%) showed acute behavioural problems following parental
divorce. While no objective measures of children's behaviour
were used, McDermott felt that the majority of these children
were sad and angry and that these upset feelings were primarily
manifested in aggressive behaviour, especially for the boys.

In a second study, McDermott (1970) compared 116 children
whose parents were divorced with 1349 children from intact
families, all of whom were seen at a children's psychiatric
hospital. He found that the children of divorce showed significantly more anti-social behaviour at home and at school, and that
the appearance of such behaviour was of shorter onset than the
presenting problems for children from intact families.

Tuckman and Regan (1966) found that boys, but not girls,
whose parents were separated or divorced had significantly
higher rates of referral for psychiatric treatment for aggression
and anti-social behaviour than children from all other family
statuses. These differences were found only for school-aged
children (ages 6 to 17).

Similarly, Felner, Stolberg, and Cowen (1975) found that
of those primary grade children referred for psychological help,
children whose parents were separated or divorced were rated
by their teachers as displaying significantly more acting-out

behaviour problems at school than children whose parents were either married or widowed. Hetherington (1972) found that the adolescent daughters of divorced women were similar to the adolescent daughters of widows in that they were anxious in their interactions with men. However, the daughters of divorced women coped with this anxiety through attention-seeking from males and early heterosexual behaviour, whereas the daughters of widows were more shy and inhibited in their interactions with men.

Santrock (1975) compared matched groups of fifth and sixth grade boys from intact families and father-absent families due to death or divorce. Teachers rated boys from divorced families as showing significantly higher levels of anti-social behaviour than boys from widowed families, and divorced women were reported as using power assertive discipline significantly more frequently than widows, according to their sons.

In a study of 387 cases seen at a children's psychiatric service, Kalter (1977) compared the referral problems of children from different types of families. He found that children whose parents had separated or divorced showed significantly more aggressive behaviour towards their parents, drug involvement, and sexual behaviour than children whose parents were married and never divorced.

The study of Hetherington, Cox, and Cox (1978) on family adaptation to divorce also reported significantly more anti-social behaviour for pre-school children whose parents were married. These findings were most pronounced for boys whose parents were divorced, as they showed high rates of non-compliance to parental directions and aggressive behaviour. While the children of divorced parents became less anti-social two years following divorce, they still remained significantly more anti-social than children whose parents were married after two years.

In a study of college women, Young and Parish (1977) found that women from father-absent families, either because of death or divorce, reported greater insecurity and more negative self-evaluations than women from either intact families or step-parent families. Parish and Taylor (1979) studied elementary and junior high school students and found lower self-concepts in children from other-headed divorced families than in children from intact families. These findings were replicated in another study of children in grades five to eight (Parish & Dostal, 1980).

In a study of pre-school children, Hodges et al. (1979) found no differences in aggressive behaviour between children from intact families and children from mother-headed divorced families who had separated an average of two years ago. Hess and Camara (1979) studied grade four and five children from intact families and mother-headed divorced families who had separated two to three years ago. They found that children whose parents were divorced were rated by their parents and teachers as showing more stress symptoms and problems in work effectiveness at school than children from intact families. The groups did not differ though in terms of aggressive behaviour and social relations.

Santrock and Warshak (1979) observed parent-child inter-actions in mother-headed and father-headed divorced families and intact families. The groups were well matched on several variables and the children were all in elementary school. There were few differences between children from divorced and intact families on a variety of observational measures of social behaviour. However, they found that children living with the opposite sex parent (mother custody boys and father custody girls) showed more problems in interacting with the opposite sex parent than children living with the same sex parent. Ambert (1982) found that custodial fathers reported that their children were better behaved than did custodial mothers, especially when the mothers were poor. Ambert did not examine the interaction between sex of the child and sex of the custodial parent, as did Santrock and Warshak (1979).

In a study of 2,351 children who ranged in age from preschool to 18 years of age and who were clients in a psychiatric clinic, Schoettle and Cantwell (1980) found higher rates of socialization and behaviour disorders in children from divorced families than in children from intact families. In two studies of elementary school children, one focussing on children referred for mental health problems and the other focussing on normal children, Felner, Ginter, Boike, and Cowen (1981) found that children from divorced families showed more acting out behaviour problems and fewer social skills, as judged by teacher ratings, than children from either intact families or children who had experienced the death of a parent. In contrast, Nelson (1982) found no significant differences in either mothers' or teachers' ratings of antisocial behaviour or shyness-withdrawal between elementary school children from recently separated (within the past two years) mother-headed families, mother-headed families in which the father had recently died, and intact families. However, children from intact families reported higher levels of happiness and self-esteem than children from either of the other two groups.

In a study of preschool children, Hodges, Buchsbaum, and Tierney (1983) found that children from divorced families were rated by their teachers as showing more aggression, poorer task orientation, and more general maladaptation at school than children from intact families. In another study, Hodges and Bloom (in press) examined the behaviour of 107 children from one to 18 years of age at two months following their parents' separation and again six to 18 months later. According to parents' ratings of their children's behaviour, younger children showed more acting-out behaviour problems than older children, while older children showed more depression than younger children. Boys showed more behaviour problems than girls at each of the three assessment periods. Children under age seven showed more behaviour problems at the 18 month follow-up than they did initially, but there were no changes over time for older children.

In summary, most of research on children's adaptation to separation/divorce of their parents has shown that children from divorced families display more problems, particularly anti-social and aggressive behaviour, and lower self-esteem than children from intact families. However, most of the studies comparing children from divorced families with children from intact families have not controlled for the influence of other variables, particularly the crucial variable of SES (Blechman, 1982; Herzog & Sudia, 1973). Several recent studies which have matched divorced families and intact families on several variables have tended to find few differences in adaptation between children from these two different family types (Hodges et al., 1979; Hess & Camara, 1979; Nelson, 1982; Santrock & Warshak, 1979). Also, research on the children of divorce has overwhelmingly focussed on pathology rather than growth. Moreoever, from the existing research it is difficult to determine whether the reported problems of the children of divorce are transitory stress reactions or potentially long-term problems in adaptation.

A substantial amount of the research on the children of divorce has examined factors that moderate the relationship between the stresses and strains of parental separation/divorce and children's adaptation. Beginning with gender differences, research on marital discord and divorce has consistently shown that pre-school and elementary school-aged boys show more problems in adaptation than do girls (Emery, 1982; Emery & O'Leary, 1982; Hess & Camara, 1979; Hetherington et al., 1978; Hodges & Bloom, in press; Hodges et al., 1983; Kurdeck & Berg, 1983; Porter & O'Leary, 1980; Tuckman & Regan, 1966; Wallerstein & Kelly, 1980). However, Santrock and Warshak (1979) found that problems existed only when the custodial parent was the opposite sex of the child. Also, there is some evidence that girls show more adaptation problems in adolescence, in the form of verbal aggressiveness, lying, early sexual activity, truancy, etc., than boys (Hetherington, 1972; Kalter, 1977; Kalter & Rembar, 1981; Schoettle & Cantwell, 1980).

Age is another moderator of children's adaptation to parental separation/divorce. Older children differ significantly from younger children in cognitive and social competence. These differences in developmental status should help older children to better adapt to parental separation/divorce. The research by Kurdeck and his colleagues has shown that older children adapt better to parental separation/divorce than do younger children, and that these age differences are mediated by social and cognitive developmental factors such as locus of control and level of interpersonal knowledge and understanding (Kurdeck & Berg, 1983; Kurdeck, Blisk, & Siesky, 1981; Kurdeck & Siesky, 1980b). Hetherington (1979) has argued that age and developmental status affects the quality of the child's adaptation to divorce. Evidence in support of this argument is provided by Hodges and Bloom (in press) who found that younger children showed more disruptive behaviour in response to their parents' divorce than older children, while older children showed more depression. Kalter and Rembar (1981) also argued that the child's age at the time of parental separation may be an important moderator of children's adaptation. They found that the most vulnerable time for children to experience parental separation was between three and five and a half years. Boys respond immediately to this stress with behaviour problems at school and later with aggression towards parents and siblings. Girls, on the other hand, do not show an immediate reaction to separation at this stage, but in adolescence, aggression towards parents and peers, and academic problems begin to emerge.

Another important stress-meeting resource for families who have undergone separation/divorce is income. A low level of income and drops in income for mothers following separation/divorce has been shown to relate to problems in parents' child rearing behaviour and children's behaviour problems (Ambert, 1982; Colletta, 1979; Desimone-Luis, O'Mahoney, & Hunt, 1979; Hodges & Tierney, in press; Hodges et al., 1979).

Other research has attempted to determine whether family tension and discord surrounding and following the marital separation or separation from and loss of time with father is more strongly related to children's problems in adaptation. One way of examining this question is to compare children whose parents have separated or divorced with children who have experienced death of a parent. Research making these comparisons

125

has found differences in the quality of adaptation with separated and divorced children showing higher rates of acting
out behaviour and delinquency (Brown, 1966; Douglas, Ross,
Hammon, & Mulligan, 1966; Felner et al., 1975; Felner, et al.,
1981; Gibson, 1969; Glueck & Glueck, 1950; Gregory, 1965;
Tuckman & Regan, 1966), while children who have experience
parental death show more shy, anxious, and withdrawn behaviour
(Felner et al., 1975; Felner et al., 1981; Tuckman & Regan, 1966).
Moreover, it has been consistently found that the level of marital
discord, unhappiness, and conflict is associated with acting out
behaviour in children both in intact and separated families
(Emery, 1982; Emery & O'Leary, 1982; Glueck & Glueck, 1962;
Hess & Camara, 1979; Jacobson, 1978b; McCord, McCord, & Thurber,
1962; Nelson, 1981; Rutter, 1971).

Three studies have shown family conflict to be more
strongly associated with children's adaptation than father
presence or absence. Nye (1957) found significantly higher rates
of anti-social behaviour for children from unhappy intact
families than for children from homes in which the father was
absent. Raschke and Raschke (1979) found no differences in self-
esteem for school-aged children from intact, single-parent,
and reconstituted families. However, level of family conflict
was significantly inversely related to self-esteem for children
from both intact and single-parent families.

In the Hetherington, Cox, and Cox (1979) study, children
from intact families were subdivided into high conflict and low
conflict groups and compared with the children from divorced
families. During the first year after divorce, children from
divorced families showed significantly more anti-social behaviour
than children from high conflict intact families, who in turn
showed significantly more anti-social behaviour than children
from low conflict intact families. However, by two years after
divorce, the pattern had reversed with children from high conflict
intact families showing significantly more anti-social behaviour
than children from divorced families.

While there is considerable research documenting the
importance of parental harmony for children's adaptation, there is
also evidence indicating the importance of attachment to and
separation from the non-custodial parent. Jacobson (1978a)
found that loss of time with father was associated with a variety
of behavioural problems for children between the ages of seven to
13. Lowenstein and Koopman (1978) found that the frequency of
interaction with the non-custodial parent was positively correlated
with boys' level of self-esteem. Hess and Camara (1979) found
that the duration, not frequency, of visits with the non-custodial
parent was associated with less stress in children.

126

In addition to the amount of time children spend with parents, the quality of parent-child relationships has been found to be very important for children's adaptation following parental separation/divorce. With one parent leaving the household, there is a change in the roles and responsibilities of the parents vis-à-vis the children. The custodial parent, usually the mother, has the lion's share of discipline thrust upon her, while the non-custodial parent, usually the father, is more at a distance from the children on a day-to-day basis.

Wallerstein and Kelly (1980) found that one year after the separation almost half of the fathers had developed better relationships with their children, while almost half of the mothers, most of whom had custody of the children, had developed more conflicted, unsatisfying relationships with their children. Furthermore, the deterioration in the quality of mother-child relationships following divorce was associated with children's adaptation problems. Continued parental conflict was also related to poor adaptation for the children.

Within the first year following divorce, the more mothers communicated with their children about the divorce, the better the adaptation of children in Jacobson's study (1978c). Children who brought problems to their mothers and who had mothers who spent some time explaining divorce to them showed the best adaptation.

By far the most exemplary study of interaction patterns of families in which the parents have divorced is that by Hetherington, Cox and Cox (1978). Using direct observation of family interaction, the authors found significant problems in parent-child interactions during the first year of divorce compared with a matched control group of intact families. However, after two years, interaction patterns between divorced parents and their children had improved considerably.

Compared to married parents, divorced parents made fewer maturity demands of and were less affectionate and consistent with their children one year after divorce. The children of divorced parents, particularly boys, were also less compliant to their parents than the children from intact families. Divorced mothers and fathers differed significantly in their methods of managing their children. Divorced mothers tended to be restrictive, as reflected in their frequent use of negative commands and sanctions, while divorced fathers tended to be permissive, using fewer commands and more positive sanctions in the management of their children. These findings are consistent with Wallerstein and Kelly's (1976) observations that divorced fathers tend to indulge their children during visits, while divorced mothers suffer the brunt of the conflict with their children from day-to-day.

The most significant interactional problems were observed between divorced mothers and their sons. Divorced mothers communicated less well with, were less consistent with, and used more negative commands and sanctions and fewer positive commands and sanctions with their sons than with their daughters. However, boys whose parents had divorced showed high rates of non-compliance and other adversive behaviours in interactions with their mothers. On the other hand, girls whose parents had divorced tended to be more whiny, complaining, and dependent. Problems in family interaction were significantly correlated both with rates of deviant child behaviours and with mothers' feelings of self-esteem, competence, anxiety, and depression. Hetherington et al. (1978) argued that the relationship between divorced mothers' adaptation and that of their children is bi-directional in nature. That is, the dysfunctional inter-action patterns appeared to be reciprocally maintained by divorced mothers and their children.

The authors reported two factors that were associated with mother-child interaction patterns in divorced families. First, an amicable relationship with the ex-husband, as reflected in agreement on child management, little conflict between the divorced partners, maturity of the father and mother, and frequent contact between mature fathers and their children, was found to be most strongly associated with positive mother-child interactions. Secondly, the positive support provided by relationships with close friends, relatives, and intimate boyfriends was also associated with good mother-child relationships in this study.

Another study of divorced families using direct obser-vation of parent-child interactions found that the more parents used an authoritative style of discipline, as opposed to authoritarian or laissez-faire style, the more socially competent was the behaviour of their children (Santrock & Warshak, 1979). In a self-report study of parent-child relationships following separation/divorce, Hodges et al. (1983) found that the more parental warmth, as opposed to reserve, the less acting-out, distractability, and total adaptation problems for the children; while the more parental restrictiveness, as opposed to permissiveness, the more fearful, withdrawn, and depressed were the children. Finally, Rutter (1971) and Hess and Camara (1979) have found that children who maintain a good relationship with both parents have fewer adaptation problems than children who have a good relationship with only one parent, who, in turn, have fewer problems than children who have a poor relationship with both parents. While Hetherington et al. (1979) found the same pattern with children from intact families, they found that in divorced families, only a good relationship with the

128

the mother, the custodial parent, was related to positive
adaptation of the children.

Research on extra-familial social supports has focussed
on the support provided to adults, with little attention to
support provided to children (Hetherington 1979; Kurdeck, 1981).
The only study of which I am aware that has examined the
influence of extra-familial social support on the adaptation
of children in that of Santrock and Warshak (1979). They
found that the total amount of time children spent with other
adult caretakers was positively correlated with their
adaptation. Further research is needed to examine the influence
of peers, teachers, relatives, family, friends, etc. who could
play an important role in mitigating the stress of parental
separation/divorce for children.

In summary, parental separation/divorce is a stressful
life event for children, as it is for adults. Furthermore,
evidence has been reviewed which has shown that the amount of
stress, children's perceptions of the separation/divorce, the
post-separation/divorce context, and the stress-meeting resources
of the child and family are related to children's adaptation.
Separation/divorce leads to many changes for the family,
including role redefinition, loss of income, role strain for
the custodial parent, changes in residences, etc. All of these
changes affect post-separation/divorce family relationships,
which are the key factors mediating children's adaptation.
The quality and quantity of parent-child relationships and the
relationship between the divorced partners have been shown to
bear a strong relationship to children's adaptation. The
mechanisms by which changes in family relationships following
separation/divorce affect children's adaptation have been
proposed from different theoretical frameworks.

Patterson (1976) has proposed a social learning view
of the development and maintenance of anti-social behaviour of
children which appears to be particularly applicable to the
situation of families in which the parents have divorced with
its emphasis on the role of the family system. According to
this view, children from conflict-ridden families learn to be
anti-social in their relations with others by modelling the
maladaptive interactions of their parents. Furthermore, the
anti-social behaviour of children is reinforced by the parents
in disturbed family systems. Patterson has used the term
"coercive interactions" to describe and to explain the manner
in which anti-social behaviours of children and maladaptive
parent management styles are mutually reinforced and, hence,
maintained in dysfunctional family interaction patterns.

In "coercive interactions", one party terminates the
aversive behaviour of the other through the use of aversive

behaviour. Thus, the aversive behaviour of each party is
reinforced by the termination of aversive behaviour in the
other. Positive behaviours, on the other hand, are mutually
ignored in such interactions and thus remain at a low
frequency of occurrence because they are not reinforced.
The results of the Hetherington et al. (1978) study, using the
family interaction coding system developed by Patterson,
support this social learning view of "coercive interactions"
in divorced families.

Tooley (1976) has presented a psychoanalytic formulation
of the anti-social behaviour of boys whose parents are divorced
that considers the dynamics of the family system. According
to this view, parental conflict culminating in the departure
of the father from the family is a stressor that arouses the
anxiety of boys. Perceiving the world as hostile and themselves
as vulnerable, boys use aggressive behaviour as a defense
mechanism in an attempt to control an unpredictable environment
and their own feelings of insecurity. Mothers' problems
following divorce and their difficulties in controlling their
children tend to confirm boys' upset and their perceived
needs to defend themselves.

When divorce occurs during the oedipal stage of development, boys assume the posture of "man in the house", according
to Tooley. Boys at this stage fail to develop internalized
superego controls because of a lack of fear of retaliation
from father and the lack of a father figure with which to
identify. Thus, boys externalize sexual and aggressive
impulses. However, Roberts and Roberts (1974) argue that
the costs far outweight the gains in this "oedipal victory",
because boys emerge with feelings of fear and arrested
personality development which will lead to future conflict
with authority figures, the law and societal norms and
expecations. While this psychoanalytic view is generally
similar to Patterson's social learning view in its emphasis
on family dynamics, it lacks the parsimony, specificity, and
supporting empirical data base of Patterson's formulation.

PREVENTIVE INTERVENTIONS

Since marital separation/divorce is a stressful life
event that is associated with difficulties in psychosocial
adaptation for both parents and children, there has been a
variety of attempts at preventive intervention with this
"high risk" population. Most of these programs have both a
social support and educational focus and are conducted on a
group basis (Fisher, 1973; Sheffner & Suarez, 1975;
Vogelsang, 1982; Welch & Granvold, 1977; Young, 1978a&b).
Social support is provided by group members who have undergone the same experience, while the educational aspects of
such programs usually cover topics such as legal and
financial issues, parenting and child care, career planning

and employment problems, socializing and personal identity, etc. The rationale for such programs is that social support and coping skills are important stress-meeting resources which can offset some of the adverse consequences of separation/divorce.

There have been outcome evaluations of a few of these programs for newly separated or divorced adults in recent years. In one study, Kessler (1978) randomly assigned recently divorced adults to either a structured group, an unstructured group, or a control group. Group leaders for the unstructured group used a non-directive style to facilitate group discussion and to promote group cohesion. Leaders for the structured groups were more directive and focused on assertiveness and coping skills training for specific problematic situations for divorced persons. The results showed that after eight weeks of intervention, those who had participated in the treatment groups reported significantly higher self-esteem than those in the control group. Furthermore, divorced persons in the structured group reported significantly higher self-esteem and consumer satisfaction with treatment than divorced persons in the unstructured group.

In another study, Thiessen, Avery, and Joanning (1980) evaluated the effectiveness of a communication skills training program for recently separated women. Compared to a no-treatment control group, those who participated in the program showed significant improvement in their level of empathy, self-esteem, and overall adaptation to separation/divorce.

By far the most exemplary piece of research in this area is that conducted by Bloom and his colleagues (Bloom, Hodges, & Caldwell, 1982; Bloom, Hodges, Kern, & McFaddin, 1984). Adults who had been separated for two months on the average were randomly assigned to a six-month intervention program ($n=100$) or a no treatment control group ($n=50$). The program consisted of study groups on several problem areas facing newly separated people and nonprofessional program representatives who provided social support, crisis intervention, and referrals to other services. At the conclusion of the program, program participants showed significantly more improvement than controls on several measure of adaptation. Furthermore, follow-up evaluations at 18 months, 30 months, and four years after the conclusion of the program showed that these gains were not only maintained, but that the differences between the experimental and control groups became even greater at successive follow-up intervals.

There have also been several descriptions of social support groups and school-based interventions for children whose parents have separated or divorced. Cantor (1977) developed a school-based support group for elementary school children whose parents were divorced. While teachers reported that they did not observe any behaviour changes following the end of the group, parents felt that their children had become more open in discussing the divorce at home. Guerney and Jordon (1979) have described a community-sponsored support group for school-aged children from divorced families. Group leaders were trained in a non-directive, client-centred approach with a focus on promoting discussion about the divorce process. Informal evaluation of the group by the children, parents, observers, and group leaders suggested that the children participated actively and openly shared their feelings about their parents' divorce with the group. Kalter, Pickar, and Lesowitz (1984) have also developed school-based social support groups for grade five and six children and are in the process of evaluating their program.

There are other programs which do not focus exclusively on adults or exclusively on children. These programs are multi-faceted and provide such activities as family life education or crisis intervention for the whole family, parenting skills training, educational and social support groups for parents, and educational and social support groups for children (Kelly & Wallerstein, 1977; Stolberg & Cullen, 1983; Wallerstein & Kelly, 1977; Warren, Grew, Konanc, Ilgen & Amara, 1982). However, there have been no reported outcome evaluations of these programs to date.

In summary, intervention programs for adults, children, and families who have recently experienced separation/divorce have been developed. Evaluations of the preventive potential of these programs for adults has already been demonstrated, and several promising programs for children and families have evaluations in progress.

CONCLUSION

In conclusion, there is a good deal of research indicating that adults, children, and families experience short-term adaptation problems following separation/divorce. However, much of the literature on the adaptation of adults and children to separation/divorce has followed a pathology model in its focus on the problems of such families. The pathology orientation of this research is related to the fact that many of the investigations in this area have examined deviant

samples of adults and children (i.e., those undergoing psychiatric treatment). Furthermore, cross-sectional research on
the short-term problems of adults and children following
separation/divorce has added to the pathology focus. The
two-parent family has long been cherished as one of the back-
bones of the social and moral fibre of North American Society.
Thus, the rising incidence of marital separation/divorce is
a change that many be viewed as threatening to the status quo
and as requiring condemnation as pathological.

Rather than condemning or condoning the rise in marital
separation/divorce, one can alternatively conceptualize this
phenomenon as a stressful life event that requires change and
a process of adaptation with both positive and negative aspects
for all family members. The psychosocial adaptation of parents
and their children from separated/divorced families is viewed
in the context of their social situation, according to this
perspective. Several writers (Blechman & Manning, 1976;
Kohen, Brown & Feldberg, 1979; Levinger, 1979) have presented
social learning or social psychological analyses of single-
parent families, arguing that the status of becoming a single-
parent family is associated with both social rewards and
social costs.

From this perspective, the psychosocial adaptation
problems of separated or divorced adults and their children are
a reflection of the special problems of their new social
situation. First of all, parents and children must disengage
themselves emotionally from previously strong attachments to
another person. During this time of separation anxiety and
stress, the family is downwardly economically mobile and must
realign family roles. Women must often assume the dual roles
of sole parent and provider. The many women who previously
played emotionally expressive, nurturing roles in the family
must now learn to assert themselves as an authority figure
in interactions with their upset children and in their interactions in a male-dominated society. Having to assume multiple
role functions means that the single-parent mother has less
time for herself and, thus, that she and her family will become
more socially isolated. Being from a separated or divorced
family may be a social stigma and relationships with old
friends may fade.

On the other hand, marital separation/divorce presents
opportunities for positive, growth experiences for parents and
their children. The loss of a close, emotional relationship
forces one to re-examine one's priorities in life and thus
may lead to a new direction and sense of identity. Becoming
the sole parent and sharing the loss with children may initially

133

present problems, but it may also eventually lead to closer mother-child relationships. Finally, both women and children from separated or divorced families must become more independent and assume more responsibility for tasks previously performed by the father. Thus, women and their children may learn new skills following separation/divorce.

Future research is needed then to examine both the positive and negative life changes experienced by parents and children following separation/divorce. Studies using longitudinal designs will allow for a focus on the processes of change in the family system, as well as examining the short-term and long-term outcomes in adaptation. Finally, there is a need for more research on factors that moderate the relationship between the stress of marital separation/divorce and the adaptation of adults and children. Such research should provide valuable information for the design and evaluation of preventive intervention programs which seek to augment the stress-meeting resources of the family. Future research should help to clarify the pros and cons of single-parent family life and to stimulate the development of necessary social and institutional supports that can prevent problems and ensure the quality of life of families which have experienced marital separation/divorce.

REFERENCES

Ahrons, C.R. (1980). Divorce: A crisis of family transition & change. Family Relations, 29, 533-540.

Albrecht, S.L. (1980). Reactions and adjustments to divorce: Differences in the experiences of males and females. Family Relations, 29, 59-68.

Ambert, A.M. (1980). Divorce in Canada. Don Mills, Ontario: Academic Press.

Ambert, A.M. (1982). Differences in children's behaviour toward custodial mothers and custodial fathers. Journal of Marriage & the Family, 44, 73-84.

Anspach, D.F. (1976). Kinship & divorce. Journal of Marriage & the Family, 38, 343-350.

Anthony, E.J. (1974). Children at risk from divorce: A review. In E.J. Anthony & C. Koupernik (Eds.), The child in his family: Children at psychiatric risk, Vol. 3. New York: John Wiley & Sons.

Asher, S.J., & Bloom, B.L. (1983). Geographic mobility as a factor in adjustment to divorce. Journal of Divorce, 6, 69-84.

Baker, M. (1983). Divorce: Its consequences and meanings. In K. Ishwaran (Ed.), The Canadian family. Toronto: Gage.

Bane, M.J. (1979). Marital disruption and the lives of children. In G. Levinger & O.C. Moles (Eds.), Divorce and separation: Context, causes and consequences. New York: Basic Books.

Barrera, M. (1981). Social support in the adjustment of pregnant adolescents. Assessment issues. In B.H. Gottlieb (Ed.), Social networks & social support. Beverly Hills: Sage.

Barrera, M., & Ainlay, S.L. (1983). The structure of social support: A conceptual and empirical analysis. Journal of Community Psychology, 11, 133-143.

Beal, E.W. (1979). Children of divorce: A family systems perspective. Journal of Social Issues, 35, 140-154.

Berman, W.H., & Turk, D.C. (1981). Adaptation to divorce: Problems & coping strategies. Journal of Marriage & the Family, 43, 179-189.

Billings, A.G., & Moos, R.H. (1981). The role of coping responses and social resources in attenuating the stress of life events. Journal of Behavioral Medicine, 4, 139-157.

Blanchard, R.W., & Biller, H. B. (1971). Father availability and academic performance among third-grade boys. Developmental Psychology, 4, 301-305.

Blechman, E.A. (1982). Are children with one parent at psychological risk? A methodological review. Journal of Marriage & the Family, 44, 179-195.

Blechman, E.A., & Manning, M. (1976). A reward-cost analysis of the single-parent family. In E.J. Mash, L.A. Hamerlynck, L.C. Handy (Eds.), Behavior modification and families. New York: Brunner/Mazel.

Bloom, B.L., Asher, S.J., & White, S.W. (1978). Marital disruption as a stressor: A review and analysis. Psycholgocial Bulletin, 85, 867-894.

Bloom, B.L., & Clement, C. (in press). Marital sex role orientation and adjustment to separation and divorce. Journal of Divorce.

Bloom, B.L., & Hodges, W.F. (1981). The predicament of the newly separated. Community Mental Health Journal, 17, 277-293.

Bloom, B.L., Hodges, W.F., & Caldwell, R.A. (1982). A preventive intervention program for the newly separated: Initial evaluation. American Journal of Community Psychology, 10, 251-264.

Bloom, B.L., Hodges, W.F., & Caldwell, R.A. (1983). Marital separation: The first eight months. In E.J. Callahan & K.A. McKluskey (Eds.), Life-span developmental psychology: Non-normative events. New York: Academic Press.

Bloom, B.L., Hodges, W.F., Kern, M.B., & McFaddin, S.C. (1984). A preventive intervention program for the newly separated: Final evaluations. Manuscript submitted for publication.

Blumenthal, M. (1967). Mental health among the divorced. Archives of General Psychiatry, 16, 603-608.

Bowen, P.A., & Gerritsen, G.W. (1978). Marital disruption & psychopathology: Causes & effects. Unpublished manuscript.

Brandewein, R.A., Brown, C.A., & Fox, E.M. (1974). Women and children last: The Social Situation of divorced mothers and their families. Journal of Marriage and the Family, 36, 498-514.

Briscoe, C.W., & Smith, J.B. (1974). Psychiatric illness: Marital units and divorce. Journal of Nervous and Mental Disease, 158, 440-445.

Briscoe, C.W., Smith, J.B., Robins, E., Marten, S., & Gaskin, F. (1973). Divorce and psychiatric disease. Archives of General Psychiatry, 29, 119-125.

Brown, F. (1966). Childhood bereavement and subsequent psychiatric disorder. British Journal of Psychiatry, 112, 1035-1041.

Brown, P., Felton, B.J., Whiteman, V., & Manela, R. (1980). Attachment and distress following marital separation. Journal of Divorce, 3, 303-317.

Brown, P., & Manela, R. (1978). Changing family roles: Women and divorce. Journal of Divorce, 1, 315-327.

Brown, P., Perry, L., & Harburg, E. (1977). Sex role attitudes and psychological outcomes for black and white women experiencing marital dissolution. Journal of Marriage & the Family, 39, 549-561.

Burr, W.R. (1973). Theory construction and the sociology of the family. New York: Wiley.

Caldwell, R.A., & Bloom, B.L, (1982). Social support: Its structure and impact on marital disruption. American Journal of Community Psychology, 10, 647-667.

Campbell, D.T., & Stanley, J.C. (1966). Experimental and quasi-experimental designs for research. Chicago: Rand McNally.

Cantor, D.W. (1977). School-based groups for children of divorce. Journal of Divorce, 1, 183-187.

Caplan, G. (1974). Support systems and community mental health. New York: Behavioral Publications.

Chiriboga, D.A., & Cutler, L. (1977). Stress responses among divorcing men and women. Journal of Divorce, 1, 95-106.

Chiriboga, D.A., Roberts, J., & Stein, J.A. (1978). Psychological well-being during marital separation. Journal of Divorce, 2, 21-36.

Cline, D., & Westman, J. (1971). The impact of divorce in the family. Child Psychiatry and Human Development, 2, 78-83.

Cochrane, R., & Robertson, A. (1973). The live events inventory: A measure of the relative severity of psychosocial stressors. Journal of Psychosomatic Research, 17, 135-139.

Coddington, R.D. (1972). The significance of life events as etiological factors in the diseases of children. II. A study of a normal population. Journal of Psychosomatic Research, 16, 205-213.

Colletta, A. (1979). Support systems after divorce: Incidence & impact. Journal of Marriage & the Family, 41, 837-846.

Colletta, N.D. (1983). Stressful lives: The situation of divorced mothers and their children. Journal of Divorce, 6, 19-31.

Cook, T.D., & Reichardt, C.S. (1976). Statistical analysis of non-equivalent control group designs: A guide to some current literature. Evaluation, 3, 136-138.

Dasteel, J.C. (1982). Stress reactions to marital dissolution as experienced by adults attending courses on divorce. Journal of Divorce, 5, 37-47.

Despert, J.L. (1962). Children of divorce. Garden City, N.Y.: Dolphin Books.

Dohrenwend, B.P., & Dohrenwend, B.S. (1969). Social status and psychological disorder: A causal inquiry. New York: Wiley.

Dohrenwend, B.P., & Dohrenwend, B.S. (1981). Socio-environmental factors, stress, and psychopathology. American Journal of Community Psychology, 9, 128-159.

Dohrenwend, B.S., & Dohrenwend, B.P. (1978). Some issues in research on stressful life events. Journal of Nervous and Mental Disease, 166, 7-15.

Dohrenwend, B.S., & Martin, J.L. (1979). Personal versus situational determination of anticipation and control of the occurrence of stressful life events. American Journal of Community Psychology, 7, 453-468.

Douglas, J.W.B., Ross, J.M., Hammond, W.A., & Mulligan, D.G. (1966). Delinquency and social class. British Journal of Criminology, 6, 294-302.

Ehrenreich, B., & Stallard, K. (1982). The nouveau poor. Ms. Magazine, 217-224.

Emery, R.E. (1982). Interparental conflict and the children of discord and divorce. Psychological Bulletin, 92, 310-330.

Emery, R.E., & O'Leary, K.D. (1982). Children's perceptions of marital discord and behavior problems of boys and girls. Journal of Abnormal Child Psychology, 10, 11-24.

Desimone-Luis, J., O'Mahoney, K., & Hunt, D. (1979). Children of separation & divorce: Factors influencing adjustment. Journal of Divorce, 3, 37-42.

Espenshade, T.J. (1979). The economic consequences of divorce. Journal of Marriage & the Family, 41, 615-625.

Farrant, R.H. (1977). Can after-the-fact designs test functional hypotheses and are they needed in psychology? Canadian Psychological Review, 18, 359-364.

Felner, R.D., Farber, S.S., & Primavera, J. (1980). Children of divorce, stressful life events, & transitions: A framework for preventive efforts. In R.H. Price, R.F. Ketterer, B.C. Bader, & J. Monahan (Eds.), Prevention in mental health: Research, policy, & practice. Beverly Hills: Sage.

Felner, R.D., Ginter, M.A., Boike, M.F., & Cowen, E.L. (1981). Parental death or divorce and the school adjustment of young children. American Journal of Community Psychology, 9, 181-191.

Felner, R.D., Stolberg, A., & Cowen, E.L. (1975). Crisis events and school mental health referral patterns of young children. Journal of Consulting and Clinical Psychology, 43, 305-310.

Felton, B.J., Brown, P., Lehman, S., & Liberatos, P. (1980). The coping function of sex-role attitudes during marital disruption. Journal of Health & Social Behaviour, 21, 240-248.

Finkel, N.J. (1975). Stress, traumas, and trauma resolution. American Journal of Community Psychology, 3, 173-178.

Fisher, E.O. (1973). A guide to divorce counseling. Family Coordinator, 22, 55-61.

Folkman, S., & Lazarus, R.S. (1980). An analysis of coping in a moddle-aged community sample. Journal of Health & Social Behavior, 21, 219-239.

Gersten, J.C., Langner, T.S., Eisenberg, J.G., & Orzek, L. (1974). Child behavior and life events: Undesirable change or change per se? In B.S. Dohrenwend & B.P. Dohrenwend (Eds.), Stressful life events: Their nature and effects. New York: John Wiley & Sons.

Gibson, H.B. (1969). Early delinquency in relation to broken homes. Journal of Child Psychology and Psychiatry, 10, 195-204.

Glueck, S., & Glueck, E. (1950). Unravelling juvenile delinquency. Cambridge, Mass.: Harvard University Press.

Glueck, S., & Glueck, E. (1962). Family environment and delinquency. Boston: Houghton Mifflin.

Gongla, P.A. (1982). Single parent families: A look at families of mothers and children. Marriage & Family Review, 5, 5-27.

Goode, W.J. (1956). After divorce. New York: Free Press.

Grant, I., Gerst, M., & Yager, J. (1976). Scaling of life events by psychiatric patients and normals. Journal of Psychosomatic Research, 20, 141-150.

Granvold, D.K., Pedler, L.M., & Schellie, S.G. (1979). A study of sex role expectancy and female postdivorce adjustment. Journal of Divorce, 2, 383-394.

Gray, G.M. (1978). The nature of the psychological impact of divorce upon the individual. Journal of Divorce, 1, 289-301.

Gregory, I. (1965). Anterospective data following childhood loss of a parent. I. Delinquency and high school dropout. Archives of General Psychiatry, 13, 99-109.

Guerney, L., & Jordan, L. (1979). Children of Divorce - A community support group. Journal of Divorce, 2, 283-294.

Hansen, D.A., & Johnson, V.A. (1979). Rethinking family stress theory: Definitional aspects. In W.R. Burr, R. Hill, F.I. Nye, & I.L. Reiss (Eds.), Contemporary theories about the family. New York: Free Press.

Herzog, E., & Sudia, C.E. (1973). Children in fatherless families. In B.M. Caldwell & H.N. Ricciuti (Eds.), Review of child development research. Chicago: University of Chicago Press.

Hess, R.D., & Camara, K.A. (1979). Post-divorce family relationships as mediating factors in the consequences of divorce for children. Journal of Social Issues, 35, 79-96.

Hetherington, E.M. (1979). Divorce: A child's perspective. American Psychologist, 34, 851-858.

Hetherington, E.M. (1972). Effects of father absence on personality development in adolescent daughters. Developmental Psychology, 7, 313-326.

Hetherington, E.M., Cox, M., & Cox, R. (1976). Divorced fathers. Family Coordinator, 25, 417-428.

Hetherington, E.M., Cox, M., & Cox, R. (1978). The aftermath of divorce. In J.H. Stevens, Jr., & M. Matthews (Eds.), Mother-child, father-child relations. Washington, D.C.: NAEYC.

Hetherington, E.M., Cox, M., & Cox, R. (1979). Family interaction and the social, emotional, & cognitive development of children following divorce. In V. Vaughn III & B. Barzelton (Eds.), The family: Setting priorities. New York: Science & Medicine.

Hill, R. (1949). Families under stress. New York: Harper.

Hodges, W.F., & Bloom, B.L. (in press). Parents' report of children's adjustment to marital separation: A longitudinal study. Journal of Divorce.

Hodges, W.F., Buchsbaum, H.K., & Tierney, C.W. (1983). Parent-child relationships and adjustment in preschool children in divorced and intact families. Journal of Divorce, 7, 43-48.

Hodges, W.F., Tierney, C.W., & Buchsbaum, H.K. (in press). The cumulative effect of stress on preschool children of divorced and intact families. Journal of Marriage & the Family.

Hodges, W.F., Wechsler, R.C., & Ballantine, C. (1979). Divorce & the preschool child: Cumulative stress. Journal of Divorce, 3, 55-67.

Hollingshead, A.B., & Redlich, F.C. (1958). Social class and mental illness. New York: Wiley.

Holmes, T.H., & Masuda, M. (1974). Life change and illness susceptibility. In B.S. Dohrenwend & B.P. Dohrenwend (Eds.), Stressful life events: Their nature and effects. New York: John Wiley & Sons.

Holmes, T.H., & Rahe, R.H. (1967). The social readjustment rating scale. Journal of Psychosomatic Research, 11, 213-218.

Hunt, M. (1966). The world of the formerly married. New York: McGraw-Hill.

Ilgenfritz, M.P. (1961). Mothers on ther own - widows and divorcees. Marriage and Family Living, 23, 38-41.

Jacobson, D.S. (1978). The impact of marital separation/divorce on children: I. Parent-child separation & child adjustment. Journal of Divorce, 1, 341-360. (a)

Jacobson, D.S. (1978). The impact of marital separation/divorce on children: II. Interparent hostility and child adjustment. Journal of Divorce, 2, 3-19. (b)

Jacobson, D.S. (1978). The impact of marital separation/divorce on children: III. Parent-child communication and child adjustment, and regression analysis of findings from overall study. Journal of Divorce, 2, 175-194 (c)

Kalter, N. (1977). Children of divorce in an outpatient psychiatric population. American Journal of Ortho-psychiatry, 47, 40-51.

Kalter, N., Pickar, J., & Lesowitz, M. (1984, April). School-based developmental facilitation groups for children of divorce: A preventive intervention. Paper presented at the Annual Meeting of the American Orthopsychiatric Association.

Kalter, N., & Rembar, J. (1981). The signficiance of a child's age at the time of parental divorce. American Journal of Orthopsychiatry, 51, 85-100.

Kanner, A.D., Coyne, J.C., Schaefer, C., & Lazarus, R.S. (1981). Comparison of two modes of stress measurement: Daily hassles and uplifts versus major life events. Journal of Behavioral Medicine, 4, 1-39.

Kellam, S.G., Ensminger, M.E., & Turner, R.J. (1977). Family structure and the mental health of children: Concurrent and longitudinal community-wide studies. Archives of General Psychiatry, 34, 1012-1022.

Kelly, J.B., & Wallerstein, J.S. (1975). The effects of parental divorce: I. The experience of the child in early latency. II. The experience of the child in late latency. American Journal of Orthopsychiatry, 45, 253-255.

Kelly, J.B., & Wallerstein, J.S. (1976). The effects of parental divorce: Experiences of the child in early latency. American Journal of Orthopsychiatry, 46, 20-32.

Kelly, J.B., & Wallerstein, J.S. (1977). Brief interventions with children in divorcing families. American Journal of Orthopsychiatry, 47, 23-39.

Kessler, S. (1978). Building skills in divorce adjustment groups. Journal of Divorce, 1, 209-216.

Kitson, G.C. (1982). Attachment to the spouse in divorce: A scale and its application. Journal of Marriage & the Family, 44, 379-393.

Kitson, G.C., Moir, R.N., & Mason, P.R. (1982). Family social support in crises: The special case of divorce. American Journal of Orthopsychiatry, 52, 161-165.

Kitson, G.C., & Raschke, H.J. (1981). Divorce research: What we know; What we need to know. Journal of Divorce, 4, 1-37.

Kohen, J.A., Brown, C.A., & Feldberg, R. (1979). Divorced mothers: The costs & benefits of female family control. In G. Levinger & O.C. Moles (Eds.), Divorce and separation: Context, causes and consequences. New York: Basic Books.

Kraus, S. (1979). The crisis of divorce: Growth promoting or pathogenic? Journal of Divorce, 3, 107-119.

Kurdeck, L.A. (1981). An integrative perspective on children's divorce adjustment. American Psychologist, 36, 856-866.

Kurdeck, L.A., & Berg, B. (1983). Correlates of children's adjustment to their parents' divorces. In L.A. Kurdeck (Ed.), Children and divorce. San Francisco: Jossey-Bass.

Kurdeck, L.A., Blisk, D., & Siesky, A.E. (1981). Correlates of children's long-term adjustment to their parents' divorce. Developmental Psychology, 17, 565-579.

Kurdeck, L.A., & Siesky, A.E. (1980). Children's perceptions of their parents' divorce. Journal of Divorce, 3, 339-378. (a)

Kurdeck, L.A., & Siesky, A.E. (1989). Effects of divorce on children: The relationship between parent and child perspectives. Journal of Divorce, 4, 85-99. (b)

Lamb, M.E. (1977). The effects of divorce on children's personality development. Journal of Divorce, 1, 163-174.

Lazarus, R. S. (1966). Psychological stress and the coping process. New York: McGraw Hill.

Levinger, G. (1979). A social psychological perspective on marital dissolution. In G. Levinger & O.C. Moles (eds.), Divorce and separation: Context causes and consequences. New York: Basic Books.

Longfellow, C. (1979). Divorce in context: Its impact on children. In G. Levinger & O.C. Moles (Eds.), Divorce and separation: Context, Causes and consequences. New York: Basic Books.

Lowenstein, J.S., & Koopman, E.J. (1978). A comparison of the self-esteem between boys living with single-parent mothers and single-parent fathers. Journal of Divorce, 2, 195-208.

Lumsden, D.P. (1980). Towards a systems model of stress:
Feedback from an anthropological study of the impact of
Ghana's Volta River project. In I. Sarason & C. Spiel-
berger (Eds.), Stress and anxiety, Vol. 7, Washington:
Hemisphere Publications.

Magrab, P. R. (1978). For the sake of the children: A review
of the psychological effects of divorce. Journal of
Divorce, 1, 233-245.

Masuda, M., & Holmes, T.H. (1967). Magnitude estimations of
social readjustments. Journal of Psychosomatic
Research, 11, 219-225.

McConville, B.J. (1978). The effect of non-traditional
families on children's mental health. Canada's Mental
Health, 26, 5-10.

McCord, J., McCord, W., & Thurber, E. (1962). Some effects
of paternal absence on male children. Journal of Abnormal
and Social Psychology, 64, 361-369.

McCubbin, H.I., Joy, C.B., Cauble, A.E., Comeau, J.K.,
Patterson, J.M., & Needle, R.H. (1980). Family stress
and coping decade review. Journal of Marriage & the
Family, 42, 855-871.

McCubbin, H.I., & Patterson, J.M. (1982). Family adaptation
to crises. In H.I. McCubbin, A.E. Cauble, & J.M.
Patterson (Eds.), Family stress, coping and social
support. Springfield, Illinois: C.C. Thomas.

McDermott, J.F. (1968). Parental divorce in early childhood.
American Journal of Psychiatry, 124, 1424-1432.

McDermott, J.F. (1970). Divorce and its psychiatric sequelae
in children. Archives of General Psychiatry, 23, 421-427.

McKenry, P.C., White, P.N., & Price-Bonham, S. (1978). The
fractured conjugal family: A comparison of married and
divorced dyads. Journal of Divorce, 1, 329-339.

McLanahan, S.S. (1983). Family structure and stress: A
longitudinal comparison of two-parent and female-
headed families. Journal of Marriage & the Family,
45, 347-357.

McLanahan, S.S., Wedemeyer, N.V., & Adelberg, T. (1981).
Network structure, social support and psychological
well-being in the single-parent family. Journal of
Marriage & the Family, 43, 601-612.

Menaghan, E.G. (1983). Individual coping efforts & family studies: Conceptual & methodological issues. Marriage & Family Review, 6, 113-135.

Mitchell, R.E., Billings, A.G., & Moss, R.H. (1982). Social support and well-being: Implications for prevention programs. Journal of Primary Prevention, 3, 77-98.

Moos, R.H., Insel, P.M., & Humphrey, B. (1974). Combined preliminary manual: Family, work, and group environment scales. Palo Alto: Consulting Psychologists Press.

Morrison, J.R. (1974). Parental divorce as a factor in childhood psychiatric illness. Comprehensive Psychiatry, 15, 95-102.

Nelson, G. (1981). Moderators of women's and children's adjustment following parental divorce. Journal of Divorce, 4, 71-83.

Norton, A.J., & Glick, P.C. (1979). Marital instability in America: Past, present and future. In G. Levinger & O.C. Moles (Eds.), Divorce and separation: Context, causes and consequences. New York: Basic Books.

Nye, F.L. (1957). Child adjustment in broken and in unhappy unbroken homes. Marriage and Family Living, 19, 356-361.

Olson, D.H., Russell, C.S., & Sprenkle, D.H. (1983). Circumplex model of marital & family systems. VI. Theoretical update. Family Process, 22, 69-83.

Pais, J., & White, P. (1979). Family redefinition: A review of the literature toward a model of divorce adjustment. Journal of Divorce, 2, 271-281.

Parish, T.A., & Dostal, J.W. (1980). Evaluations of self and parent figures by children from intact, divorced, & reconstituted families. Journal of Youth & Adolescence, 9, 347-351.

Parish, T.S., & Taylor, J.C. (1979). The impact of divorce and subsequent father absence on children's and adolescents' self-concepts. Journal of Youth & Adolescence, 8, 427-432.

Patterson, G.R. (1976). The aggressive child: Victim and architect of a coercive system. In L. Hamerlynck, L.C. Handy, & E.J. Mash (Eds.), Behavior modification and families. New York: Brunner/Mazel.

146

Paykel, E.S., Prusoff, B.A., & Uhlenhuth, E.H. (1971). Scaling of life events. Archives of General Psychiatry, 25, 340-347.

Paykel, E.S., & Uhlenhuth, E.H. (1972). Rating the magnitude of life stress. Canadian Psychiatric Association Journal, 17, 93-100.

Pearlin, L.I., & Johnson, J.S. (1977). Marital status, life-strains, and depression. American Sociological Review, 42, 704-715.

Pearlin, L.I., & Schooler, C. The structure of coping. Journal of Health & Social Behavior, 19, 2-21.

Peters, J.F. (1979). Divorce. Toronto: Guidance Centre, Faculty of Education, University of Toronto.

Peters, J.F. (1983). Divorce: The disengaging, disengaged and re-engaging process. In K. Ishwaran (Ed.), The Canadian family. Toronto: Gage.

Pett, M.G. (1982). Predictors of satisfactory social adjust-ment of divorced single parents. Journal of Divorce, 5, 1-17.

Porter, B., & O'Leary, K.D. (1980). Marital discord and childhood behavior problems. Journal of Abnormal Child Psychology, 8, 287-295.

Price-Bonham, S., & Balswick, J.O. (1980). The non-insti-tutions: Divorce, desertion & remarriage. Journal of Marriage & the Family, 42, 959-972.

Raschke, H.J. (1977). The role of social participation in postseparation and postdivorce adjustment. Journal of Divorce, 1, 129-140.

Raschke, H.J. & Raschke, V.J. (1979). Family conflict and children's self-concepts: A comparison of intact and single-parent families. Journal of Marriage and the Family, 41, 367-374.

Roberts, A.R., & Roberts, B.J. (1974). Divorce and the child: A pyrrhic victory? In A.R. Roberts (Ed.), Childhood deprivation. Springfield, Ill.: C.C. Thomas.

Rosenthal, R., & Rosnow, R.L. (1969). The volunteer subject. In R. Rosenthal & R.L. Rosnow (Eds.), Artifact in behavioral research. New York: Academic Press.

147

Rutter, M. (1971). Parent-child separation: Psychological effects on the children. Journal of Child Psychology and Psychiatry, 12, 233-260.

Sandler, I.N., & Ramsay, T.B. (1980). Dimensional analysis of children's stressful life events. American Journal of Community Psychology, 8, 285-302.

Santrock, J.W. (1975). Father absence, perceived maternal behavior, and moral development in boys. Child Development, 46, 753-757.

Santrock, J.W., & Warshak, R.A. (1979). Father custody & social development in boys and girls. Journal of Social Issues, 35, 112-125.

Sarason, I.G., Johnson, J.H., & Siegel, J.M. (1978). Assessing the impact of life changes: Development of the Life Experiences Survey. Journal of Consulting & Clinical Psychology, 46, 932-946.

Saunders, B.E. (1983). The social consequences of divorce: Implications for family policy. Journal of Divorce, 6, 1-17.

Schoettle, U.C., & Cantwell, D.P. (1980). Children of divorce - Demographic variables, symptoms, & diagnoses. American Academy of Child Psychiatry, 19, 453-475.

Sheffner, D.J., & Suarex, J.M. (1975). The postdivorce clinic. American Journal of Psychiatry, 132, 442-444.

Shinn, M. (1978). Father absence and children's cognitive development. Psychological Bulletin, 85, 295-324.

Smith, M.J. (1980). The social consequences of single parenthood: A longitudinal perspective. Family Relations, 29, 75-81.

Smith, W.G. (1971). Critical life-events and prevention strategies in mental health. Archives of General Psychiatry, 25, 103-109.

Spanier, G.B., & Casto, R.F. (1979). Adjustment to separation and divorce: An analysis of 50 case studies. Journal of Divorce, 2, 241-253.

Spanier, G.B., & Thompson, L. (1983). Relief and distress after marital separation. Journal of Divorce, 7, 31-49.

Spicer, J.W., & Hampe, G.D. (1975). Kinship interaction after divorce. Journal of Marriage & the Family, 37, 113-119.

Spivey, P.B., & Scherman, A. (1980). The effects of time lapse on personality characteristics and stress on divorced women. Journal of Divorce, 4, 49-59.

Stolberg, A.L., & Anker, J.M. (in press). Cognitive and behavioral changes in children resulting from parental divorce and consequent environmental changes. Journal of Divorce.

Stolberg, A.L., & Cullen, P.M. (1983). Preventive interventions for families of fivorce: The divorce adjustment project. In L.A. Kurdeck (Ed.), Children and divorce. San Francisco: Jossey-Bass.

Sugar, M. (1970). Children of divorce. Pediatrics, 46, 591.

Thiessen, J.D., Avery, A.W., & Joanning, H. (1980). Facilitating postdivorce adjustment among women: A communication skills training approach. Journal of Divorce, 4, 35-44.

Tooley, K. (1976). Antisocial behavior and social alientation post divorce: The "man of the house" and his mother. American Journal of Orthopsychiatry, 46, 33-42.

Tuckman, J., & Regan, R.A. (1966). Intactness of the home and behavioral problems in children. Journal of Child Psychology and Psychiatry, 7, 225-233.

Turner, R.J., Frankel, B.G., & Levin, D. (1983). Social support: Conceptualization, measurement, and implications for mental health. In J.R. Greenley (Ed.), Research in community mental health, Vol. III, Greenwich: JAI Press.

Vinokur, A., & Selzer, M.L. (1975). Desirable versus undesirable life events: Their relationship to stress and mental distress. Journal of Personality & Social Psychology, 32, 329-337.

Vogelsang, J.D. (1982). Working with the separated and divorced. Journal of Religion & Health, 21, 325-330.

Wallerstein, J.S., & Kelly, J.B. (1974). The effects of parental divorce: The adolescent experience. In E.J. Anthony & C. Koupernik (Eds.), The Child in his family: Children at psychiatric risk. New York: John Wiley & Sons.

Wallerstein, J.S., & Kelly, J.B. (1976). The effects of parental divorce: Experiences of the child in later latency. American Journal of Orthopsychiatry, 26, 256-269.

Wallerstein, J.S., & Kelly, J.B. (1975). The effects of parental divorce: Experiences of the preschool child. Journal of the American Academy of Child Psychiatry, 14, 600-616.

Wallerstein, J.S., & Kelly, J.B. (1977). Divorce counseling: A community service for families in the midst of divorces. American Journal of Orthopsychiatry, 47, 4-22.

Wallerstein, J.S., & Kelly, J.B. (1980). Surviving the breakup: How children and parents cope with divorce. New York: Basic Books.

Warren, N.J., Grew, R.S., Konanc, J.T., Ilgen, E.R., & Amura, I. (1982, August). Parenting after divorce: Evaluation of preventive programs for divorcing families. Paper presented at the Annual Meeting of the American Psychological Association.

Weiss, R.S. (1975). Marital separation. New York: Basic Books.

Welch, G.J., & Granvold, D.K. (1977). Seminars for separated/divorced: An educational approach to postdivorce adjustment. Journal of Sex and Marital Therapy, 3, 31-39.

Westman, J.C. (1971). The psychiatrist and child custody contests. American Journal of Psychiatry, 27, 123-124.

Westman, J., Cline, D.W., Swift, W.J., & Kramer, D.A. (1970). Role of child psychiatry in divorce. Archives of General Psychiatry, 23, 416-421.

White, S.W., & Bloom, B.L. (1981). Factors related to the adjustment of divorcing men. Family Relations, 30, 349-360.

White, S.W., & Mika, K. (1983). Family divorce and separation: Theory and research. Marriage & Family Review, 6, 175-192.

Wilcox, B.L. (1981). Social support in adjusting to marital disruption: A network analysis. In B.H. Gottlieb (Ed.), Social networks and social support. Beverly Hills: Sage.

Woodruff, R.A., Guze, S.R., & Clayton, P.J. (1972). Divorce among psychiatric outpatients. British Journal of Psychiatry, 121, 289-292.

Young, D.M. (1978). Consumer satisfaction with the divorce workshop: A follow-up. Journal of Divorce, 2, 49-56. (a)

Young, D.M. (1978). The divorce experience workshop: A consumer evaluation. Journal of Divorce, 2, 37-47. (b)

Young, D.M. (1983). Two studies of children of divorce. In L.A. Kurdeck (Ed.), Children and Divorce. San Francisco: Jossey-Bass.

Young, E.R., & Parish, T.S. (1977). Impact of father absence during childhood on the psychological adjustment of college females. Sex Roles, 3, 217-227.

Zeiss, A.M., Zeiss, R.A., & Johnson, S.M. (1980). Sex differences in initiation of and adjustment to divorce. Journal of Divorce, 4, 21-33.

A. ONE PARENT FAMILIES: OVERVIEW

1. Armstrong-Dillard, P. "Developing Services for Single Parents and their Children in the School," Social Work in Education, 3(1): 1980, 44-57.

    A comprehensive approach to providing supportive services to children and their parents may include the following: (1) counseling on an individual basis, (2) working with groups of single parents, (3) leading children's groups, (4) founding programs of professional development for teachers, and (5) developing innovative alternative ways of serving children and parents affected by divorce.

2. Atlas, S.L. Single Parenting: A Practical Resource Guide. Englewood Cliffs, N.J.: Prentice-Hall, 1981.

    Practical advice, based on personal experiences and insights are presented in this book.

3. Bureau of the Census. Household and Family Characteristics: March 1981. Washington, D.C.: U.S. Department of Commerce, 1982.

    This report presents detailed demographic information on the characteristics of households and families including one-parent families in the United States.

4. Cunningham, D. The One-Parent Family Research Study. London, Ontario: London Council of Women, 1979.

    A study of one-parent families in London, Ontario. The sample comprised 191 adults and 374 children.

5. Dietl, L.K. and M.J. Nett. Single Parent Families: Choice or Chance, New York: Teachers College, Columbia University, 1983.

    This is part of the Human Needs and Social Welfare Curriculum Project. It is intended for students studying this area in their curriculum.

6. Edwards, D.W. "A Pilot investigation of 40 single parent families and 40 intact families." Journal of Humanics, 9(1): 1981, 28-36.

    A study attempted to identify common problems encountered by single-parent families resulting from desertion, separation, divorce, or death of

153

a spouse or parent. Forty intact families were compared with forty single-parent families who participated in a self-help organization. The most common problems experienced by the single parents were economic, social, and psychological in nature, all of which were closely interrelated. A brief discussion of how the self-help organization for single parents was developed is provided. The conclusion focuses on the implications of the study's findings for practice and future research.

7. Espinoza, R. and N. Naron. Work and Family Life Among Anglo, Black and Mexican American Single-Parent Families. Austin, Texas: Southwest Educational Development Laboratory, December 1983.

This report summarizes a research project which examines how families adapt and function in relation to workplace policies. Attention is paid to the parents' child care arrangements and socialization of their children.

8. Esses, L. and R. Rachlis. "Single Parent and Remarried Families: Reasons for Reconsidering Traditional Models of the Family." (in) D.S. Freeman and B. Trute (eds) Treating Families with Special Needs. Ottawa: Canadian Association of Social Workers, 1981, 113-130.

The special circumstances of single parents are considered as becoming more prevalent and that challenge traditional norms on evaluating family functioning.

9. Fischer, J.L. "Mothers Living Apart From their Children." Family Relations, 32 (July 1983), 351-357.

This paper discusses the situations of mothers who live apart from their children. Negative societal evaluations of mothers in this lifestyle are contrasted with the findings based on empirical research. The various processes by which mothers come to live apart from their children are discussed. Finally implications for family life educators and family therapists are identified.

10. Fowler, E. Single Parent Family Study Report. Niagara Falls, Ontario: The Social Planning Council of Niagara Falls, 1983.

A study of the needs and problems faced by the single parent families in Niagara Falls, Ontario, Canada. In Niagara there are 2320 single parent families, of whom 350 are headed by a father.

11. Fulmer, R.H. "A Structural Approach to Unresolved Mourning
     in Single Parent Family Systems", Journal of Marital
     and Family Therapy, 9 (July 1983), 259-269.

     The mother's depression is considered as a special
     problem in the family therapy of single parent families.
     It is seen as resulting from unresolved mourning
     that is maintained by the family system. Several
     reasons why the single parent family's structure
     seems inherently vulnerable to unresolved mourning
     are offered. Some techniques of Structural Family
     Therapy are proposed in a specific order to
     facilitate mourning in such families.

12. Giovannoni, J.R. and A. Billingsley. "Family: One Parent",
     in Encyclopedia of Social Work (Vol. 1) Washington,
     D.C.: National Association of Social Workers, 1978,
     397-408.

     An overview of the one-parent family.

13. Gonder, J. and S. Gordon. The Housing Needs of 'Non-
     Traditional' Households. Washington: Department
     of Housing and Urban Development (H.U.D.), 1979.

     The authors discuss the problems which single parents
     face in dealing with housing and urban arrangements
     planned and built with the two-parent nuclear family
     in mind. They argue that discrimination against
     children, combined with low income makes it
     extremely difficult for single parents to find
     suitable housing. They describe three non-
     traditional housing projects built to cater to
     single parents.

14. Hanson, S.M.H. and J.A. Trilling. "A Proposed Study of
     the Characteristics of the Healthy Single-Parent
     Family", Family Perspective, 17 (Spring 1983),
     79-88.

     The proposed study will investigate single-parent
     families and describe the characteristics which make
     this family unit strong and healthy. In addition,
     a comparison will be made between healthy single-
     parent families according to the sex of the
     custodial parents and the custodial arrangements
     which have been made on behalf of the children.

15. Heath, J. A Report on Single Parents. Vancouver:
     Vancouver School Board, 1980.

     A demographic analysis of the 1976 Census data
     related to single parents in British Columbia.

16. Hofstein, S. "Perspectives on the Jewish Single-Parent Family," J. of Jewish Communal Services, 54 (Spring 1978), 229-240.

This paper examines the contemporary single parent family in the Jewish community in the United States.

17. Hogan, M.J., Buehler, C. and B. Robinson. "Single Parenting: Transitioning Alone", (in) H.I. McCubbin and C.R. Figley (eds) Stress and the Family: Coping With Normative Transitions, New York: Brunner-Mazel, 1983, 116-132 (Vol. 1).

Most single-parent families experience a pile-up of changes and demands. Single parents must take on several roles combining nurturing and earning responsibilities, roles which are assumed by two parents in most families. The children, depending on their developmental stage, may acquire new responsibility. Single parents may be separated, with or without legal sanction, divorced, widowed, or never-married. The family may be headed by a mother, a father, or parents may have joint custody of their children. The larger the family, the more complex the organization; children may be at different developmental stages such as preschool, adolescent, and/or adult.

18. Klodawsky, F., Spector, A.N., and C. Hendrix. Housing and Single Parents: An Overview of the Literature. Toronto: Centre for Urban and Community Studies, University of Toronto, 1984.

This 48 page monograph reviews the literature related to housing and single parents in Canada and the United States. There is also a 50 item annotated bibliography.

19. Li, Selina. Options for Single Mothers. Toronto: Social Planning Council of Metropolitan Toronto, Project Child Care, Working Paper #4, 1978.

An examination of working single-parent mothers in Toronto.

20. McLanaham, S.S., Wedemeyer, N.V. and T. Adelberg. "Network Structure, Social Support, and Psychological Well-Being in the Single-Parent Family," J. of Marriage and the Family, 43 (August 1981), 601-612.

This research examines the relationship among network structure, social support, and psychological well-being in the single-parent family. Three network types are identified: the family or origin network, the extended network, and the conjugal network.

21. Mendes, H.A. "Single Parent Families: A Typology of Life Styles", _Social Work_ 24 (May 1979), 193-200.

This article presents a beginning conceptualization of five distinct life-styles of single-parent families. Social workers can help such families anticipate and deal with the psychosocial risks and make maximum use of the unique opportunities of the life-style they adopt.

22. Miller, J.B. "Psychological Recovery in Low-Income Single Parents", _American J. of Orthopsychiatry_, 52 (April 1982), 346-352.

A small group of low-income single parents, seen several years after marital separation, was found to be functioning well psychologically. Although they had suffered distress at the time of marital separation, they had overcome formidable economic and social obstacles and had incorporated positive developments in their self-representations and object relationships.

23. Murdock, C.V. _Single Parents are People Too_. New York: Butterick, 1980.

A single parent herself, the author includes in her book pointers from various helping professions on living as a single parent.

24. Orthner, D.K. _Families in Blue: A Study of Married and Single Parent Families in the U.S. Air Force_. 1980.

An examination of one-parent families in the Air Force which comprise 1% of the total American Air Force.

25. Paynton, I.S. "Single Parent Households: An Alternative Approach", _Family Economics Review_ 3 (Winter 1982), 11-16.

This paper focuses on differences in structure and composition of households headed by single parents. A typology for classification of such households into 12 categories is presented and then applied to data.

26. Riley, B. "Education and One-Parent Families", _Education Manitoba_, 8 (December 1981), 9-16.

The purpose of this background paper is to provide

educators in Manitoba with information on the
incidence, effects, counselling techniques, and
practical considerations associated with children of
one-parent families.

27. Schlesinger, B. The One Parent Family: Perspectives and
     Annotated Bibliography. Toronto: University of
     Toronto Press, 1978, (4th edition).

     Six essays discuss various aspects of one-parent
     families. The annotated bibliography contains 750
     items up to March 1978.

28. Schlesinger, Benjamim. "Single Parent Adoptions,"
     J. of the Ontario Association of Children's Aid
     Societies, 21 (February 1978), 3-5, 12-14.

     A review of the literature related to single parent
     adoptions.

29. Schlesinger, B. (ed) One in Ten: The Single Parent in
     Canada. Toronto: Guidance Centre, Faculty of
     Education, University of Toronto, 1979.

     Twenty-one papers discuss the various categories of
     one-parenthood related to the Canadian scene.

30. Schlesinger, B. "One Parent Families: Knowns and
     Unknowns", Conciliation Courts Review, 17 (Sept.
     1979), 41-44.

     Twenty factors are discussed about our present
     knowledge and gaps in the area of one-parent families.

31. Schlesinger, B. "One Parent Families and their Children
     in Canadian Society," (in) D. Radcliffe (ed) The
     Family and Socialization of Children: Report of a
     Workshop. Ottawa: Social Sciences and Humanities
     Research Council of Canada, 1980, 82-114.

     A discussion of one-parent families and their
     children in Canadian society.

32. Schlesinger, B. "Jewish One-Parent Families: A Growing
     Phenomenon in the 1970's", J. of Psychology and
     Judaism, 7 (Spring-Summer 1983), 89-100.

     A review of the existing literature in Canada and
     the United States related to Jewish one-parent
     families.

33. Schlesinger, B. Canadian Family Studies: A Selected
     Annotated Bibliography, 1970-1982. Chicago:
     Council of Planning Librarians, 1983.

     This bibliography contains 88 items including
     those related to single-parent families in Canada.

34. Schlesinger, B. "One-Parent Families: Coping in a Two-
     Parent Family System," (in) D.P. Lumsden (ed).
     Community Mental Health Action. Ottawa: The
     Canadian Public Health Association, 1984, 119-127.

     A short overview of the various categories of single
     parent families found in Canada. Some of their
     problems and positive aspects of family life are
     discussed.

35. Schorr, A.L. and P. Moen. "The Single Parent and
     Public Policy", Social Policy, 9 (March-April 1979),
     15-21.

36. Smith, M.J. "The Social Consequences of Single Parent-
     hood: A Longitudinal Perspective," Family Relations,
     29 (Jan. 1980), 75-81.

     Loneliness and the lack of social support have been
     described as the more serious social consequences
     of the single-parent family status. Secondary
     analysis of interviews with a national sample of
     families over six years revealed many shifts in the
     household composition of one parent families over
     time, a slightly lower level of community partici-
     pation, and a feeling of powerlessness among single-
     parent, family heads.

37. Smith, M.J. "Economic Conditions in Single Parent
     Families," Social Work Research Abstracts, 16
     (Summer 1980), 20-24.

     This secondary analysis of a longitudinal sample of
     families reveals the pervasive negative effects of
     single parenthood on the income and employment of
     never-married, widowed, separated and divorced
     parents. Despite the common plight of all single-
     parent families, a unified approach to income
     maintenance for this group remains lacking.

38. Smith, M.J. and B. Moses. "Social Welfare Agencies and
     Social Reform Movements: The Case of the Single
     Parent Family," Sociology and Social Welfare, 7 (1),
     1980, 125-136.

     To a greater extent than before, social welfare

agencies are emphasizing social change over direct
services. A social reform movement is a mechanism
by which societal and institutional change may be
accomplished. The relationship between social
welfare organizations and social movements has not
been clearly defined.

The single parent group is discussed as a group
with the potential to generate into a social reform
movement.

39. Snyder, L.M. "The Deserting, Non Supporting Father:
     Scapegoat of Family Non Policy," The Family
     Co-ordinator, 28 (Oct. 1979), 594-598.

     This study of the impact of the criminal justice
     system on the deserting, nonsupporting father in
     relation to the fulfillment of his role as provider
     provides data for rethinking our approach in aiding
     the nonsupporting father to cope with his dilemma
     as well as our own.

40. Social Planning Council of Metropolitan Toronto. Metro's
     Suburbs in Transition, Part I, (Background Report)
     Toronto: 1979.

     The concentration of single parent households in
     suburban public housing projects is described and
     evaluated. Problems of social isolation and of
     dependence upon inadequate public transportation
     are noted. As well, a reluctance on the part of
     municipal governments to meet the needs of
     'solitary' parents is identified and attributed to
     the perception of them as problem tenants in public
     housing.

41. Social Planning Council of Metropolitan Toronto. Metro's
     Suburbs in Transition (Part II), Planning Agenda
     for the Eighties, Toronto: 1980.

     This report puts forth concrete suggestions as to
     how Toronto's suburbs could be made more flexible
     in order to better meet the needs of its citizens.
     One target group it considers is single parents
     and it discusses ways in which suburban environ-
     ments might be made more accessible to those
     without a car, and to those with a loss of income
     who want to remain in their old suburban neighbour-
     hoods. It also argues an increase in subsidized
     day care spaces.

42. Social Planning Council of Metropolitan Toronto, and
     Ontario Welfare Council. <u>And the Poor Get Poorer</u>.
     Toronto: 1981.

     This study analyzed the impact of government trans-
     fers in terms of their impact upon the poverty
     status of recipients. Among other results, it
     found that a mother with one child receiving Family
     Benefit support and in public housing would achieve
     poverty line income level. It also pointed out
     that the availability of public housing throughout
     Ontario was such that only a minority would be
     able to take advantage of it.

43. Soper, M. "Housing for Single-Parent Families: A Women's
     Design" (in) <u>New Space for Women</u>, G. Wekerle et al.
     (eds) Boulder, Colorado: Westview Press, 1980.

     Soper describes the development of a conceptualization
     for public housing in LeBreton Flats, Ottawa, which
     specifically attempted to incorporate facilities
     geared to women. Single parents were identified
     as an important group to be considered and two
     phases of housing need, in the transition from
     marriage to single parenthood, were identified. The
     first consisted of short-term emergency facilities
     and the second was to be geared to longer-term
     transition needs.

44. Statistics Canada. <u>Canada's Families</u>. Ottawa: 1979.

     In this bulletin based upon 1976 Census material,
     female lone parents were identified as a group
     which is particularly concentrated among the poor.
     Also noted was the growth of female lone-parents
     and a decline in the proportion of male lone parents.

45. Steele, M. <u>The Demand for Housing in Canada</u>. Ottawa:
     Statistics Canada, 1979.

     In this study based upon 1971 Census material,
     Steele finds that the ownership and household
     expenditure patterns of widowed, separated and
     divorced heads are significantly different than
     their married counterparts. While the expenditure
     patterns of the latter are usually explained in
     terms of current income, for the former, especially
     middle-aged females, the family income at the time
     of the dissolution of the marriage is a more
     important predictor.

46. Thompson, E.H., and P.A. Gonzola. "Single Parent Families: In the Mainstream of American Society," in Contemporary Families and Alternative Lifestyles, edited by E.M. Macklin and R.R. Rubin, Beverly Hills, California: Sage, 1983, 97-124.

A comprehensive review of the American literature related to one-parent families. These families are becoming to be recognized in society.

47. Todres, R. (ed) Self-Help Groups: An Annotated Bibliography, 1970-1982. New York: National Self-Help Clearing House, 1983.

This annotated bibliography of articles and books contains all the self-help group items related to one-parent families.

48. Trost, J. "The Concepts of One-Parent Family," J. of Comparative Family Studies, 9 (Winter 1980), 129-138.

The concept of one parent family is a heterogenous concept and in this article the phenomenon of the existing bonds after the dissolution of a primary group are hinted at. A property space analysis including some of the most important variables when looking upon the transmission from a two parent family into a one parent family is presented and discussed.

49. Turow, R. Daddy Doesn't Live Here Anymore. New York: Anchor Books, 1978.

A practical and understandable guide for parents who are dissolving their marriage.

50. Wargon, S. Canadian Households and Families. Ottawa: Statistics Canada, 1979.

This survey of recent demographic trends is based on the results of Canadian census data from 1931 to 1971. She notes that husband-wife families are always more likely than single parent families to be maintaining their own households, and also discusses differences between types of single parent families. Female heads are making up an increasing share of family heads not maintaining their own households.

51. Waxman, C.I. <u>Single-Parent Families: A Challenge to the Jewish Community</u>. New York: American Jewish Committee, Institute of Human Relations, 1980.

A short overview of the situation of single parent families in the Jewish community.

52. Weiss, R. "Housing for Single Parents," <u>Policy Studies Journal</u>, 8 (No. 2, 1979).

Weiss' article is based on conversational interviews with over two hundred single parents. Respondents were ambivalent about moving at the time of marital dissolution, but for many, a reduced income makes it impossible for homeowners to remain in their homes. This also seems to be true for renters. Weiss outlines the problems faced by single parents in finding adequate housing and notes that single parents often move several times before suitable housing is found.

53. Weiss, R.S. <u>Going It Alone</u>. New York: Basic Books, 1979.

The author discusses the family life and the social situation of the woman or man who is left to care for the children.

54. Weiss, R.S. "Growing Up a Little Faster: The Experience of Growing Up in a Single-Parent Household," <u>J. of Social Issues</u>, 35 (Fall 1979), 97-111.

On the basis of interviews with single parents, and with adolescent children living with single parents, a theory of the structure and functioning of single-parent households is proposed.

55. Weltner, J.S. "A Structural Approach to the Single-Parent Family," <u>Family Process</u>, 21 (June 1982), 203-210.

Structural theory, with its emphasis on subsystems, generational boundaries, and organizational patterns, provides a framework for viewing the built-in vulnerability of the single-parent family unit. Minuchin's emphasis on generational boundaries and the problem of enmeshment underlies the theoretical and therapeutic approach presented here.

56. Blechman, E.A. "Are Children with One Parent at Psychological Risk? A Methodological Review," J. of Marriage and the Family, 44 (Feb. 1982), 179-196.

Is the child reared by one parent at risk for psychological maladjustment? Four decades of research have not provided conclusive information. Design errors include poor control over extraneous natural covariates of family type, particularly socioeconomic status; unrepresentative samples; and invalid dependent measures.

57. Brown, B.F. "A Study of the School Needs of Children from One-Parent Families," Phi Delta Kappan, 61 (April 1980), 537-540.

Nearly half of U.S. children born in 1980 will live "a considerable time" with only one parent. This study shows that many of them will have special academic and behavior problems. What are the implications for education?

58. Earl, L. and N. Lohmann. "Absent Fathers and Black Male Children," Social Work, 23 (September 1978), 413-415.

In the research reported in this article, the availability of male role models was examined in the lives of fifty-three black latency age boys in Knoxville, Tennessee. The study focused on whether these children, raised in homes from which the fathers were absent, had access to their fathers or other black males as potential role models and male images.

59. Gardner, R.A. The Boys and Girls Book About One-Parent Families. New York: Bantam Books, 1983.

A guide to the many questions asked about one-parent families by children.

60. Graham-Cambrick, L., Gursky, E.J. and J. Brendler. "Hospitalization of Single-Parent Families of Disturbed Children," Family Process, 21 (June 1982), 141-152.

In this paper, six years of experience with well-planned, short-term family hospitalization is described. Each family has at least one identified patient who is a child. The approach to treatment is systemic and structural. Areas discussed are selection of families, planning of the hospitalization, stages of the hospitalization, and the organization of the staff.

61. Grossberg, S.H. and L. Crandall. "Father Loss and Father Absence in Preschool Children," Clinical Social Work Journal, 6 (Summer 1978), 123-134.

The role of the father in child development is discussed. Children's reactions to the death, separation, or divorce of their fathers are explored. Implications for diagnosis are stated along with specific recommendations for treatment.

62. Hetherington, E.M., Camara, K.A. and D.L. Featherman. Cognitive Performance, School Behavior and Achievement of Children of One-Parent Families. Medford, Mass.: Child and Family Study, Tufts University, 1981.

In this report, the authors have reviewed the research literature on the effects of divorce and one-parent childrearing on academic achievement and intellectual functioning. Life changes accompanying the decision to separate are described. At each stage following divorce, family members face different challenges and different stresses. Through the analysis of available studies on family life after divorce, the experience of living in a one-parent household, and achievement during and beyond the school years, the authors reach several major conclusions.

63. Hetherington, E.M., Camara, K.A. and D.L. Featherman. "Achievement and Intellectual Functioning of Children in One-Parent Households," (in) J.T. Spence ed. Achievement and Achievement Motives: Psychological and Sociological Approaches, San Francisco: W.H. Freeman, 1983, 208-284.

In this chapter, the authors have set themselves the important tasks of reviewing the voluminous and often methodologically flawed research literature to discern what is known about the relationship between children's academic achievements and their rearing in a one-parent home and of developing a social-psychological model that describes the relationships this research has revealed.

64. Holman, T.B. "Marital Instability, Maternal Stress, and Sex-Role Development in Children," Family Perspective, 17 (Spring 1983), 89-100.

Research on the effects of marital instability on sex-role development in children has been contra-dictory and often confusing. This paper shows that there is theoretical and empirical justification

165

for proposing that marital instability affects
children's sex-role development through the inter-
vening variables of maternal stress and maternal
interaction techniques. The theoretical model that
is developed, in essence, ties together two more
abstract theories—crisis theory and parent-child
socialization theory.

65. Horner, C.T. The Single-Parent Family in Children's
Books: An Analysis and Annotated Bibliography,
with an Appendix on Audiovisual Material. Metuchen,
N.J.: Scarecrow, 1978.

Horner's study of 100 years of fiction books for
children portrays one-parent families. Adults
guiding children through traumatic family upheavals
and librarians building collections to support their
efforts could use this comprehensive view. The 215
available titles were perused and analyzed according
to such factors as the moralistic or bibliotherapeutic
message, setting, identification of the single parent,
portrayal of the absent parent, and the economic
status of the family.

66. Houts, P.L. (ed). When the Family Comes Apart. The
National Elementary Principal, 59 (October 1979).
Special Issue.

This special issue deals with children of one-
parent families in the school system.

67. Jacobson, D.S. "The Impact of Marital Separation/Divorce
on Children: I Parent-Child Separation and Child
Adjustment," J. of Divorce, 1 (Summer 1978), 341-
360.

This is a report of the findings from one of several
dimensions of study of the impact of divorce on
children. Other dimensions will be reported in
subsequent articles. This portion of the study
examined the association between the child's psychosocial adjustment and the amount of time and
activity list with each parent after the parental
separation. The sample consisted of 30 families
(51 children) all of whom had experienced a parental
separation within 12 months prior to the research
interview.

68. Jacobson, D.S. "The Impact of Marital Separation/Divorce
     on Children: II Interparent Hostility and Child
     Adjustment," J. of Divorce, 2 (Fall 1978), 3-19.

     This is the second of a series of three papers
     that report on a study of the impact of marital
     separation/divorce on children aged 3-17 during
     the 12-month period following the parental
     separation. The focus of the overall study is on
     factors that affect the psychosocial adjustment
     of children within 12 months after the marital
     separation, a specific period when the child is
     adjusting to a life situation of having only one
     parent in the home.

69. Jacobson, D.S. "The Impact of Marital Separation/Divorce
     on Children: III Parent Child Communication and
     Child Adjustment," J. of Divorce, 2 (Winter 1978),
     175-194.

     This is the third of a series of reports on the
     findings from a study directed at further under-
     standing the impact of marital separation/divorce
     on children during the 12-month period following
     the parental separation. The focus of the overall
     study is on factors that affect the adjustment of
     children within this 12-month period after
     parental separation, a specific period when the
     child is adjusting to a life situation that involves
     having only one parent in the home.

70. Lebowitz, M.L. "The Organization and Utilization of a
     Child-Focused Facility for Divorcing, Single-
     Parent, and Remarried Families," Conciliation
     Courts Review, 21 (December 1983), 99-104.

     Teachers and physicians can play important roles
     as they interact with members of divorcing,
     single-parent, and remarried families, however,
     when parents in these families turn to teachers
     and physicians as their primary initial resource,
     the experience can be frustrating for everyone
     involved. The responses of teachers and physicians
     can vary greatly, depending upon the individual's
     own comfort and feeling of competency, assessment
     of the situation, availability of time, and
     familiarity with appropriate community resources.

167

71. Lerner, Samuel. "Services to the Child in the Single Parent Family," J. of Jewish Communal Service, 55 (June 1979), 369-374.

    The author outlines key programs that should be considered by Jewish family agencies in working with single parent families.

72. Lindsay, J.W. Do I Have a Daddy? Buena Park, California: Morning Glory Press, 1982.

    Part of the Morning Glory Press series on single parents, this book is written as a children's story and intended for use by single parents. Contains special section for single mothers and fathers.

73. Raschke, Helen J., and Vernon J. Raschke. "Family Conflict and Children's Self Concepts: A Comparison of Intact and Single-Parent Families," J. of Marriage and the Family, 41 (May 1979), 367-374.

    A sample of 289 3rd, 6th and 8th grade children were used in this study. Self concept scores were significantly lower for children who reported higher levels of family conflict.

74. Schlesinger, B. "One-Parent Families - Children's Viewpoint." Education Manitoba, 8 (May 1982), 4-10.

    Children from one-parent families were interviewed (N=40). This involved open-ended questions. The average length of time they had been living in a single-parent family was 4.7 years.

75. Schlesinger, B. "Children's Viewpoint of Living in a One-Parent Family," J. of Divorce, 5 (Summer 1982), 1-23.

    A review of American and Canadian studies dealing with children in one-parent families.

76. Turner, P.H. and R.H.M. Smith. "Single Parents and Day Care," Family Relations, 32 (April 1983), 215-226.

    This study assessed the day care needs, attitudes, and practices of 252 single parents with dependent children. The sample was diverse in terms of age, income, educational level, and number and ages of dependent children. The study suggests that single parents need: Adequate day care services

that are affordable and convenient to either their
home or work.

Treatment and Services to One-Parent Families

77. Hajal, F. and Rosenberg, E.B. "Working with the One-
    Parent Family in Family Therapy," J. of Divorce,
    3 (Spring 1978), 259-269.

    This paper describes the particular problems that
    arise in the treatment of one-parent families.
    These problems are seen as stemming from the
    experience of disruption in the life of the family
    and the resulting special family structure.
    Techniques of handling the various resistances and
    issues that surface are presented and discussed.
    A case report illustrating many of the points made
    in the body of the paper is included.

78. Handelman, E.R. "Developing Networks of Services to
    Single Parents: A Population at Risk," J. of
    Jewish Communal Service, 58 (Fall 1981), 36-41.

    The author describes the steps the Jewish Community
    Centre of Greater Rochester took in establishing
    a Single Parent Department.

79. Morawetz, A. and G. Walker. Brief Therapy with Single-
    Parent Families. New York. Brunner-Mazel, 1983.

    Provides a theoretical and practical framework by
    examining every aspect of this family constellation.
    Based on a three-year project conducted at the
    Ackerman Institute for Family Therapy, it covers
    basics in theory and practice, presents detailed
    cases illustrating successful treatment strategies
    for working with families at different stages of
    separation, and discusses desertion, marriage,
    divorce, and death.

80. Parks, A.P. "Mutual Help for Single Parents: Parents
    Without Partners, Inc.," Conciliation Courts
    Review, 19 (June 1981), 73-76.

    A description of the work of Parents Without
    Partners (PWP).

81.   Porter, B.R. and R.S. Chatelain. "Family Life Education
       For Single Parents," Family Relations, 30 (October
       1981), 517-525.

       Approximately one out of five children in the
       United States under the age of 18 now lives in a
       one-parent family. The emotional, social, and
       financial problems that often affect parents and
       children deserve the serious attention of family
       life educators who can develop and offer programs
       that will assist involved individuals in coping
       with these problems. Challenges that may be
       unique to single parents and their children have
       been identified and means of dealing with these
       challenges are discussed.

82.   Schlesinger, B. and R. Todres. "Characteristics of
       Canadian Members of Parents Without Partners."
       In One in Ten: The Single Parent in Canada,
       B. Schlesinger, ed. Toronto: Guidance Centre,
       Faculty of Education, University of Toronto, 1979,
       107-11.

       Parents Without Partners offers both an educational
       program and the opportunity to single parents to
       meet with one another to discuss common interests.
       This study looked at the nature of the members of
       P.W.P. in Canada in 1974. Questionnaires were
       sent to members of P.W.P. throughout Canada. The
       response rate was 13% (N=386).

83.   Stark, R. "The Fatherless Boys Project of the Jewish
       Board of Guardians: Some Therapeutic Implications,"
       J. of Jewish Communal Service, 53 (Winter 1976),
       200-207.

       A description of a project which offers service to
       fatherless boys.

84.   Srong, J. "A Human Communications Model and Its Influence
       on Six Single Parents," Family Perspective, 17
       (Spring 1983), 67-68.

       The new Human Communication Model has included a
       number of concepts which have allowed these six
       single parents to understand what was going on in
       their own lives and in their relationships with
       their children and others.

B.   DIVORCE

Children and Divorce

85.   Ahrons, C. and S. Arnn. "When Children From Divorced
       Families are Hospitalized: Issues for Staff,"
       Health and Social Work, 6 (August 1981), 21-27.

       This article presents major issues for social
       workers and other personnel in hospitals to
       consider when working with divorced families whose
       children become hospitalized.

86.   Beal, E.W. "Children of Divorce: A Family Systems
       Perspective," J. of Social Issues, 35 (Fall 1979),
       140-154.

       This paper is a report of a study of marriage and
       divorce as processes through which emotional
       attachments are established and resolved. The
       concepts of family systems theory and therapy are
       used to describe the ways in which emotional
       attachments in general, and child focus in
       particular, operate in families undergoing
       separation or divorce.

87.   Benedek, R.S. and E.P. Benedek. "Children of Divorce:
       Can We Meet their Needs?" J. of Social Issues, 35
       (Fall 1979), 155-169.

                                                    301.105/5

88.   Bienenfeld, F. "What the Children Say About Divorce,"
       Conciliation Courts Review, 18 (December 1980),
       47-50.

       A concilation counselor gives some guidelines on
       how to talk to children about divorce.

89.   Bilgé, B. and G. Kaufman. "Children of Divorce and One-
       Parent Families: Cross-Cultural Perspectives,"
       Family Relations, 32 (January 1983), 59-71.

       One-parent families, particularly female-headed
       households, are found to be widespread in cross-
       cultural data. By examining such families in
       diverse societies, insights can be gained which
       give a broader perspective to the situation of one-
       parent households in our own society. When viewed
       cross-culturally, the one-parent family is found
       to be neither pathological nor inferior.

90. Black, K.N. "Children and Divorce," Single Parent, 21 February 1978), 16-39.

A description of how divorce affects children by a divorced psychologist.

91. Bumpass, L. and R.R. Rindfuss. "Children's Experience of Marital Disruption," American J. of Sociology, 85 (January 1979), 49-65.

This paper uses life-table procedures and data from the 1973 Family Growth Survey to ask three basic questions: (1) What is the cumulative probability that by a given age a child will have experienced a single-parent family as a consequence of marital disruption? (2) Given a marital disruption, what is the cumulative proportion of children either experiencing parental remarriage or reaching age 18 within a given number of years following disruption? (3) What is the average duration of experience in a single-parent family? Estimates based on the early 1970's suggest that about one-third of all children will spend some time in a single-parent family before age 16 as a consequence of marital disruption.

92. Cantor, D.W. "Divorce: A View From the Children," J. of Divorce, 2 (Summer 1979), 357-361.

A play, written by a third-grade boy, is presented to illustrate the awareness of children during the preseparation phase of divorce. The "Divorce Play" was written by a member of an elementary school group for children of divorce, and performed by group members for their parents and teachers. The parents are reported to have found the play an embarrassing and sobering experience, and were overwhelmed to learn how much their children had perceived during the preseparation period. Cantor presents this play to dispel the notion that children are ignorant of the fact that family disruption is occuring.

93. Cantor, D.W. and E.A. Drake. Divorced Parents and Their Children. New York: Springer Publishing Co., 1983.

This book is a guide to mental health professionals who are involved in counselling and treating divorced parents and their children.

94. Cassetty, J. "Child Support: Emerging Issues for
         Practice," Social Casework, 65 (February 1984),
         74-80.

         Providing adequate parental support for children
         is an increasing problem because of the growth in
         divorces, single-parent families, and stepfamilies.
         The dilemmas are complex and difficult. This
         article explores present solutions and suggests
         ways of improving them.

95. Drake, E.A. "Helping the School Cope with Children of
         Divorce," J. of Divorce, 3 (Fall 1979), 69-75.

         Children of divorce may manifest problems at school
         while none is observable in the home setting.
         Parents, therefore, cannot be relied upon to always
         identify problems resulting from the divorce.
         School personnel, and especially teachers who have
         the most contact with the students, need to be aware
         of the common problems associated with divorce seen
         within the school setting and how to intervene.
         The effects of learning and school performance,
         peer relationships, relationships with teachers and
         other adult school personnel are explored and
         literature is cited to clarify the educational and
         social effects of divorce as seen within the
         school. Intervention methods are proposed.

96. Effron, A.K. "Children and Divorce: Help from an
         Elementary School," Social Work, 61 (May 1980),
         305-312.

         Short-term group work in an elementary school
         provided an outlet for preadolescents undergoing
         the stress of their parents' divorce. Contact with
         peers in similar situations and the opportunity to
         play out their family dramas in a structured
         setting provided the catharsis needed for better
         management of classroom tasks.

97. Farber, S.S., Primavera, J. and R.D. Felner. "Older
         Adolescents and Parental Divorce: Adjustment Problems
         and Mediators of Coping," J. of Divorce, 7 (Winter
         1983), 59-76.

         This study explores the problems associated with
         parental divorce for adolescents of college age
         and examines some of the factors which mediate
         adaptation to this life transition. Analyses of
         the responses of 83 clinical directors of college
         mental health counseling centers revealed that
         parental divorce may be a highly stressful life
         transition for older adolescents.

98. Fulton, J.A. "Parental Reports of Children's Post-
    Divorce Adjustment," J. of Social Issues, 35
    (Fall 1979), 126-139.

    Two years after the final decree, 560 divorced
    parents, fathers as well as mothers, were asked to
    assess the impact of the divorce on their
    children. Their responses to this question--as
    well as to other questions--seemed to divide into
    a "his" and "hers" perspective. Other variables
    having to do with the parents and their children,
    the marriage, the divorce and the changes
    necessitated by the divorce were analyzed in
    relation to these parental assessments.

99. Glick, P.C. "Children of Divorced Parents in Demo-
    graphic Perspective," J. of Social Issues, 35
    (Fall 1979), 170-182.

    The rise in the number of children with divorced
    parents has been associated with many other demo-
    graphic changes. Among the changes discussed are
    the increasing proportion of children under 18
    who are of school age; who live with a stepparent;
    who spend some time in a one-parent family; whose
    divorced parent has a college education; and who
    live with an unmarried couple.

100. Hetherington, E.M. "Divorce: A Child's Perspective,"
    American Psychologist, 34 (October 1979), 851-858.

    The average length of time spent by children in a
    single-parent home as a result of marital disruption
    is about six years. The majority of these children
    reside with their mothers, with only 10% living with
    their fathers even though this proportion has
    tripled since 1960. Living with the father is most
    likely to occur with school-aged rather than pre-
    school children.

    This article first presents an overview of the
    course of divorce and its potential impact on
    children and then uses research findings as a basis
    for describing the process of divorce as it is
    experienced by the child.

101. Hetherington, E.M., Cox, M., and R. Cox. "Play and
     Social Interaction in Children Following a
     Divorce," J. of Social Issues, 35 (Fall 1979),
     26-49.

     This paper presents the results of a longitudinal
     study of the effects of divorce on play and social
     interaction in children. Forty-eight middle class
     white preschool children from divorced families
     and a matched group of forty-eight non divorced
     families were studied at 2 months, 1 year and 2
     years after divorce.

102. Hodges, W.F., R.C. Wechsler, and C. Ballantine. "Divorce
     and the Preschool Child: Cumulative Stress," J. of
     Divorce, 3 (Fall 1979), 55-67.

     A comparative study is presented in which 26 pre-
     school children from divorced homes and 26 from
     intact homes were studied by means of parent report,
     teacher report and direct observation. A discussion
     of the literature shows some consensus that divorce
     leads to developmental problems in young children.
     The literature review forms the basis for the
     research hypotheses identified. The two voluntary
     populations were controlled for sex of child, type
     of preschool or daycare centre, and the combined
     income of the parents. The children from divorced
     homes were all living in the custody of their
     mothers.

103. Hodges, W.F., Buchsbaum, H.K., and C.W. Tierney.
     "Parent-Child Relationships and Adjustment in
     Preschool Children in Divorced and Intact Families,"
     J. of Divorce, 7 (Winter 1983), 43-58.

     Quantitative and qualitative aspects of child
     rearing as a function of the marital status of
     parents were investigated in terms of how they
     affected child adjustment. Custodial divorced
     mothers and mothers of intact families described
     the frequency and quality of contact with their
     preschool children and both parents and preschool
     teachers described the child's adjustment. Quantity
     of contact with parents was unrelated to adjust-
     ment in children of divorce, while numerous
     relationships were found for children in intact
     families.

104. Kalter, N. and J. Rembar. "The Significance of a Child's
          Age at the Time of Parental Divorce," American J. of
          Orthopsychiatry, 51 (January 1981), 85-100.

      The literature on children of divorce presents three
      theories on the relationship between a child's age
      at divorce and subsequent adaptation. Outpatient
      evaluations of 144 children of divorce, ranging in
      age from seven to 17 years, were coded for nature
      of emotional-behavioral problems and overall degree
      of psychological adjustment.

105. Kanoy, K. and Miller, B.C. "Children's Impact on the
          Parental Decision to Divorce," Family Relations,
          29 (July 1980), 309-315.

      Although many theorists and researchers have
      examined variables related to divorce, little
      attention has been given to how children may affect
      their parents' decision to divorce. Since over
      60% of divorces involve children, the popular
      notion that they prevent divorce should be re-
      examined. The evidence indicates that in some
      instances children may facilitate the parental
      decision to divorce.

106. Kulka, R.A. and H. Weingarten. "The Long-Term Effects
          of Parental Divorce in Childhood on Adult
          Adjustment," J. of Social Issues, 35 (Fall 1979),
          50-79.

      Relationships between experiencing a parental
      divorce or separation prior to age 16 and a variety
      of measures of adult adjustment and psychological
      functioning are examined using data from two
      national cross-sectional surveys conducted nearly
      20 years apart.

107. Kurdek, L.A. and A.E. Siesky. "Effects of Divorce on
          Children. The Relationship Between Parent and
          Child Perspectives," J. of Divorce, 4 (Winter
          1980), 85-99.

      Seventy-one divorced single custodial parents and
      their 130 5- to 19- year-old children were
      administered open-ended questionnaires dealing
      with various aspects of how the children reacted
      and adjusted to the divorce. Positive reactions
      and adjustments were found to be related to
      children's (a) defining divorce in terms of
      psychological separation between the parents, (b)
      sharing divorce-related concerns with friends,

(c) holding positive evaluations of both parents, and (d) have acquired strengths and responsibilities as a result of the divorce experience.

108. Levitin, T.E. (ed.) "Children of Divorce," J. of Social Issues, 35 (Fall 1979). Special Issue. 186 pp.

Ten papers discuss the social problems related to divorce and its effects on children. This issue presents some of the most current research findings in this area of family life.

109. List, J.A. The Day the Loving Stopped: A Daughter's View of her Parents' Divorce. New York: Seaview Books, 1980.

A 23-year-old woman discusses her childhood diaries, kept after the divorce of her parents.

110. Luepnitz, D.A. "Children of Divorce: A Review of Psychological Literature," Law and Human Behavior, 2(2), 1978, 167-179.

The purpose of this paper is to contrast the popular myths with results of the best research on children of divorce. Principal questions addressed are: What are the typical reactions of children to the divorce of their parents? To what degree has divorce been shown to harm children, and which aspect of divorce is the major stressor? What are the implications of these findings for clinicians, researchers, and lawyers?

111. Luepnitz, D.A. "Which Aspects of Divorce Affect Children," Family Coordinator 28 (January 1979), 79-85.

An exploratory study of a non-clinical population of college students, whose parents had divorced before they were sixteen years of age, provides a retrospective opportunity to gain insight into the duration of the effects of divorce. By exploring experiences before, during and after divorce, this study looks at the major stressors, enduring effects and coping strategies of children of divorce.

177

112. Mitchell, A.K. <u>When Parents Split Up: Divorce Explained to Young People</u>. Edinburgh, Scotland: Macdonald Publishers, 1982.

A sensitive explanation of divorce written for children who are under the age of 16 years.

113. Peterson, G.W., Leigh, G.K., and R.D. Day. "Family Stress Theory and the Impact of Divorce on Children," <u>J. of Divorce</u>, 7 (Spring 1984), 1-20.

A middle-range theory is presented that describes the potential impact of divorce on children. Concepts from family stress theory are integrated with research findings from the divorce literature to accomplish this goal. The proposed theoretical model is concerned especially with variations in the "definition of the situation" assigned to the crisis of divorce by children and custodial parents.

114. Robson, B. <u>My Parents are Divorced Too</u>. Toronto: Dorset, 1979.

A psychiatrist interviews 28 young people who underwent separation and divorce.

115. Rofes, E (ed). <u>The Kids' Book of Divorce</u>. Lexington, Mass.: Lewish Publishing Co., 1981.

Twenty children aged 11-14 wrote this book "for and about kids" in divorce.

116. Rosen, R. "Some Crucial Issues Concerning Children of Divorce," <u>J. of Divorce</u>, 3 (Fall 1979), 19-25.

This paper considers two crucial aspects of the post-divorce situation affecting children, namely, awarding of custody and access arrangements. The effects of these factors upon the ultimate adjustment of children are examined. Ninety-two white, middle-class, English-speaking children of divorced parents were interviewed and their general adjustment level assessed clinically. Age range of the sample was 9 to 28 years. Findings revealed no difference in the ultimate adjustment of children reared by mothers and those reared by fathers.

117. Rosen R. "Children of Divorce: An Evaluation of Two Common Assumptions," _Canadian J. of Family Law_, 2 (October 1979), 403-415.

Courts have commonly held that the mother should be the preferred custodian when spouses separate and that divorce results in disturbed children. The author examines the psychological literature in this regard and reports on her own empirical studies in which children of divorced parents were interviewed and psychological tests administered. She suggests that the "tender years" doctrine is not an appropriate yardstick to determine custody disputes, but that regard should be had to the unique circumstances of each case.

118. Stolberg, A.L. and J.M. Anker. "Cognitive and Behavioral Changes in Children Resulting from Parental Divorce and Consequent Environmental Changes," _J. of Divorce_, 7 (Winter 1983), 23-42.

Operationalizing divorce as environmental change helps to understand the processes leading to the development of psychopathology in some children of divorce. Children living with their divorced mothers and children living with their married, natural parents completed change measures (Recent Life Changes Questionnaire, Environmental Change Questionnaire), a behavior checklist (Child Behavior Checklist) and a cognitive/perceptual characteristics measure (Semantic Differential).

119. Troyer, W. _Divorced Kids_. Toronto: Clarke, Irwin, 1979.

A divorced father interviews children of divorce. The children reply with candour and with humour about their adjustment to divorce.

120. Vess, J.D., Schwebel, A.I., and J. Moreland. "The Effects of Early Parental Divorce on the Sex Role Development of College Students," _J. of Divorce_, 7 (Fall 1983), 83-95.

The present study examined the long-term effects of early parental divorce on the sex role development of college students. Two hundred and nineteen undergraduates served as subjects; 84 from families where the parents divorced prior to the subject's tenth birthday, and 135 from families in which the parents had never divorced or separated.

121. Wallerstein, J. "Children of Divorce: The Psychological Tasks of the Child," American J. of Orthopsychiatry, 53 (April 1983), 230-243.

Long-range outcomes for the child of divorce are related to factors within the family following divorce, and to the child's mastery of specific threats to development, which are here conceptualized as six interrelated hierarchical coping tasks. Beginning at the separation and culminating in young adulthood, these tasks add substantially to the normal challenges of growing up.

122. Wallerstein, J.S. and J.B. Kelly. "Children and Divorce: A Review," Social Work, 24 (Nov. 1979), 468-475.

The authors review the literature related to the emotional impact of divorce on children.

123. Wallerstein, J.S. and J.B. Kelly. "California's Children of Divorce," Psychology Today, 14 (January 1980), 67-76.

Five years after the breakup, 34 percent of the children are happy and thriving, 29 percent are doing reasonably well, and 37 percent are depressed. An in-depth study of 60 families taces patterns in these different outcomes. As in married families, what counts most are the two parents' attitudes.

Custody

124. Ahrons, C.R. "Predictors of Paternal Involvement Postdivorce: Mothers' and Fathers' Perceptions," J. of Divorce, 6 (Spring 1983), 55-70.

Recent research on the effects of divorce on children indicates the relationship of the non-custodial father both to the former spouse and to the children are critical factors affecting the child's adjustment. Guided by a family systems perspective, this study examined the relationship between paternal involvement postdivorce, the divorced coparental relationship and feelings of the former spouses' toward each other. Data were obtained from intensive interviews with 54 pairs of ex-spouses one year after divorce.

125. Alexander, S.J. "Influential Factors on Divorced
     Parents in Determining Visitation Arrangements,"
     J. of Divorce, 3 (Spring 1980), 223-239.

     A group of divorced parents were asked how
     important certain considerations were when they
     determined visitation arrangements: visiting
     parent's best interests, custodial parent's best
     interests, child's best interest, and parental
     relationship. The child's and visiting parent's
     best interests were significantly more important
     than all other factors; the custodial parent's
     best interests was significantly more important
     than the personal relationship.

126. Ambert, A.M. "Differences in Children's Behavior Toward
     Custodial Mothers and Custodial Fathers," J. of
     Marriage and the Family, 44 (Feb. 1982), 73-86.

     One important gap in the literature on the one-
     parent family is the lack of empirical and
     theoretical focus on children's behavior toward
     their custodial parents. This article reports the
     results of in-depth interviews with twenty
     custodial mothers and seven custodial fathers.

127. Bartz, K.W. and W.C. Witcher. "When Father gets
     Custody," Children Today, 7 (Sept.-Oct. 1978),
     2-6.

     What happens when a father gets custody of his
     children after divorce? Until recently the question
     was seldom asked. When it was, the answer generally
     contained dire warnings of crises and maladjust-
     ment for both father and children.

     But times are changing. More fathers are actively
     seeking and receiving custody of their children.
     In part, this is due to a revolution in our
     definitions of male and female roles. Active
     involvement in the day-to-day lives of children
     is no longer the exclusive domain of mothers.

128. Branson, M.L. "Resource Management: Divorced Custodial
     Fathers Compared to Divorced Custodial Mothers,"
     Family Perspective, 17 (Spring 1983), 101-108.

     Divorce has been increasing steadily during the
     last decade in the United States, In 1981,
     according to the U.S. census figures, there were
     63 million children under eighteen in the United
     States. About 20 percent, or 12.6 million
     children, live with only one parent.

If statistics related to divorce are projected
at the present rate, a majority of children born
this year will have experienced life in a one-
parent family prior to the attainment of age
eighteen. Many Americans now married will become
single heads of households.

129. Dominic, K.T. and B. Schlesinger. "Weekend Fathers:
     Family Shadows," J. of Divorce, 3 (Spring 1980),
     241-247.

     Very little attention has been focused on the
     weekend or part-time fathers related to divorced
     one-parent families in the United States and Canada.
     Nine part-time fathers were interviewed and some
     selected findings are present. The scant literature
     to the topic is also reviewed.

130. Ericsson, M. "Some Empirical and Theoretical Reflections
     on the Conditions of the Non-Guardian," J. of
     Comparative Family Studies, 9 (Winter 1980), 87-
     114.

     In this article the importance of also studying
     the parent not having custody of the child is
     emphasized. Data are presented from a study in
     Sweden of the economic conditions of non-guardians.

131. Everett, C.A. and S.S. Volgy. "Family Assessment in
     Child Custody Disputes," J. of Marital and Family
     Therapy, 9 (October 1983), 343-353.

     This paper has operationalized family systems theory
     to explicate the interfacing dynamics between
     family dissolution and child custody disputes.
     The authors suggest that clinical assessment and
     intervention in these matters which focus solely on
     individual and marital, or child dimensions, fail
     to recognize the powerful influences of systemic
     family process.

132. Grief, G.L. "Custodial Dads and their Ex-Wives," Single
     Parent, 26 (Jan.-Feb. 1984), 17-20.

     The results of a study of 1100 fathers who belonged
     to "Parents Without Partners" completed in 1982.
     In this paper the author focuses on the ex-wives'
     involvement with the children.

133. Hanson, S. "Single Custodial Fathers and the Parent-
      Child Relationship," Nursing Research, 30 (July-
      Aug. 1981), 202-204.

      The single-parent family has become a major family
      structure over the last two decades. According
      to the Census Bureau, 11 million of 60 million
      children in the United States lived in single-
      parent homes in 1978; 10 million lived with
      single mothers and one million lived with single
      fathers. In addition, the number of single-
      father homes is rising rapidly.

      The purpose of this study was to investigate the
      social status on single custodial fathers, their
      histories, the reasons they were granted custody,
      and to see if a relationship exists between each
      of these characteristics and the parent-child
      relationship as perceived by the fathers and the
      children.

134. Kelly, C. "Assessment of Potential Single Parent
      Family Units for Child Custody Purposes,"
      Conciliation Courts Review, 18 (Dec. 1980), 21-26.

      The purpose of this paper is to develop: 1) a con-
      ceptual framework for assessing a parent's strengths
      and deficits; and 2) a procedure for making and
      conveying such an assessment when a consultation
      is requested. The same format should also be use-
      ful for assessing treatment needs; however, this
      paper does not concentrate specifically on
      treatment.

135. Koehler, J.M. "Mothers Without Custody," Children
      Today, 11 (March-April 1982), 12-15, 35.

      Mothers who actively choose not to have custody
      of their children are at a vanguard in the United
      States. Research has rarely addressed the role
      or position of mothers without custody. In a
      discussion, the author, who chose to give custody
      to her then 4-year-old daughter to her husband
      when their marriage broke up two and a half years
      ago, shares her feelings and experiences as well
      as those of some other women similarly situated
      whom she met as founder of Offspring, a local
      support group for noncustodial mothers.

136. Kurdek, L.A. and A.E. Siesky. "Sex Role Concepts of
     Single Divorced Parents and Their Children," J. of
     Divorce, 3 (Spring 1980), 247-261.

     Seventy-four single divorced custodial parents
     completed the Bem Sex Role Inventory and their
     ninety-two 10- to 19-year-old children completed
     a revised version of the same inventory. Both
     custodial mothers and fathers evidenced high levels
     of androgyny when contrasted with published norms,
     although parents' masculinity and feminity scores
     were unrelated to those of their children. The
     children themselves were classified as mostly
     either androgynous and undifferentiated, with
     boys being more androgynous and girls more un-
     differentiated when contrasted with available
     norms.

137. Luepnitz, D.A. Child Custody: A Study of Families
     After Divorce. Lexington, Mass.: Lexington Books,
     1982.

     The author compares the postdivorce experience of
     families in three custody patterns. The sample
     consists of 43 families.

138. Mendes, H.A. "How Divorced Fathers Obtain Custody:
     A Review of Research," Conciliation Courts Review,
     17 (June 1979), 27-30.

     A review of the actual processes by which fathers
     obtained custody.

139. Musetto, A.P. Dilemmas in Child Custody: Family
     Conflicts and their Resolution. Chicago: Nelson-
     Hall, 1982.

     A psychologist's guide for parents and clinicians.
     The book discusses custody and visitation issues
     and problems from the family therapy point of
     view.

140. Riechers, M. "Mothers Without Custody: Reversing
     Society's Old Stereotypes," Single Parent, 25
     (October 1981), 13-15.

     Mothers, like fathers, have mixed feelings about
     being the "visiting" parent after a divorce. But
     contrary to popular belief, it can be for the
     best when a mother has the courage to give up
     custody.

141. Santrock, J.W. and R.A. Warshak. "Father Custody and
      Social Development in Boys and Girls," J. of
      Social Issues, 35 (Fall 1979), 112-125.

      The effects of father custody on children's social
      development are being studied by comparing children
      whose fathers have been awarded custody, children
      whose mothers have been awarded custody, and
      children from intact families. Half of the subjects
      are boys, and half are girls aged 6-11 years.
      Families are matched on SES, family size, and
      sibling status.

142. Watson, M.A. "Custody Alternatives: Defining the Best
      Interests of Children," Family Relations, 30
      (July 1981), 474-479.

      Whereas in the recent past the majority of child
      custody decisions have favored the mother, an
      increasing number of decisions are presently
      rendered in favor of the father or in favor of a
      shared custodial arrangement. This study presents
      interview data on a non-clinical population of 17
      adults and 3 children who have lived in alternate
      custody arrangements: joint custody and father
      custody.

Divorce and the Family System

143. Ahrons, C.R. "Divorce: A Crisis of Family Transition
      and Change," Family Relations, 29 (October 1980),
      533-540.

      This paper presents a conceptualization of a
      normative process of divorce as a crisis of family
      transition. With the integration of family stress
      and systems theories, a series of five transitions
      are identified as normative. Within each of these
      transitions, stresses associated with major role
      transitions and common family coping strategies
      are identified.

144. Ahrons, C.R. "Redefining the Divorced Family: A
      Conceptual Framework," Social Work, 25 (November
      1980), 437-441.

      The author presents a conceptual framework for
      the family's reorganization after divorce, in
      which divorce is viewed as a crisis of family
      transition resulting in changes in the family
      system.

145. Ahrons, C. "Divorce: Before, During and After," (in)
H.I. McCubbin and C.R. Figley, eds. Stress and
the Family: Coping with Normative Transitions.
New York: Brunner-Mazel, 1983, 102-115. (Vol. 1).

In this chapter the author reviews some of the
numerous reports and studies of the effects of
divorce on the family and put forward the concept
of the binuclear family as a useful family model.
Then, using the case example of the Burke family,
she reviews the stressors associated with each
transition or phase in the divorce process,
suggesting functional and dysfunctional coping
patterns at each phase.

146. Ahrons, C.R. and M.R. Bowman. "Changes in Family
Relationships Following Divorce of Adult Child:
Grandmother's Perceptions," J. of Divorce, 5
(Fall/Winter 1981), 49-68.

This paper presents findings from interviews with
78 grandmothers whose son or daughter experienced
a divorce. Grandmothers were questioned regarding
the effects of divorce on their relationships
with their divorced child, their former in-law,
and their grandchildren. Respondents' feelings
about their child's divorce were also explored.

147. Bader, L., De Frain, J., and A. Parkhurst. "What
Parents Feel When Their Child Divorces," Family
Perspective, 16 (Spring 1982), 93-100.

A study of 66 parents whose child divorced. The
authors present in anecdotal form the results
of their study.

148. Brown, E.M. "Divorce and the Extended Family: A
Consideration of Services," J. of Divorce, 5
(Fall/Winter 1981), 159-171.

The impact of divorce on the extended family is
extensive. Relatives, especially parents,
experience feelings of disappointment, failure,
and helplessness. They frequently provide
extensive practical and economic support to the
divorcing spouse who is related, often at a
sacrifice. Except in regard to access to grandchildren, extended family members seldom request
help from clinicians. If the needs of extended
family members are to be met, clinicians will need
to expand their definition of the divorcing

family, and take an active role in reaching out
to members of the extended family.

149. Colletta, N.D. "Support Systems After Divorce:
      Incidence and Impact," J. of Marriage and the
      Family, 41 (November 1979), 837-846.

      In order to specify more exactly the impact of
      support systems on post-divorce family functioning,
      the support available to 72 one- and two-parent
      families was examined. Divorced and married mothers
      were found to differ in the amount and sources of
      the support they received and in their satisfaction
      with their support systems. The amount of support
      received and the mother's satisfaction with that
      support were found to be significantly related to
      a number of childrearing practices.

150. Duffy, M. "Divorce and the Dynamics of the Family
      Kinship System," J. of Divorce, 5 (Fall/Winter
      1981), 3-18.

      Little research exists on the dynamics of relation-
      ships within the extended family after divorce and
      remarriage. Several related methodological/con-
      ceptual issues are presented in explanation of
      this gap in research: the persistence of a nuclear
      mythology surrounding the family, differences in
      the focus of sociological and psychological
      research, and the neglect of research on qualita-
      tive aspects of family interactions.

151. Fischer, E.O. (ed). "Impact of Divorce on the Extended
      Family," J. of Divorce, 5 (Fall and Winter 1981).
      Special Issue.

      Eleven papers written by psychologists, sociologists,
      lawyers, and clinicians focus on the extended
      family and divorce.

152. Goldman, J. "Can Family Relationships Be Maintained
      After Divorce?", J. of Divorce, 5 (Fall/Winter
      1981), 141-158.

      In this paper, the current functioning of extended
      families is described, as well as how that
      functioning is altered at the family level by the
      adjustment required when separation and divorce
      occur. A case study of a large and functional
      Jewish family is presented in order to explore
      changes in membership inclusion after divorce.

153. Goldsmith, J. "The Postdivorce Family System," (in)
F. Walsh, ed. Normal Family Processes, New York:
Guilford Press, 1982, 297-330.

In this chapter the post divorce family is seen
essentially as a normal family form. Data from
several studies support this viewpoint.

154. Green, R.G. and M.J. Sporakowski. "The Dynamics of
Divorce: Marital Quality, Alternative Attractions
and External Pressures," J. of Divorce, 7 (Winter
1983), 77-88.

This study tested Lewis and Spanier's theory of
marital quality and marital stability by utilizing
a sample of 131 married and 166 divorced social
survey respondents. It empirically examined the
relationship between the quality and stability
of their marriages and assessed the manner in which
alternative attractions and external pressures to
remain married influenced the strength of this
relationship.

155. Johnson, E.S. "Older Mothers' Perceptions of Their
Child's Divorce," The Gerontologist, 21 (No. 4)
1983, 395-401.

This study of 212 women age 50 or over, selected
at random from census lists in a small city-
suburb in the Boston area reported on their own
experience and on the experience of friends with a
divorced child. Most of the mothers of divorced
children indicated that the event had been
negative--traumatic, painful, and sad--for them.
Almost one-third said their feelings about the
event were still negative. The emotional effects
on the divorce on the mothers suggest that
supportive alternatives should be made available
for parents of the divorcing couple.

156. Johnson, E.S. and B.H. Vinick. "Support of the
Parent When An Adult Son or Daughter Divorces,"
J. of Divorce, 5 (Fall/Winter 1981), 69-78.

The impact of a son or daughter's divorce on the
older parent has been neglected by researchers
and practitioners. Because of the greater needs
of the divorcing couple, the impact of divorce
on their parents has been largely ignored. Such
a divorce may have far reaching implications for
the older parent-adult child relationship. Support

to the parent primarily from individual friends,
other family or clergy may be affected by the
view of divorce that these groups hold.

157. Kalish, R.A. and E. Visher. "Grandparents of Divorce
      and Remarriage," J. of Divorce, 5 (Fall/Winter
      1981), 127-140.

      Among the individuals affected by divorce are the
      parents of the divorcing persons. Their role must
      be seen through three perspectives: that of the
      older persons themselves, that of the divorcing
      couple, and that of the children of the divorcing
      couple. A dozen grandparent-of-divorce settings
      are outlined and their implications discussed.

158. Kaslow, F.W. "Divorce: An Evolutionary Process of
      Change in the Family System," J. of Divorce, 7
      (Spring 1984), 21-40.

      This article approaches divorce from a combined
      family systems, individual life cycle and stage
      theory of development perspective. It posits that
      the choice of what kind of therapy is apt to be
      most efficient and most efficacious for any
      patient/couple should be made after identifying
      at what stage in the divorce process the person(s)
      is/are in when they enter treatment and what their
      respective ego strengths, cognitive functioning,
      and social and resource networks are.

159. Kaslow, F. and R. Hyatt. "Divorce: A Potential Growth
      Experience for the Extended Family." J. of Divorce,
      5 (Fall/Winter 1981), 115-126.

      This article discusses some of the ways in which
      divorce, usually conceived of as a primarily
      negative and painful experience, can be turned
      to positive advantage, and have a beneficial impact
      on the divorcing person's extended family. The
      authors indicate that when the divorcing one
      copes well, his behavior serves as a model for
      handling difficulty well and diminishes others'
      fears about losses and embarking on new relation-
      ships.

160. Khleif-Anderson, S. Divorced but Not Disastrous,
      Englewood, N.J.: Prentice-Hall, 1982.

      A sociologist interviews 76 divorced parents with
      and without custody to examine this pattern of
      family life.

161. Kitson, G.C., Moir, R.N. and P.R. Mason. "Family Social
      Support in Crises: The Special Case of Divorce,"
      American J. of Orthopsychiatry, 52 (January 1982),
      161-165.

      Using data from a survey of divorced and separated
      men and women, this study suggests that family help
      is less likely to be provided when the families are
      themselves experiencing life change events or dis-
      approve of the divorce decision. Family help does
      tend to be forthcoming, however, when respondents
      are simultaneously undergoing other life stressors
      in addition to the divorce experience.

162. Kurdek, L.A. and D. Blisk. "Dimensions and Correlates
      of Mothers' Divorce Experiences," J. of Divorce,
      6 (Summer 1983), 1-24.

      Twenty-five single divorced mothers who had been
      separated an average of about 6 years provided
      evaluations of: (a) the difficulty of various
      aspects of the divorce; (b) reasons for the divorce
      decision; (c) their estimation of their ex-spouses'
      reasons for the divorce decision; (d) individuals
      of support in the post-separation period; (e)
      problems experienced in the current post-separation
      period; (f) the degree and nature of contact with
      the ex-spouse; and (g) the degree and nature of
      environmental change occasioned by the divorce.
      These divorce experience dimensions were not
      highly intercorrelated and are described in detail.

163. Lero, D.S. Divorce: The Family Crisis. Toronto: TV
      Ontario, 1981.

      This booklet studies the effects of divorce on
      the four members of a family.

164. Matthews, S.H. and J. Sprey. "The Impact of Divorce
      on Grandparenthood: An Exploratory Study," The
      Gerontologist, 24 (February 1984), 41-47.

      Nineteen grandparent couples with no divorced
      children and 18 with at least one divorced child
      were interviewed about their relationships with
      their children, in-law children, and grandchildren.
      Neither group was well informed about their
      children's marriages. Following divorce, whether
      own child or in-law child was awarded custody of
      the grandchildren was found to affect the like-
      lihood of maintaining contact with former in-law

children, as well as the grandparental style adopted and relationship with grandchildren.

165. Smyer, M.A. and B.F. Holland. "Divorce and Family Support in Later Life: Emerging Concerns," J. of Family Issues, 3 (March 1982), 61-77.

Two patterns are among the most important considerations in planning services for the elderly of the future: (1) the current role of family members in supporting older adults and (2) the present high rate of divorce. If forecasts of increasing demands for service by older adults are correct, service planners must consider what resources will be available to the elderly of the future. In the report presented, the literature from a variety of areas is reviewed, focusing on one question: How will the currently high rate of divorce affect the family support system of older adults in the future?

166. Willison, M.M. Diary of a Divorced Mother. New York: Bantam Books, 1981.

The diary of a 27-year-old woman left to raise two sons on her own.

Divorce Mediation

167. Barsky, M. "Stratégies and Techniques of Divorce Mediation," Social Casework, 65 (February 1984), 102-108.

Divorce mediation requires strategies to achieve the objectives of the process and techniques to effect those strategies. Case examples illustrate specific strategies and techniques in this report of the experiences of a mediator who has worked in private and agency practice.

168. Brown, D.G. "Divorce and Family Mediation: History, Review, Future Directions," Conciliation Courts Review, 20 (Dec. 1982), 1-44.

This review covers the studies related to family mediation. It contains a 275-item bibliography.

169. Haynes, J.M. "Divorce Mediator: A New Role," Social Work, 23 (January 1978), 5-9.

In response to soaring divorce rates and liberalized divorce laws, the author proposes a

new role for social workers--divorce mediator.
Social work skills can be used to lessen the pain
and frustration of couples who are dissolving an
unsuccessful marriage at the same time that husband
and wife are helped to face the future.

170. Irving, H.H. Divorce Mediation: A Rational Alternative
to the Adversary System. New York: Universe Books,
1980.

The author, a social worker, presents a cogent
argument for mediation as an alternative to
adversarial divorce.

171. Kressel, K., Jaffee, N., Tuchman, B., Watson, C. and
M. Deutsch. "A Typology of Divorcing Couples:
Implications for Mediation and the Divorce Process,"
Family Process, 19 (June 1980), 101-116.

An experimental mediation procedure for the
negotation of divorce settlement agreements was
studied through the intensive analysis of nine
completed mediation cases. The audio recordings
of mediation sessions and postdivorce interviews
with both of the former marital partners provided
the material on which the analysis is based,
Five additional couples, drawn from a similar
population but who used the traditional adversarial
system, provided a comparative perspective.

172. Vanderkooi, L. and J. Pearson. "Mediating Divorce
Disputes: Mediator Behaviors, Styles and Roles,"
Family Relations, 32 (October 1983), 557-586.

Despite the growing popularity of divorce
mediation, there has been little systematic research
on the process of mediation and the roles and
skills of mediators. This article reviews 35
cases involving contested child custody and visitation and generalizes about the techniques used
by experienced divorce mediators to help couples
reach resolutions to their differences. The
article discusses different ways mediators orient
couples to mediation, gain their commitment,
identify the issues in dispute, overcome emotional
and substantive obstacles and generate agreements.

192

173. Abarbanel, A. "Shared Parenting After Separation and Divorce: A Study of Joint Custody," American J. of Orthopsychiatry, 49 (April 1979), 320-329.

Intensive case studies of four families in which divorced parents have maintained joint custody of their children suggest that this arrangement works well under certain conditions. Components of a successful joint custody arrangement are considered, limitations are discussed, and support is urged for divorcing parents interested in establishing joint custody.

174. Ahrons, C.R. "Joint Custody Arrangements in the Post-Divorce Family," J. of Divorce, 3 (Spring 1980), 189-205.

Interviews with forty-one divorced parents who have court-awarded joint custody reveal several characteristics of shared parenting arrangements. Although some parents divided parenting respon- sibilities fairly equally, most exhibited a variety of shared parenting patterns, with differential involvement of the nonresidential parents. The majority (86 percent) of the sample reported satisfaction with their joint custody arrangements.

175. Ahrons, C.R. "The Continuing Coparental Relationship Between Divorced Spouses," American J. of Orthopsychiatry, 5 (July 1981), 415-428.

Findings are reported from an empirical investi- gation of the relationship between divorced spouses one year following the divorce. Interviews cover- ing a wide range of topics were conducted with 54 pairs of divorced parents. It was found that the majority continued to interact with one another; those who interacted the most frequently were the supportive and cooperative coparents.

176. Clingempeell, W.G. and N.D. Reppucci. "Joint Custody After Divorce," Psychological Bulletin, 91(1), 1982, 102-127.

A comprehensive review of the research literature dealing with joint custody.

177. Ernst, I. and R. Altis. "Joint Custody and Co-Parenting:
      Not By Law But By Love," Child Welfare, 60
      (December 1981), 669-677.

      In recent years, joint custody and co-parenting of
      children after divorce or separation has received
      considerable attention. The authors advocate wider
      recognition of this option to sole custody and
      visitation. They review pertinent legal and other
      literature, identify indications and contra-
      indications, and briefly discuss the implications
      for social workers.

178. Folberg, H.J. and M. Graham. "Joint Custody of Children
      Following Divorce," (in) H. Irving ed. Family
      Law: An Interdisciplinary Perspective. Toronto:
      The Carswell Co., 1981, 71-124.

      This article analyzes the law of joint custody as
      well as its history, terminology, and use.

179. Galper, M. Co-Parenting. Philadelphia: Running Press,
      1978.

      A sourcebook for the separated or divorced family.
      The book describes an alternative to the
      traditional forms of custody arrangements.

180. Green D. "Joint Custody and the Emerging Two-Parent
      Family," Conciliation Courts Review, 21 (June
      1983), 65-75.

      When the two-parent family does break down,
      estranged parents soon discover that our legal
      system has not kept pace with social change.
      Family law in most American states, and through-
      out Canada, is still based on the single-parent
      concept. Moreover, the single parent is usually
      assumed to be the mother.

181. Greif, J.B. "Fathers, Children, and Joint Custody,"
      Amer. J. of Orthopsychiatry, 49 (April 1979),
      311-319.

      This survey of 40 middle-class divorced fathers,
      focusing on father's perceptions of their relation-
      ship with their children, suggests that those with
      joint custody are more likely than those with
      visitation rights to continue to have a high degree
      of involvement in and influence on their children's
      growth and development.

194

182. Nehls, N. and M. Morgenbesser. "Joint Custody: An
     Exploration of the Issues," Family Process, 19
     (June 1980), 117-125.

     Joint custody, an increasingly popular custody
     decision, allows both divorced parents to share
     equally the rights and responsibilities of child
     rearing following their divorce. The potential
     positive and negative effects of this new and
     highly controversial custody decision are dis-
     cussed by reviewing relevant research and theo-
     retical concepts. Suggestions for further
     research are offered.

183. Ricci, I. Mom's House, Dad's House: Making Shared
     Custody Work. New York: Collier Books, 1980.

     Deals with the complex issues of shared custody
     after the divorce.

184. Roman, M. and W. Haddad. The Disposable Parent. New
     York: Penguin Books, 1978. The authors make a
     point for joint custody.

185. Rothberg, B. "Joint Custody: parental problems and
     satisfactions," Family Process, 22 (March 1983)
     43-52.

     Joint custody, the total care of children by each
     parent part of the time, enables both parents to
     be "custodial" parents after divorce. Increasingly,
     it has become a solution to custody problems,
     allowing both parents major involvement in their
     children's lives as well as freedom for themselves.
     A study addressed joint custody from the parents'
     perspective, exploring the salient issues. The
     problems and satisfactions are discussed, and the
     sex differences are highlighted.

186. Schreiber, R.F. "Sharing Children of Divorce: Duration
     and Development," Conciliation Courts Review,
     21 (June 1983), 53-64.

     The sharing of children of divorce, particularly
     with the new emphasis upon joint custody, is one
     of the most frustrating and complicated problems
     we all face. Almost everyone now accepts the
     premise that a solid, consistent and continuing
     relationship between the child and both parents
     after divorce is very beneficial, even necessary,
     for the child's well-being.

187.   Steinman, S. "The Experience of Children in a Joint
        Custody Arrangement: A Report of a Study,"
        American J. of Orthopsychiatry, 51 (July 1981),
        403-414.

        The psychological experience of 32 children living
        in a joint-custody arrangement with their parents
        is examined. This report is part of a larger study,
        begun in 1978, of 24 families in which parents have
        shared child-rearing responsibilities and physical
        custody of their children following marital sep-
        aration. Findings suggest that joint custody is
        not a simple solution, and that the reaction of
        children is highly individual. The need for further
        study is emphasized.

188.   Trombetta, D. and B.W. Lebbos. "Co-Parenting: Everyone's
        Best Interest." Conciliation Courts Review, 17
        (Dec. 1979), 13-23.

        A comprehensive review of articles and books
        related to co-parenting after a divorce.

Legal Aspects: Divorce

189.   Bala, N. and K.L. Clarke, The Child and the Law.
        Toronto: McGraw-Hill Ryerson, 1981.

        Two Canadian experts discuss laws that effect
        children. Chapter 3 discusses the child in the
        family including families in crisis.

190.   Dixon, R.B. and L.J. Weitzman. "Evaluating the Impact
        of No-Fault Divorce in California," Family
        Relations, 29 (July 1980), 297-307.

        The adoption of a no-fault divorce law in
        California in 1970 was accompanied by a number of
        changes--some intended, some unintended--in the
        nature of the legal process of divorce and in the
        patterns of requests and settlements regarding
        alimony, property, and child custody. Analysis
        of five samples of 500 decress of divorce drawn
        from Los Angeles and San Francisco counties in
        1968 and 1972, and from Los Angeles in 1977,
        suggests that although the process of marital
        dissolution under the no-fault law is less
        litigious and perhaps less acrimonious than under
        the old adversary system, the new law raises some
        interesting questions about equity in spousal
        support and property settlements when no one is
        at fault.

191. Dixon, R.B. and L.J. Weitzman. "When Husbands File
     For Divorce," J. of Marriage and the Family, 44
     (Feb. 1982), 103-116.

     One immediate consequence of the adoption of the
     1970 no-fault divorce law in California was a
     significant increase in the percentage of husbands
     who files for divorce. This paper explores the
     effects of a change in the law on the motivations
     of husbands who file for divorce.

192. Eisenstein, I. "A New Approach to Jewish Divorce,"
     J. of Divorce, 6 (Summer 1983), 85-90/

     The traditional Jewish law of divorce, which
     permits a husband to divorce his wife, but does
     not sanction the wife's divorcing him, has created
     hardship for Jewish women for centuries. In view
     of the new attitudes toward the equality of women,
     the rabbis of the Reconstructionist Movement in
     Judaism have innovated an egalitarian "get"
     (divorce), a bold effort to prevent Jewish women
     from becoming agunot (abandoned wives). By means
     of the new type of divorce, the Jewish woman takes
     the initiative and divorces the husband.

193. Elkin, M. "The Missing Links in Divorce Law: A Re-
     Definition of Process and Practice," J. of
     Divorce, 6 (Fall-Winter 1982), 37-63.

     Challenging the traditional and outmoded approach
     to divorce, the author, using a systems approach,
     proposes interrelated changes (the missing links)
     in the divorce process and related legal practices.
     The resulting new and interprofessional structure
     for the divorce experience would provide for a
     more humanistic approach to divorce, create a system
     of non-adversarial practices that would enable
     the law itself to become a more effective support
     system, maximize client self-determination, re-
     define the role of the judge and attorney in divorce,
     and would recognize that parents are forever and
     families are forever.

194. Foster, H.H. and D.J. Freed, "Grandparent Visitation:
     Vagaries and Vicissitudes," J. of Divorce, 5
     (Fall/Winter 1981), 79-100.

     Examination is made of the attitude of the law
     toward the visitation rights of grandparents in
     divorce and adoption and state statutes which

197

permit an award of visitation when found to be
beneficial to the child. The law tends to have
more flexible attitudes toward custody claims of
grandparents than those for visitation.

195. King, L. <u>What Every Woman Should Know About Marriage,
      Separation and Divorce</u>. Toronto: James Lorimer,
      1980.

      A lawyer answers questions women ask about
      marriage, separation and divorce.

196. McKie, D.C., Prentice, B., and P. Reed. <u>Divorce: Law
      and the Family in Canada</u>. Ottawa: Ministry of
      Supply and Services, 1983.

      A history of marriage and divorce in Canada since
      pioneer times, with an examination of social and
      legal aspects of divorce during the 1970's.

197. Welch, C.E. and S. Price-Bonham. "A Decade of No-Fault
      Divorce Revisited: California, Georgia, and
      Washington," <u>J. of Marriage and the Family</u>, 45
      (May 1983), 411-418.

      A previous study of property settlements under the
      adversary and no-fault systems of divorce for San
      Diego County, California, concluded that such
      settlements had become more unfavorable for
      divorcing mothers since the advent of no-fault
      divorce. That study was replicated for divorces
      granted in Clarke County, Georgia and in Spokane
      County, Washington.

Parenting After Divorce

198. Booth, A., Brinkerhoff, D.B., and L.K. White. "The
       ᐧ Impact of Parental Divorce on Courtship," <u>J. of
      Marriage and the Family</u>, 46 (February 1984), 85-94.

      Drawing on the large sample of college students
      that includes 365 cases of parental divorce, the
      authors examine the impact of the amount of
      parental conflict during and after divorce, change
      in the quality of parent-child relations, and
      parent's remarriage on the level and evaluation
      of courtship relations. Our analysis shows that
      parental divorce increases courtship activity
      among offspring.

199. Coletta, N.D. "The Impact of Divorce: Father Absence or Poverty?", J. of Divorce, 3 (Fall 1979), 27-35.

This study sought to determine if the often-described differences in the child-rearing practices of divorced and married mothers are related to the father's absence, or if they are largely related to the low income which so often occurs with divorce. Seventy-two mothers varying along the dimensions of father absence, income, number of children, and sex of the target child were interviewed. The results suggest that income is a key factor; child-rearing practices were more restrictive and demanding at the lower but not at the higher income levels.

200. Coletta, N.D. "Stressful Lives: The Situation of Divorced Mothers and Their Children," J. of Divorce, 6 (Spring 1983), 19-32.

This study sought to determine if the often-described situation of divorced mothers and their children is in fact related to the father's absence or if it is largely a function of the low income that so often follows a divorce. Seventy-two divorced and married mothers at two income levels were interviewed. The results suggest that income is the key factor.

201. Cottle, T.J. Divorce and the Jewish Child. New York: American Jewish Committee, Institute of Human Relations, 1981.

This monograph describes interviews with Jewish families with whom the author was working. The focus is on the parents' divorce and the effect on the children.

202. Crosby, J.F., Gage, B.A., and M.C. Raymond. "The Grief Resolution Process in Divorce," J. of Divorce, 7 (Fall 1983), 3-18.

The process of grief resolution is divorce is compared to the Kubler-Ross model of grief resolution in bereavement. A sample of seventeen divorced persons wrote detailed essays giving the account of their progression through divorce. The results suggest a conceptual model based on three chronological stages; First Serious Thought to Separation and/or Filing, Separation and/or Filing to Final Decree, Final Decree to Penultimate Closure. Each stage considers three factors;

Affective, Cognitive, and Behavioral. Respondents are further divided between "more Active" and "more Passive."

203. De Frain, J. and R. Eirick. "Coping as Divorced Single Parents: A Comparative Study of Fathers and Mothers." Family Relations, 30 (April 1981), 265-274.

A study of 33 divorced single-parent fathers and 38 divorced single-parent mothers found almost no statistically significant differences between the two groups on a large number of measures. Fathers held a slight edge over the mothers in income, education, and the tendency not to move from their home and community after the divorce.

204. Goldstein, S. Divorced Parenting: How to Make it Work. Toronto: McGraw-Hill Ryerson, 1982.

A child psychiatrist talks about divorce and its impact on children.

205. Hess, R.D. and K.A. Camara. "Post-Divorce Family Relationships as Mediating Factors in the Consequences of Divorce for Children," J. of Social Issues, 35 (Fall 1979), 79-96.

In this study, the psychological structure of the family after divorce is seen as mediating the impact of divorce upon children. Divorce affects primary bonds with parents, presents challenges to conceptions of social reality, and creates stress which interferes with normal development. The effects of divorce upon child behaviour (peer relations, stress, aggression, work effectiveness at school) were examined through two contrasting research strategies: 1) a comparison of the behavior of children in divorced and intact families, and 2) analysis of the association between family processes and child outcomes in intact and divorced families.

206. Nelson, G. "Moderators of Women's and Children's Adjustment Following Parental Divorce," J. of Divorce, 4 (Spring 1981), 71-83.

This research sought to determine the strongest moderators of the relationship between the crisis of parental divorce and the psychosocial adjust-ment of divorced women and their dependent children.

200

The current relationship with the ex-husband was
the best predictor of divorcees' adjustment, while
divorcees' happiness in their former marriages was
most strongly related to their children's adjustment.

Process of Divorce

207.   Albrecht, S.L.   "Reactions and Adjustments to Divorce:
       Differences in the Experiences of Males and
       Females," Family Relations, 29 (Jan. 1980), 59-68.

       Divorce rates in the United States have increased
       significantly in recent years, and the trend shows
       no tendency toward reversal. Consequently, an
       increasing number of persons is going to confront
       the problems associated with adjusting to the termi-
       nation of a marriage. Past research on divorce
       adjustment has concentrated primarily on female
       subjects. In this analysis, the divorce experien-
       ces of males are compared with those of females for
       a sample of 500 over-divorced persons from eight
       Rocky Mountain states.

208.   Albrecht, S.L. and P.R. Kunz, "The Decision to Divorce:
       A Social Exhcange Perspective," J. of Divorce, 3
       (Summer 1980), 319-337.

       In this paper the authors review the process
       through which a sample of 500 respondents reached
       the decision to obtain a divorce. Specifically,
       major problems that existed in their relationship
       that prompted them to finally seek a legal term-
       ination of their union are considered. In
       addition, the authors will examine barriers that
       had to be overcome before that decision was
       finally reached as well as major sources of social
       support that encouraged the decision.

209.   Ambert, A.M. Divorce in Canada. Toronto: Academic
       Press, 1980.

       The first monograph on divorce in Canada. It
       contains an overview of the topic, focusing on
       the Canadian scene.

210.   Ambert, A.M. "Marriage Dissolution: Structural and
       Ideological Changes" (in) M. Baker ed. The Family:
       Changing Trends in Canada. Toronto: McGraw-Hill
       Ryerson, 1984, 85-103.

       A discussion of the current Canadian situation
       related to divorce.

211.   Bahr, S.J.   "The Pains and Joys of Divorce: A Survey
       of Mormons," Family Perspective, 16 (Fall 1982),
       191-200.

       Interviews with 89 recently-divorced individuals
       were conducted.   The study was completed in Utah
       County, Utah.

212.   Beal, E.W.   "Separation, Divorce and Single-Parent
       Families," (in) The Family Life Cycle: A Framework
       for Family Therapy, ed. by E.A. Carter and M.C.
       McGoldrick.   New York: Gardner Press, 1980, 241-
       264.

       This chapter focused on divorce as a process that
       occurs in a family over a period of time and that
       has far-reaching effects throughout the extended
       family sytem.

213.   Berman, W.H. and D.C. Turk.   "Adaptation to Divorce:
       Problems and Coping Strategies," J. of Marriage
       and the Family, 43 (February 1981), 179-189.

       Through multivariate techniques, the present
       study first examines the effect of divorce-
       related problems on perceived distress.   Second,
       the role of various coping strategies in mediating
       distress is examined.   The results indicate that
       only interpersonal and familial problems have a
       major effect on overall mood state.

214.   Booth, A., and L. White.   "Thinking about Divorce,"
       J. of Marriage and the Family, 42 (August 1980),
       605-616.

       Using interview data from 1,364 married people, a
       study compared people who indicated they were
       thinking about divorce with those who were not.
       The analysis showed that thinking about divorce, while
       it has some of the same correlates as marital
       dissatisfaction and divorce itself, exhibits
       unique patterns as well.

215.   Deckert, P. and R. Langelier.   "The Late-Divorce
       Phenomenon: The Causes and Impact of Ending 20-Year-
       Old or Longer Marriages," J. of Divorce, 1
       (Summer 1978), 381-390.

       The escalating divorce rate in Canada is mirrored
       by the Province of Quebec where divorce has in-
       creased by 270% in the past 5 years.   This study

examined late divorce occuring after 20 years or
more of marriage. Late divorce was found to result
from the breakdown of the traditional type of
marriage which legally ended because of adultery.
Multiple causes, including sexual satisfaction,
were the primary "real" reasons.

216. De Shane, M.R. and K. Brown-Wilson. "Divorce in Late
Life: A Call for Research," J. of Divorce, 4
(Summer 1981), 81-91.

In spite of the potential consequences of late
life divorce on adjustment to old age, almost no
attention has been paid to the subject. Social,
psychological and economic consequences of late
life divorce are discussed and areas of needed
research are explicated.

217. Goetting, A. "Divorce Outcome Research: Issues and
Perspectives," J. of Family Issues, 2 (September
1981), 350-378.

The effects of divorce on adults are summarized
and analyzed in terms of (a) practical problems,
(b) the consequences for social life and intimate
relationships, and (c) health and safety. The
effects of parental divorce on children are
reviewed in terms of (a) cognitive performance and
school success, (b) personality, (c) interpersonal
relationships, (d) health, and (e) juvenile
delinquency.

218. Hall, S. "Trading Down but Not Out," The Single Parent,
24 (Jan.-Feb. 1981).

This article describes the situation of many
divorced people who have to sell the marital home.
The necessity of moving is described as very
stressful, for parents and children, especially
when the new housing is smaller and children must
cope with relocation. Many newly-divorced women
find it difficult to qualify for mortgage money.

219. Hancock, E. "The Dimensions of Meaning and Belonging
in the Process of Divorce," American J. of
Orthopsychiatry, 50 (January 1980), 18-27.

Emotional reactions to divorce are described, with
particular reference to the loss of social
definition faced by members of the separating family.

It is suggested that, for children in particular, disruption of the famly matrix constitutes a crisis of meaning and belonging that may be central to the impact of divorce.

220. Ibrahim, A.I. "The Process of Divorce," Conciliation Courts Review, 22 (June 1984), 81-88.

The process of divorce consists of ten steps: threat, separation, denial, shock, anger, bargaining, depression, isolation, acceptance, and new beginning. It is more important to note that not all divorcees pass through each of these stages. The possibility exists that some divorcees may complete the whole process successively and successfully, some may skip some of the steps mentioned, and some may repeat the process, or some of its stages, several times.

221. Isaacs, M.B. "Helping Mom Fail: A Case of a Stalemated Divorcing Process," Family Process, 21 (June 1982), 225-234.

This article describes a systems approach to the problem of a child who had become symptomatic as a result of her parents' separation. Elements of the divorcing process that can create a symptomatic child are highlighted. Family members cope with separation and divorce by devising strategies for navigating the divorcing process.

222. Jorgensen, S.R. and A.C. Johnson. "Correlates of Divorce Liberality," J. of Marriage and the Family, 42 (August 1980), 617-626.

Current theorizing about causes of the increasing rate of marital instability in the United States has pointed to increasingly liberal attitudes toward divorce as a key explanatory variable. An investigation attempted to identify significant correlates of divorce liberality by testing a series of hypotheses derived from cognitive dissonance, social learning, and social exchange theories. Based on interviews of a sample of 240 spouses (120 couples), data included that husbands and wives differ in terms of the variables influencing the degree of divorce liberality.

223. Kitson, G.C. "Attachement to the Spouse in Divorce: A
     Scale and its Application," J. of Marriage and the
     Family, 44 (May 1982), 379-398.

     A scale to assess continuing affectional bonds, or
     attachment, in divorce is described. In a sample
     of suburban Cleveland men and women going through
     divorce, 86% indicate some signs of attachment to
     their ex-spouses. Greater feelings of attachment
     are likely when the decision to divorce was
     recently decided upon and when the spouse asked
     for the divorce. Feelings of attachment are less
     affected by resources and social supports than is
     subjective distress.

224. Kitson, G.C. and H.J. Raseke. "Divorce Research: What
     We Know; What We Need to Know," J. of Divorce, 4
     (Spring 1981), 1-37.

     This paper reviews research on the antecedents and
     the consequences of divorce for adults. Divorce is
     discussed as part of a continuum of marital in-
     stability. Research on historical and socio-
     logical causes of divorce and theoretical models
     for the study of divorce are reviewed. The
     changes in health status and the role re-definitions
     experienced by the divorced are discussed.

225. Kitson, G.C. and M.B. Sussman. "Marital Complaints,
     Demographic Characteristics, and Symptoms of
     Mental Distress in Divorce," J. of Marriage and the
     Family, 44 (Feb. 1982), 87-102.

     Patterns of marital complaints in a sample of
     divorcing men and women in metropolitan Cleveland
     are explored. Two codes of complaints are used:
     William Goode's code developed for his 1948
     study of Detroit women's adjustment to divorce and
     a second code developed for the Cleveland study.
     Approximately half of the respondents made com-
     plaints which were either infrequently mentioned
     or not mentioned at all by Goode's respondents.

226. Kolevson, M.S. and S.J. Gottlieb. "The Impact of Divorce:
     A Multivariate Study," J. of Divorce, 7 (Winter
     1983), 80-98.

     A survey of members of a local chapter of Parents
     Without Partners was conducted in an attempt to
     assess the validity of existing theories regarding
     the phases of emotional adjustment experienced
     attendant with the divorce process. The study's

205

findings provided no evidence to suggest that
particular dimensions of emotional adjustment
represent challenges that are unique to particular
stages of divorce.

227. Lewis, P.H. "Innovative Divorce Rituals: Their Psycho-
      Social Functions," J. of Divorce, 6 (Spring 1983),
      71-81.

      The purpose of this paper is 1) to describe rituals
      currently in use which facilitate the psycho-social
      transitions of a divorcing pair and their family;
      and 2) to suggest new practices which may enable
      a healthy, adaptive response to these life changes,
      while maintaining the integrity of the family.

228. Newman, H.M. and E.J. Langer. "Post-Divorce Adaptation
      and the Attribution of Responsibility," Sex Roles,
      7 (No. 3) 1981, 223-231.

      A study was conducted to explore the possible
      relationship between post-divorce adjustment and
      the attributions divorced women give for the
      failure of their marriages. The study revealed that
      significantly more subjects who attributed their
      divorces to interactive rather than personal
      factors were more active, more socially skilled,
      happier, more optimistic, and less likely to blame
      themselves rather than outside forces for failures.

229. Norton, A.J. "The Influence of Divorce on Traditional
      Life-Sycle Measures," J. of Marriage and the
      Family, 42 (February 1980), 63-70.

      This paper presents data and discussion which
      compare life-cycle measures of women whose
      marriages have dissolved by divorce with those of
      women who had never divorced. The findings
      indicate that differences do exist in the timing
      of life cycle events according to marital history,
      race, and education but that birth cohort associa-
      tion represents an overriding source of
      differential timing.

230. Perlman, J.L. "Divorce--A Psychological and Legal
      Process," J. of Divorce, 6 (Fall-Winter 1982),
      99-114.

      Divorce is examined as a psychological and legal
      process. Etiological factors believed to be con-
      tributing to divorce and the psychological
      sequelae of divorce are critically explored.

Legal issues surrounding court-based interventions, the impact of the "no-fault" law, and
the role of lawyers are reviewed. The role of
mental health professionals, lawyers, and courts
in a divorce are discussed in terms of individual
contributions as well as interdisciplinary "team"
approaches.

231. Peters, J.F. <u>Divorce</u>. Toronto: Faculty of Education,
Guidance Centre, University of Toronto, 1979.

This booklet discusses divorce in Canada.

232. Saul, S.C. and A. Scherman. "Divorce Grief and Personal
Adjustment in Divorced Persons Who Remarry or
Remain Single," <u>J. of Divorce</u>, 7 (Spring 1984),
75-86.

This study hypothesized that there would be no
significant differences on measures of grief or
adjustment between those who have remarried and
those who have remained single. The 114 subjects
between the ages of 25-35 included males without
live-in children, females with children, and
females without children. They had been divorced
either 6-18 months or 19-36 months.

233. Saunders, B. "The Social Consequences of Divorce:
Implications for Family Policy," <u>J. of Divorce</u>, 6
(Spring 1983), 1-18.

This paper is presented as "research for family
policy." Its purpose is to outline the social
consequences of divorce to the divorcing person
for use by social policymakers at both the micro
and macro levels. An integrative review of the
available research concerning the social situation
of divorced persons, five meta-policy guidelines,
and examples of possible policy implementations
relating to divorced persons are presented.

234. Sell, K.D. (ed) <u>Divorce in the 70s: A Subject
Bibliography</u>. Phoenix: The Oryx Press, 1981.

This bibliography lists the majority of materials,
excluding fiction written on divorce in the
United States during the 1970-1979 period.

235. Tcheng-Laroche, F. and R.H. Prince. "Middle Income,
      Divorced Famale Heads of Families: Their Lifestyles,
      Health and Stress Levels," Canadian J. of Psychiatry,
      24 (January 1979), 35-42.

      According to health professionals and the mass
      media, an increasing number of well educated and
      economically viable women are actively choosing
      to dissolve their marriages to assume the role of
      heads of families--and are enjoying it.

      In this report, the authors describe a group of
      such women, whom they were able to identify in
      Montreal.

236. Thurnher, M., Fenn, C.B., Melichar, J. and D.A. Chiriboga.
      "Sociodemographic Perspectives on Reasons for
      Divorce," J. of Divorce, 6 (Summer 1983), 25-36.

      This paper examines reasons for divorce reported by
      a sample of 333 men and women, aged 20 to 79.
      Reasons for divorce, which ranged from lack of
      personal self-fulfillment to nonfulfillment of
      marital role obligations, were shown to be in-
      fluenced by sex, age, education, income, and
      number of children.

237. Wallerstein, J.S. and J.B. Kelly. Surviving the Breakup.
      New York: Basic Books, 1980.

      The results of a five-year study of sixty
      families in their post-divorce stage. The study
      focuses especially on the children ranging in age
      from three to 16 years.

238. White, S.W. and B.L. Bloom. "Factors Related to the
      Adjustment of Divorcing Men," Family Relations, 30
      (July 1981), 347-360.

      In order to examine the effects of marital dis-
      ruption upon divorcing men, a sample of 40 men
      separated between one and six months and involved
      in a divorce petition was interviewed. All but
      three were reinterviewed between three and four
      months later. There was relatively little
      improvement during the time interval.

208

239. Cherlin, A.J. Marriage, Divorce, Remarriage: Social
      Trends in the United States. Cambridge, Mass.:
      Harvard University Press, 1981.

      The author discusses family change over the past
      35 years, and explains the latest research findings.

240. Crosby, J.F. "A Critique of Divorce Statistics and
      Their Interpretation," Family Relations, 29
      (Jan. 1980), 51-58.

      Increasingly, appeals to the divorce statistics
      are employed to substantiate the claim that the
      family is in a state of breakdown and marriage is
      passe. This article contains a consideration of
      reasons why the divorce statistics are invalid
      and/or unreliable as indicators of the present
      state of marriage and family.

241. Davids, L. "Divorce and Remarriage in Canadian Jews,"
      J. of Comparative Family Studies, 13 (Spring 1982),
      37-47.

      The traditional self-image of the Jews and their
      culture includes the belief that Jewish family life
      is stable and happy. If would be expected that
      divorce rates as a result would be lower among
      Jews than Canadians in general. Traditionally,
      divorce among this group was legitimate but
      regarded as a tragedy. It was discouraged and
      attempts were made to keep the couple together at
      the expense of their own personal happiness in some
      cases. This was done with children and society's
      interests in mind. This paper investigates the
      differences in the number of divorces; the amount
      of increase in divorce rate and the rate of re-
      marriage between Jews and all Canadians.

242. Malcabe, T. "Provincial Variations in Divorce Rates:
      A Canadian Case," J. of Marriage and the Family,
      42 (February 1980), 171-176.

      It has become clear that since the enactment of
      new divorce legislation in 1968 that divorce rates
      vary between the provinces in Canada. The eastern
      provinces have the lowest divorce rates, while the
      west (excluding Saskatchewan) have the highest.
      This study investigates the different social and
      economic conditions in the provinces with reference
      to their divorce rates.

209

243. Price-Bonham, S. and J.O. Balswick. The Noninstitutions:
      Divorce, Desertion and Remarriage," J. of Marriage
      and the Family, 42 (November 1980), 959-972.

      Selected research and theoretical writings, pub-
      lished in the 1970s, on divorce, remarriage, and
      desertion were reviewed. Particular emphasis was
      focused on variables (demographic and inter-
      personal) related to divorce, divorce adjustment,
      probability of remarriage, and the dynamics of re-
      marriage. Data presented confirm some previous
      findings but challenge others. Implications of
      the noninstitutional status of divorce, remarriage,
      and desertion, and suggestions for research in the
      1980s are included.

244. Rowe, G.K. "A Comparative Analysis of Divorce Rates in
      Canada and the United States, 1927 to 1967." J. of
      Divorce, 4 (Fall 1980), 61-71.

      A comparative analysis of the divorce rates in
      Canada and the United States between 1927 and 1967
      was performed. The association between divorce
      rates in these two nations and economic prosperity
      (national income), depression, and war was
      investigated.

245. Wilkinson, K.P., Reynolds, R.R., Thompson, J.G. and
      L.M. Ostresh. "Divorce and Recent Net Migration
      into the Old West," J. of Marriage and the Family,
      45 (May 1983), 437-446.

      A positive association between change in the
      divorce rate and net immigration has been suggested
      in discussions of recent rural population growth,
      particularly in areas affected by rapid development
      of energy resources. Previous research findings
      suggest that the divorce rate is affected by stress
      and by effectiveness of constraints to divorce
      and that these might be influenced by net immigra-
      tion. Data on change in divorce rates of 292
      counties of the Old West region from 1970 to 1975
      were examined. Multiple regression results
      indicate that new immigration had little effect on
      change in the divorce rate.

246. Bonkowski, S.W. and B. Wanner-Westly. "The Divorce Group: A New Treatment Modality," Social Casework, 60 (November 1979), 552-557.

Participation in a group of others with similar concerns is an effective treatment method for people dealing with divorce. This time-limited experience aids understanding and provided needed information and support. Professional leadership facilitates managing the complex interactions of the differing personalities.

247. Bonkowski, S.W., Bequette, S.Q. and S. Boomhower. "A Group Design to Help Children Adjust to Parental Divorce," Social Casework, 65 (March 1984), 131-137.

Children of divorce are a vulnerable and largely unreached population. An eight-week semi-structured group intervention was designed to mitigate the effects of divorce on latency-age children. The group's objectives, format, and interventive techniques are discussed.

248. Camiletti, Y. and V. Quant. "Anticipating Counselling for Adolescents of Divorced Parents," The School Guidance Worker, 39 (September 1983), 20-23.

This article reviews the difficulties of adolescent children of divorced parents and the coping strategies they use. The author focuses attention on a mode of intervention initiated in a high school setting and the findings of a pilot group consisting of eight students in London, Ontario.

249. Cantor, D.W. "The Psychologist as Child Advocate with Divorcing Families," J. of Divorce, 6 (Fall-Winter 1982), 77-86.

Each year over a million children in the United States are involved in the break-up of their families by divorce. Most of them are left to deal with the stress produced by the family trauma on their own. Children need someone to respond to them when their parents are divorcing. This article proposes that psychologists assume an active role as child advocate with divorcing families to reduce the stress for the children.

250.   Coche, J. and J. Goldman. "Brief Group Psychotherapy
        for Women after Divorce: Planning a Focused
        Experience," J. of Divorce, 3 (Winter 1979),
        153-160.

        Divorce is a period of personal turbulence for
        women experiencing the separation process. A
        model for a brief, focused group psychotherapy
        experience for women, led by women therapists,
        is suggested as an effective means to ease the
        transition from marriage and to allow a re-
        definition of the self as a single individual.
        Case material and follow-up information is
        described.

251.   Dreyfus, E.A. "Counseling the Divorced Father," J. of
        Marital and Family Therapy, 5 (October 1979),
        79-85.

        Counseling divorced fathers brings with it many
        special concerns unique to the divorced father.
        Four phases of counseling with these men are
        discussed. Phase I deals with the immediate crisis
        bringing the client into counseling; Phase II
        examines the various losses and dependency needs;
        Phase III centers around beliefs, values, and
        social realities; Phase IV focuses on issues of
        being an unmarried parent.

252.   Felner, R.D., Primavera, J., Farber, S.S., and T.A.
        Bishop. "Attorneys as Caregivers during Divorce,"
        Amer. J. of Orthopsychiatry, 52 (April 1982),
        323-336.

        In a survey of the emotional and practical problems
        presented by divorce clients, 74 attorneys
        reported spending one-fifth of their time in such
        cases dealing with clients' extralegal problems.
        While most attorneys reported feeling generally
        effective in this caregiving role, an overwhelming
        majority would welcome mental health consultation.

253.   Freeman, R. "Children and Divorce: Evaluating a Model
        of Brief Treatment," (in) Changing Structures of
        Families: Adaptation and Fragmentation. Ottawa:
        Family Service Canada, 1983, 137-150.

        A child-fcoused treatment of the Family Service
        Association of Metropolitan Toronto is described.
        This paper highlights the approach to treatment.
        The research currently in process is briefly
        described and some preliminary results are

                            212

presented. To conclude, issues relevant to program implementation are addressed.

254. Goldmeier, J. "Intervention in the Continuum from Divorce to Family Reconstitution," Social Casework, 61 (January 1980), 39-47.

Caseworkers increasingly see clients moving through phases from separation to the establishment of new family units. A framework for working with these persons identifies the predictable phases and common impediments to coping faced by these clients and suggests that a flexible approach to timing interventions is most appropriate.

255. Gverney, L. and L. Jordon. "Children of Divorce: A Community Support Group," J. of Divorce, 2 (Spring 1979), 283-294.

The purpose of Children of Divorce, which is a community-based and community-sponsored education-support group, is to assist children in adjusting to separation or divorce in their families. Intended as a primary preventive effort, the program is open to all child volunteer participants. Children meet with volunteer group leaders for a series of six weekly sessions.

256. Hassall, E. and D. Madar. "Crisis Group Therapy with the Separated and Divorced," Family Relations, 29 (October 1980), 591-597.

This paper examines the use of crisis intervention techniques in a group setting as an effective modality for meeting the social and emotional needs of separated and divorced people and helping them to deal with their relationship loss trauma. The authors have drawn on their own experience with groups of separated and divorced people.

257. Kitson, G.C., Graham, A.V. and D.D. Schmidt. "Troubled Marriages and Divorce: A Prospective Suburban Study," The J. of Family Practice, 17(2), 1983, 249-258.

A longitudinal survey of adjustment to divorce in Cleveland, Ohio, suburbs was conducted with a matched sample of married persons in order to identify some of the common complaints, feelings, concerns, and health hazards among separated and divorced

213

persons. The study findings show that substantial
numbers of divorced and married people turn to
their physicians for help with personal problems,
suggesting that physicians need to be prepared to
help them appropriately.

258. Kraus, S. "The Crisis of Divorce: Growth Promoting or
Pathogenic?", J. of Divorce, 3 (Winter 1979), 107-
119.

Divorce and separation are considered highly
stressful life events, as indicated by the high
weighting for these items on the Holmes & Rahe
Social Readjustment Rating Scale. Previous to
the 1970s, most of the research examining the
emotional impact of divorce focused on the relationship between divorce and psychopathology. This
report critically examines the pathogenic perspective on divorce, pointing out its methodological and conceptual shortcomings.

259. Kressel, K. "Patterns of Coping in Divorce and Some
Implications for Clinical Practice," Family
Relations, 29 (April 1980), 234-240.

On the basis of a three-year research project on the
social-psychological aspects of divorce and a
selective summary of recent empirical studies on
the divorcing process, characteristic patterns
of individual and marital coping response to the
stresses of divorce are described. Implications
for clinical practice are discussed in terms of
the need for active, concrete, practically focused
forms of assistance and the therapist's role in
the decision-making process, including the
decision to divorce.

260. Lang, J. "Divorce and the Jewish Woman: A Family
Agency Approach," J. of Jewish Communal Service,
54 (Spring 1978), 220-228.

The author discusses the experience of Jewish
Agencies in New York in working with divorced
women.

261. Langelier, R. and P. Deckert. "Divorce Counseling
Guidelines for the Late-Divorced Female," J. of
Divorce, 3 (Summer 1980), 403-411.

This paper offers divorce counseling guidelines
for the female who divorces after 20 years or more
of marriage. It is based on a 1977 study of 204

214

late divorced female Canadians. This research emphasized six major life adjustment areas. The six major areas are in order of suggested treatment: emotions, divorce grounds, finances and budgetting; children; life-style changes, and independence.

262. Rosenthal, P.A. "Sudden Disappearance of One Parent with Separation and Divorce: The Grief and Treatment of Preschool Children," J. of Divorce, 3 (Fall 1979), 43-54.

This paper reports on one aspect of a larger problem: the sudden departure due to divorce or separation of one parent, their pathological effect on young children and consequential treatment. It was found that the feelings that surround the loss of one parent affects the child less than the relationship the child has with the remaining parent and the facilitating and supportive environment.

263. Salts, C.J. and C.E. Zongker. "Effects of Divorce Counseling Groups on Adjustment and Self Contept," J. of Divorce, 6 (Summer 1983), 55-68.

The purpose of this study was to test whether or not self concept and adjustment of separated or divorced individuals could be enhanced by participation in group counseling. Individuals who participated in a structured group had significantly higher post-test adjustment than a casualty group.

264. Scheiner, L.S., Musetto, A.P. and D.C. Cordier. "Custody and Visitation Counseling: A Report of an Innovative Program," Family Relations, 31 (January 1982), 99-107.

An innovative approach to custody/visitation counseling developed by the Camden County Health Services Center, Community Mental Health Program in cooperation with the Juvenile and Domestic Relations Court is presented. The goals are based on Family Systems Theory and an integration of the results of clinical and current research findings. Families are seen from three to seven sessions for evaluation and counseling.

265. Seward-Patten, P. A Teacher's Guide to Helping Children of Divorce. Corning, New York: Patricia Patten Seward, 1981 (30 Brown Rd., Corning, N.Y. 14830).

215

A teacher gives classroom teachers tips on how to handle children of divorce in the schools.

266. Spira, L. "The Experience of Divorce for the Psycho-Therapy Patient--A Developmental Perspective," Clinical Social Work Journal, 9 (Winter 1981), 258-270.

In this article the dynamics of divorce are discussed from the perspective of psychoanalytic developmental psychology. This theoretical frame-work is used to highlight and to explain some typical internal and external responses of psycho-therapy patients for whom divorce is an issue. A therapeutic stance is suggested that enables the patient to understand the connection between his or her marital situation, early life experience, and past developmental problems.

267. Sprenkle, D.H. and C.L. Storm. "Divorce Therapy Outcome Research: A Substantive and Methodological Review," J. of Marital and Family Therapy, 9 (July 1983), 239-258.

Empirical studies related to divorce therapy are reviewed both substantively and methodologically. There is strong evidence for the superiority of mediation to traditional adversary methods for custody and visitation disputes. Conciliation counseling appears to increase the number of re-conciliations in the short-term.

268. Stack, S. "The effects of Marital Dissolution on Suicide," J. of Marriage and the Family, 42 (February 1980), 83-92.

Previous research on the relationship between divorce and suicide has focused on a number of case studies and the simple bivariate relationship. The present study explores the relationship more systematically through a multiple regression analysis of data from the 50 American states. The results indicate that the incidence of divorce is closely associated with the rate of suicide even after we control for the influence of the effects of age composition, percentage black, the rate of interstate migration and income.

269. Storm, C.L. and D.H. Sprenkle. "Individual Treatment in
      Divorce Therapy: A Critique of an Assumption,"
      J. of Divorce, 6 (Fall-Winter 1982), 87-98.

      This paper critically examines the maxim commonly
      held and generally supported in the divorce therapy
      literature that the preferred treatment in divorce
      therapy is individual treatment, and will consider
      conjoint and family treatment as viable alternatives.
      This assumption will be addressed by: 1) assessing
      how a therapist's theory of divorce therapy dictates
      the treatment unit adopted in divorce therapy, 2)
      reviewing individual, conjoint, and family divorce
      therapy research, and 3) discussing the significance
      of timing in divorce therapy.

270. Tessman, L.H. Children of Parting Parents. New York:
      Jason Aronson, 1978.

      The author describes many vignettes of children
      who have experienced divorce. Therapeutic
      techniques are also included in working with
      these children.

271. Titkin, E.A. and C. Cobb. "Treating Post-Divorce
      Adjustment in Latency Age Children: A Focused
      Group Paradigm," Social Work with Groups, 6
      (Summer 1983), 53-66.

      The authors have developed a unique group para-
      digm for children 7-12 whose parents are involved
      in separation or divorce. The model consists of a
      parent-child assessment system, a focused set of
      group games and exercises for the children and
      concurrent integrative parent sessions.

272. Woody, J.D. "Preventive Intervention for Children of
      Divorce," Social Casework, 59 (November 1978),
      537-544.

      The high rate of problems suffered by children of
      divorce may be ameliorated by an active pro-
      fessional stance aiming at early intervention.

273. Wylder, J. "Including the Divorced Father in Family
      Therapy," Social Work, 27 (November 1982, 479-
      482.

      Practitioners should involve the divorced father
      in family therapy, both to acknowledge the bond

that will always remain between father and child
and to deal with practical problems such as
visitation rights. The resistance of many mothers
to the idea of bringing in their former husbands
in family sessions is discussed, as is the stance
taken by the therapist to bring it about.

C.   FEMALE-HEADED ONE-PARENT FAMILIES

274. Bradburg, K., Danziger, S., Smolensky, E. and
      P. Smolensky. "Public Assistance, Female Head-
      ship, and Economic Well-Being," J. of Marriage
      and the Family, 41 (August 1979), 519-535.

      In recent years there has been a rapid growth in
      the number of households headed by women and in
      the proportion of these households receiving
      public assistance. This paper presents a model to
      test the hypothesis that changes in the public
      assistance system contributed to the increase in
      these households.

275. Buehler, C.A. and M.J. Hogan. "Managerial Behavior and
      Stress in Families Headed by Divorced Women: A
      Proposed Framework," Family Relations, 29
      (October 1980), 525-532.

      Female-headed families are vulnerable to high levels
      of stress following divorce. A framework is pro-
      posed which conceptually links economic stressors
      and family management patterns. Ecosystem and
      management perspectives are offered as an integrated
      framework.

276. Cashiou, B.G. "Female-Headed Families: Effects on
      Children and Clinical Implications," J. of Marital
      and Family Therapy, 8 (April 1982), 77-85.

      The social psychological research pertaining to
      female-headed families published between 1970-1980
      is reviewed. The literature indicates that
      theoretically children do not need the presence
      of the same-sex/opposite-sex parents in the
      family in order to develop sex-role behaviour.

277. Freeman, J. "Women and Urban Policy," Signs, 5
      (Spring 1980).

      Freeman points out that the numbers of female-
      headed families continues to rise; that these
      families are often living in poverty, and that

their concentration in cities is both the cause and
the consequence of the cities' fiscal woes.

278. Gongla, P.A. "Single Parent Families: A Look at Families
      of Mothers and Children" Marriage and Family Review,
      5 (Summer 1982), 5-28.

      Gongla's discussion of female-headed, single parent
      families shows how concept clarification and re-
      finement improves our understanding of this major
      alternative family form. Her analysis points to
      three problems that have plagued the study of
      this family type: the focus on the individual
      rather than on the family; the lack of examination
      of the family's relationship to its social envir-
      onment; and the assumption of an absent father.

279. Jordan, E. The Housing Needs of Female Led One-Parent
      Families. Ottawa: Canada Mortgage and Housing
      Corporation, 1981.

      This monograph looks at the housing needs of female-
      led one-parent families in Canada.

280. McLahan, S.S. "Family Structure and Stress: A
      Longitudinal Comparison of Two-parent and Female-
      headed Families," J. of Marriage and the Family,
      45 (May 1983), 347-358.

      This paper examines the relationship between family
      headship and stress. Three types of stressors
      are identified and examined: the presence of
      chronic life strains, the occurrence of major
      life events, and the absence of social and psycho-
      logical supports. The first part of the analysis
      compares levels of stress between two-parent,
      "male-headed" families and one-parent, female-
      headed families. The second part focuses on stress
      among different subgroups of female-headed
      families and examines stress as a function of time
      since marital disruption.

281. Roncek, D.W., Bell, R. and H.M. Choldin. "Female-
      Headed Families: An Ecological Model of Residential
      Concentration in a Small City," J. of Marriage
      and the Family, 42 (February 1980), 157-170.

      The authors explain the distribution of female-
      headed families in a small city. They propose and
      evaluate an ecological model comparing the effects

219

of the social composition of subareas to the
effects of spatial and site features. They use
data for city blocks to provide a precise picture
of the patterns of concentration of female-headed
families.

282. Slesinger, D.P. "Rapid Changes in Household
Composition Among Low Income Mothers," Family
Relations, 29 (April 1980, 221-228.

Change in family structure over a 17 month period
in a sample of 123 low-income urban and rural
Wisconsin mothers who gave birth in 1974 is
examined. One-third of the households changed
household types as measured by presence or absence
of male partner and/or extended family members.
One-third of the mothers were heads of households
at the study's outset; of these, two-thirds
remained heads over the time period. Mother's age,
education, and poverty status were characteristics
most strongly related to household composition
changes.

283. Stern, E.A. "Single Mothers' Perceptions of the Father
Role and of the Effects of Father Absence on Boys,"
J. of Divorce, 4 (Winter 1980), 77-84.

This study examined single mothers' concerns about
the effects of father absence on boys. A two-part
questionnaire covering 11 dimensions of parent
role and child development was administered to a
group of single and a group of nonsingle mothers.
Subjects rated the "importance" of a father and
a mother and the effects of a father's absence on
a boy. It would found that singles rated a father
more important than nonsingles did, but singles also
rated a mother more important--this was called the
"parenting effect."

284. Tcheng-Laroche, F.C. "Yesterday Wife and Mother, Today
Head of Household: The Experience of a Group of
Separated or Divorced Women," Canada's Mental
Health, 26 (September 1978), 6-9.

The objective of this study is to attempt to
gain a better knowledge of the situation of the
female head of household who is separated or
divorced and who belongs to a middle or higher

socio-economic group. What happens when finances are not of primary concern? How does she see her role as head of household? What are her aspirations and her problems? What strategies has she had to adopt to deal with her new situation? How does she experience this new situation? What measures or services would facilitate her "new life"? What personal or social factors give her greater satisfaction?

285. Wattenberg, E. and H. Reinhardt. "Female-headed Families: Trends and Implications," Social Work, 24 (November 1979), 460-467.

A review of current demographic trends related to fatherless families.

D. MALE-HEADED ONE-PARENT FAMILIES

286. Chang, P.N. and A.S. Dienard. "Single-Father Care-takers: Demographic Characteristics and Adjustment Processes," American J. of Orthopsychiatry, 52 (April 1982), 236-243.

Eighty single-father caretakers were surveyed, the majority of whom tended to be middle-aged, of high educational level, and earning at or above the national average income. Findings suggest that these fathers sought custody because of their love for their children and their confidence in their parenting ability. Despite some minor difficulties, most of the fathers demonstrated satisfactory adjustment.

287. Gatley, R.H. and D. Koulack. Single Father's Handbook. New York: Anchor Books, 1979.

This book is for men who are separated from their children, written by two psychologists for fathers like themselves.

288. Greif, G.L. "Dads Raising Kids," Single Parent, 25 (December 1982), 19-23.

The results of a study of 1100 single-parent fathers who are raising their children.

289. Katz, A. "Lone Fathers: Perspectives and Implications for Family Policy," Family Relations, 28 (Oct. 1979), 521-528.

The paper focuses on the general theoretical concept of the lone father family, examines

221

previous research, and then presents the
findings related to a study of 409 lone fathers.
It ends with some suggestions related both to
intervention and the need for the "helping
community" to be more aware of the unique qual-
ities of this population.

290.   Keshet, H.F. and K.M. Rosemthal. "Fathering after
       Marital Separation," Social Work, 23 (January
       1978), 11-18.

       The study described in this article deals with
       the experience of a group of separated or divorced
       fathers who chose to remain fully involved in the
       upbringing of their children. As they underwent
       the transition from married parenthood to single
       fatherhood, these men learned that meeting the
       demands of child care contributed to their own
       stability and personal growth.

291.   Keshet, H.F. and K.M. Rosenthal. "Single Fathers: A
       New Study," Children Today, 7 (May-June 1978),
       13-17.

       This article is about single-parent fathers who
       are rearing their young children after marital
       separation. It discusses what fathers do for and
       with their children and how being a single
       parent affects their lifestyles and work respon-
       sibilities.

       The article is based on interviews, conducted by
       trained male interviewers, with 49 separated or
       divorced fathers who live in the Boston area and
       have formal or informal custody of their children.

292.   Knight, B.M. Enjoying Single Parenthood. New York: Van
       Nostrand Reinhold, 1980.

       Written by a single father, this guide gives infor-
       mation on many social and personal areas of single
       parenthood.

293.   Lewis, K. "Single-Father Families: Who They Are and
       How They Fare," Child Welfare, 57 (December 1978),
       643-652.

       In this article, a single-father family is defined
       as one consisting of an unmarried male and his
       minor child or children living in the same

household. This definition includes widowers,
divorced and separated fathers, never-married
males, and single adoptive fathers. It excludes
fathers whose wives are not present in the home
for reasons such as imprisonment or hospitalization.
A single father is the parent of children under
18 years old who live in his household all of
the time or for long periods of time, and for
whom he has primary responsibility.

294. Nieto, D.S. "Aiding the Single Father," Social Work,
27 (November 1982), 473-478.

Unmarried males partially or totally responsible
for the rearing of their minor children encounter
particular and peculiar problem sets in consequence
of their status. The survey on which part of the
discussion is based indicates that most helping
practitioners are aware of single fathers as a
client group and that most such practitioners want
further information relatives to this group.
There is substantial interest in the phenomenon
of single fatherhood as a potential practice area,
and most practitioners perceive significant
deficits in terms of available support systems.

295. Oakland, T. Divorced Fathers: Reconstructing a Viable
Life. New York: Human Sciences Press, 1983.

Practical advice is offered to divorced fathers.
The psychological impact of divorce on the entire
family and the father's role adjustment are also
reviewed.

296. Orthner, D.K. and R.J. Brown. "Single-Parent Fathers:
Implications for the Military Family," (in)
E.J. Hunter and D.S. Nice, eds. Military Families:
Adaptation to Change. New York: Praeger, 1978,
88-102.

Over the last decade, the military has shown itself
to be increasingly subject to the same trends and
pressures as the society-at-large. With the
decline in an insulated environment, changes in
social values, laws, and family norms are being
felt more and more by the military personnel.
Therefore, it is important to look at the way in
which changes in parental roles and custody
arrangements may influence the military family.

297. Orthner, D.K. and K. Lewis. "Evidence of Single-Father
        Competence in Childrearing," Family Law Quarterly,
        8 (Spring 1979), 27-48.

        Over one million divorces per year are now pro-
        cessed in the courts of the United States. In
        some 60 percent of these divorce actions, children
        are involved as well. Most often the custody of
        these children is decided upon by their parents
        prior to the petition for divorce, requiring only
        the sanctioning of the court. In nine out of ten
        of these cases, the parents, often with the advice
        of counsel, decide to place the children with their
        mother--a decision bolstered by the legal and social
        presumption that mothers are more capable custod-
        ians of minor children than fathers.

        But in a growing number of divorces, demands by
        fathers for custody of their children are
        challenging this presumption of maternal preference.

298. Rosenthal. K.M. and H.F. Keshet. "The Impact of Child-
        Care Responsibilities on Part-Time or Single
        Fathers: Changing Patterns of Work and Intimacy,"
        Alternative Lifestyles, 1 (November 1978), 465-
        491.

        The study described in this article was designed
        to determine the effects of childcare involvement
        on the lifestyles of fathers with young children.
        One hundred and twenty-seven separated or divorced
        men were interviewed. Their parental responsib-
        ilities ranged from full custody or joint custody
        to weekends or monthly visits. For the most part
        these men represented a middle class, highly
        educated, urban population.

299. Rosenthal,K.M. and H.F. Keshet. Fathers Without
        Partners. Totown, New Jersey: Rowman and Little-
        field, 1981.

        This study describes the lives of fathers with
        custody, joint custody, and men who visit their
        children.

300. Schlesinger, B. "Single Parent Fathers: A Research
        Review," Children Today, 7 (May-June 1978), 12,
        18-19.

        A review of studies up to 1978, related to
        motherless families in Canada and the United
        States.

301. Smith, R.M. and C.W. Smith, "Child Rearing and Single-Parent Fathers," Family Relations, 30 (July 1981), 411-416.

This paper is based on a study of 27 single-parent fathers. The convenience sample, of predominately middle class caucasians, consisted of fathers who had sole custody of and were rearing at least one dependent child with no adult female companion living with them at the time of the interview. The interview was designed to assess the five variables of goal facilitation, transition procedures, normative change, role strain, and ease of role transition during three different phases of their lives.

302. Todres, R. "Motherless Families and Deserting Wives," In One in Ten: The Single Parent in Canada, B. Schlesinger, ed. Toronto: Guidance Centre, Faculty of Education, University of Toronto, 1979, 8-15.

The number of motherless homes has increased in Canada in recent years (40% between 1966 and 1971, and 20% between 1970 and 1973). The two studies reported here responded to the lack of research on this phenomenon. The first, carried out in 1974, investigated this history and the life-styles and problems of motherless families. The second, performed in 1975, studied the reasons for and circumstances surrounding the mother's desertion.

The first study involved 74 motherless families in the Toronto area. The second investigation involved 38 deserting mothers in the same geographic area. Both were exploratory in nature.

303. Todres, R. "Runaway Wives: An Increasing North-American Phenomenon," The Family Coordinator, 27, (January 1978), 17-21.

A study of 38 wives who left their families and children with their husbands in Metropolitan Toronto, Canada.

E. NON-MARRIED PARENTS

304. Barrera, M. "Social Support in the Adjustment of
     Pregnant Adolescents - Assessment Issues," (in)
     B.H. Gottlieb ed. Social Networks and Social
     Support. Beverly Hills, California: Sage, 1981,
     69-96.

     A review of the literature related to social
     support is followed by a discussion of support to
     pregnant adolescents.

305. Bolton, F.G. The Pregnant Adolescent: Problems of
     Premature Parenthood. Beverly Hills, California:
     Sage, 1980.

     A discussion of the existing literature on
     adolescent pregnancy.

306. Byrne, D. and W.A. Fisher. Adolescents, Sex and
     Contraception. Hillsdale, N.J.: Lawrence
     Erlbaum Associates, 1982.

     This book brings together theory, research, and
     application on the important contemporary issue
     of teenage pregnancy. The contents of this
     volume will broaden the understanding of the com-
     plexity that underlies this seemingly irrational
     behaviour on noncontraceptive intercourse.

307. Cannon-Bonventre, K. and J. Kahn. "Interviews with
     Adolescent Parents: Looking at Their Needs,"
     Children Today, 8 (September-October 1979), 17-19.

     What do teenage parents think about their lives,
     their problems and acceptable sources and forms
     of help? The literature is full of discussions
     by service providers and researchers, but we
     rarely hear from the young parents themselves.
     The authors believe that knowledge of teenage
     parents' own views and concerns is crucial to
     sensitive and effective service provision and
     policy planning.

308. Chilman, C.S. Adolescent Sexuality in a Changing
     American Society. Washington, D.C.: U.S.
     Department of Health, Education and Welfare, 1979.

     A comprehensive view of adolescent sexuality and
     parenthood which reviews existing research studies.

309. Chilman, C.S. "Teenage Pregnancy: A Research Review,"
     Social Work, 24 (November 1979), 492-498.

     On the assumption that public policy should be
     based on knowledge, the author presents a brief
     analytic summary of all readily available social
     and psychological research concerning the apparent
     causes and consequences of adolescent childbearing.
     Existing federal programs addressed to this pro-
     blem are listed with recommendations for further
     development of public policies and programs.

310. Chilman, C.S. Adolescent Pregnancy and Childbearing:
     Findings From Research. Washington, D.C.: U.S.
     Department of Health and Human Services, 1980.

     This book includes the papers given at the Con-
     ference on Determinants of Adolescent Pregnancy
     and Childbearing in 1975 and 1976.

311. Chilman, C.S. "Social and Psychological Research
     Concerning Adolescent Childbearing: 1970-1980,"
     J. of Marriage and the Family, 42 (November 1980),
     793-806.

     The author presents the major research findings
     during the 1970's.

312. Furstenburg, F.F. "Burdens and Benefits: The Impact
     of Early Childbearing on the Family," J. of
     Social Issues, 36 (Winter 1980), 64-87.

     This paper explores the impact of teenage preg-
     nancy and childbearing on the families of the
     adolescent and examines the amount and type of
     support extended by the family of origin to the
     pregnant teenager. The analysis draws on data
     from a longitudinal study of teenage childbearing
     in Baltimore and a series of intensive case
     studies of adolescents and their families carried
     out at the Philadelphia Child Guidance Clinic.

313. Furstenburg, F.F., Lincoln, R. and J. Menken. Teenage
     Sexuality, Pregnancy and Childbearing. Philadel-
     phia: University of Pennsylvania Press, 1981.

     Twenty-eight papers reprinted from "Family
     Planning Perspectives" discuss the varied issues
     dealing with teenage mothers in America.

314. Gallas, H.B. (ed). "Teenage Parenting: Social Deter-
     minants and Consequences," J. of Social Issues,
     36 (Winter 1980), Special Issue.

     Seven papers discuss adolescent parenthood as
     one form of a one-parent family.

315. Gilchrist, L.D. and S.P. Schinke. "Teenage Pregnancy
     and Public Policy," Social Service Review, 57
     (June 1983), 307-322.

     Pregnancy among teenagers has caused widespread
     concern. The number of pregnant adolescents and
     the difficulties they face are significant. This
     paper outlines what social science reveals about
     the scope and consequences of teenage pregnancy.
     The authors review the history of policies and
     legislation that have addressed the problem and
     summarize the complexities of public involvement
     in teenagers' contraception, unplanned pregnancy,
     and parenthood.

316. Hollingsworth, D.R. and A.K.K. Kreutner. "Teenage
     Pregnancy," The New England J. of Medicine, 303
     (August 28, 1980), 516-518.

     Early pregnancy has unique medical, social,
     behavioral, and emotional consequences for very
     young women. It is of critical importance to
     search for reasonable solutions to this problem,
     since these women and their children will form a
     large segment of our next generation.

317. Mott Foundation. Teenage Pregnancy: A Critical Family
     Issue. Flint, Michigan: Mott Foundation, 1982.

     A comprehensive overview of teenage pregnancy
     ˎand parenting.

318. Ross, A. Teenage Mothers, Teenage Fathers. Toronto:
     Personal Library, 1982.

     A nurse educator discusses teenage pregnancy and
     parenting. Includes a short birth-control guide.

319. Schinke, S.P., Gilchrist, L.D. and B.J. Blythe. "Role
     of Communication in the Prevention of Teenage
     Pregnancy," Health and Social Work, 5 (August
     1980), 54-59.

     Traditional intervention with young women has
     done little to reduce the incidence of unwanted

teenage pregnancy and childbearing. A new, more
promising approach helps at-risk teenagers learn
the interpersonal skills necessary to communicate
effectively and use contraceptives successfully.

320. Schinke, S.P., Gilchrist, L.D. and R.W. Small. "Pre-
venting Unwanted Adolescent Pregnancy: A Cognitive-
Behavioral Approach," American J. of Orthopsychiatry, 49 (January 1979), 81-88.

Teenage pregnancy is a growing social problem in
the United States. Past interventive failures
and current research suggest new directions for
primary prevention. A comprehensive prevention
program is outlined, and training techniques
based on a cognitive-behavioral approach are
proposed to help adolescents acquire skills
necessary to avoide unwanted pregnancies.

321. Stuart, I.R. and C.F. Wells (eds). Pregnancy in
Adolescence: Needs, Problems and Management.
New York: Van Nostrand and Reinhold, 1982.

Nineteen selections examine the situation of
pregnancy and parenthood in adolescence from a
multi-disciplinary approach.

Children of Non-Married Parents

322. Baldwin, W. and V.S. Cain. "The Children of Teenage
Parents," Family Planning Perspectives, 12
(February 1980), 34-43.

Children born to teenagers suffer intellectual
deficits, largely because of the economic and
social impact of early childbearing on the young
parents. Such children are more likely to spend
part of their childhoold in one-parent households and to have children themselves while
still adolescents.

Fathers: Non-Married

323. Barret, R.L. and B.E. Robinson. "A Descriptive Study
of Teenage Expectant Fathers," Family Relations,
31 (July 1982), 349-352.

This study reports demographic data on a sample
of 26 adolescent expectant fathers and information
about their relationships with the expectant
mothers and their families. Results indicate

that young fathers maintained positive relationships with their girlfriend's family, maintained
social contact with the expectant mother, and
desired to participate in the naming of the child
and to meet certain responsibilities toward mother
and baby.

324. Barret, R.L. and B.E. Robinson. "Teenage Fathers:
Neglected Too Long," Social Work, 27 (November
1982, 484-488.

Although adolescent pregnancy is now recognized
as a social problem of growing proportions, consideration of the teenage father is virtually
absent from the literature as well as from the
planning and implementation of social programs.
A comprehensive review of the literature on
teenage fathers is presented, along with recommendations on how services to unwed adolescent
parents of both sexes can be improved.

325. Brown, S.V. "The Commitment and Concerns of Black
Adolescent Parents," Social Work Research and
Abstracts, 19 (Winter 1983), 27-34.

Researchers and service providers have ignored
the role of unwed fathers in teenage pregnancy
experiences. This article reports on a study of
black adolescent fathers and mothers to assess
the quality of their commitment and concerns as
couples. The examination of both partners calls
into question several race-linked assumptions
about the sexual morality of black teenagers,
their attitudes, and their concerns.

326. Earls, F. and B. Siegel. "Precocious Fathers,"
American J. of Orthopsychiatry, 50 (July 1980),
469-480.

A review of current knowledge related to teenage
fathers.

327. Hendricks, L.E. "Unmarried Adolescent Fathers:
Problems and Support Systems," (in) W.T. Hall and
C.L. Young, eds. Proceedings: Integrating
Tertiary Care into Community Health Services.
Pittsburg: University of Pittsburg, Graduate
School of Public Health, 1981, 124-132.

This paper discusses two select samples of young Black fathers.

328. Hendricks, L.E. "Suggestions for Reaching Unmarried Black Adolescent Fathers," Child Welfare, 62 (March-April, 1983), 141-146.

A cross-sectional study explored ways to aid the growing population if unmarried black fathers. The sample consisted of ninety-five such fathers living in Tulsa, Chicago, and Columbus. The subjects participated in interviews and were selected by social service workers from three teenage parenting agencies. Findings revealed that almost half of the subjects had had their first coital experience at age 12 or younger. Over half were 17 years of age or younger when they became fathers. Many reported feeling closer to their mothers than to their fathers and had brothers and sisters who were also unwed parents.

329. Leushore, B.R. "Human Services and the Unmarried Father: The Forgotten Half," The Family Coordinator, 28 (October 1979), 529-534.

This paper provides a more complete view of the problem of illegitimacy by focusing on its "forgotten half," the unmarried father. It examines characteristics of unmarried fathers, their legal status, and the provision of social services for them. A policy approach utilizing several guiding principles is suggested to improve the provision of services for the unmarried father.

330. Parke, R.D., Power, T.G. and T. Fisher. "The Adolescent Father's Impact on the Mother and Child," J. of Social Issues, 36 (Winter 1980), 88-106.

The adolescent father's impact on the mother and child is the focus of this review. Research on the father-infant relationship is reviewed and the role of the father as caregiver and playmate is emphasized. The consequences of the adolescent father's participation for the development of the infant's cognitive and social-emotional development is examined. A model that distinguishes direct and indirect paths of influence for adolescent fathers is proposed.

331. Berns, J. "Denial of Pregnancy in Young Women,"
       Health and Social Work, 7 (November 1982), 314-
       319.

       Despite the increase in single mothers having and
       raising children, a small group of single women
       successfuly conceal pregnancy, obtain no prenatal
       care, and request adoption immediately after
       delivery. The author discusses the role of the
       hospital social worker with such patients and the
       need to improve access to planning and prenatal
       care.

332. Bolton, F.G., Laner, R.H. and S.P. Kane. "Child Mal-
       treatment Risk Among Adolescent Mothers: A Study
       of Reported Cases," American J. of Orthopsychiatry,
       50 (July 1980), 489-504.

       Findings from the sample of 5,098 incidents of
       child maltreatment reported over a three-year
       period indicated that the adolescent mothers
       (and their families): were involved in more than
       one-third of all reported incidents of mal-
       treatment; provided 61.7 percent of all victims
       of incidents of maltreatment; and, had a reported
       mean annual income almost 20 percent less than
       non-adolescent mothers and their families. A
       comprehensive review of offical records revealed
       that similar dynamic variables had been reported
       for both adolescent and non-adolescent mothers.
       Implications and limitations of the findings and
       suggestions for further study are presented.

333. Borowski, H. and J.G. Macdonald. The Adolescent
       Mother and Her Child: Issues and Trends.
       Toronto: Faculty of Social Work, University of
       Toronto, 1982.

       A review of the literature related to adolescent
       mothers.

334. Burden, D.S. and L.V. Klerman. "Teenage Parenthood:
       Factors that Lessen Economic Dependence,"
       Social Work, 29 (January-February 1984), 11-16.

       The literature reveals that teenage mothers
       have high rates of welfare dependence. Factors
       that lessen the long-term negative economic
       consequences of early motherhood include (1)
       deferment of marriage, (2) support from the

family of origin, (3) increased education and
career motivation, (4) decreased fertility,
and (5) comprehensive programs for teenager
mothers.

335. Cartoof, V.G. "Postpartum Services for Adolescent
Mothers," Child Welfare, 58 (October 1979), 673-
680.

The history, development, and initial findings
of a service delivery system for teenage mothers,
known as the Extended Day Program, are examined.
The program's format is based on the agency's
recognition of the need to reach out assertively
to young mothers by visiting them in their own
homes and by accompanying them to various
referral sources.

336. Fischman, S.H. and H.A. Palley. "Adolescent Unwed
Motherhood: Implications for a National Family
Policy," Health and Social Work, 3 (February
1978), 31-45.

Out-of-wedlock pregnancies among adolescents
from impoverished families and the decision of
these girls to have their babies rather than to
seek an abortion represent an adaptation to the
circumstances of poverty. The authors contend
that a national family policy might help some
of these girls avoid out-of-wedlock pregnancy
and childbearing.

337. Furstenburg, F.F. and A.G. Crawford. "Family Support:
Helping Teenage Mothers to Cope," Family
Planning Perspectives, 10 (Nov-Dec. 1978), 322-
333.

Some teenage parents do overcome the handicaps
imposed by adolescent childbearing: they complete their educations, get decent jobs, and avoid
welfare dependency. Those who continue to live
with their parents and benefit from parental
assistance--financial, psychological, and child
are--do better than those who must depend on
their own resources.

338. Gershenson, H.P. "Redefining Fatherhood in Families
with White Adolescent Mothers," J. of Marriage
and the Family, 45 (August 1983), 591-600.

Thirty white primparous adolescent mothers were
interviewed about social support and family

relationships and about the role of the child's
father. The interviews revealed that men other
than the child's biological father must be considered in any discussion of adolescent parenthood. The relationships and types of support
from four groups of fathers are described in
detail.

339. Glossop, B. "Adolescent Motherhood: The Games
         Children Play," Transition (Vanier Institute
         of the Family), June 1982, 7-9.

Denied the opportunity to genuinely participate
in and contribute to the world they will inherit,
children today are confined to playing games
in a perpetual state of role moratorium looking
for an appropriate identity.

340. Grow, L.J. "Today's Unmarried Mothers: The Choices
         Have Changed," Child Welfare, 58 (June 1979),
         363-371.

A mid-1970's study of the characteristics of
white, pregnant unmarried persons who keep their
children and those who surrender them for
adoption discloses some differences from the
characteristics of such mothers in the late
1960's and early 1970's. The present unwed
mother's decision to keep her child appears to
reflect changes in societal values and can less
easily be attributed to social deviancy or
psychological problems, which were explanations
in earlier eras. Comparisons between mothers
who surrendered and those who kept their
children were made on over 100 variables relevant
to distinguishing between the groups.

341. Grow, L.J. Early Childbearing by Young Mothers: A
         Research Study. New York: Child Welfare League
         of America, 1979.

This research study places the problem of out-of-
wedlock mothers and their children in a new
perspective. The book is based on an intensive
three-year study of young and mostly white
mothers, who are not only keeping their babies,
but raising them with reasonable success. The
author examines the physical, social and
emotional problems of unwed mothers caring for
their children.

342. Grow, L.J. "Follow-Up Study of Early Childbearing,"
      Child Welfare, 59 (May 1980), 311-313.

      Three-year follow-up interviews of white
      primiparous mothers less than 25 years old at
      the time of the birth showed that key factors
      in outcome were psychiatric impairment, lack
      of available resources, and mothers' permissive-
      ness in discipline.

343. Henderson, G.H. "Consequences of School-Age Pregnancy
      and Motherhood," Family Relations, 29 (April
      1980), 185-190.

      Consequences of school-age pregnancy and mother-
      hood are important factors in decision-making
      regarding school procedures and educational
      practices related to school-age pregnant girls
      and young mothers. Such consequences often are
      assumed by decision-makers and are seldom
      research based. School-age mothers, their
      parents, and school personnel were interviewed
      independently to determine their perceptions of
      consequences of school-age pregnancy and mother-
      hood.

344. Kinard, E.M. and L.V. Klerman. "Teenage Parenting and
      Child Abuse: Are They Related?", American J. of
      Orthopsychiatry, 50 (July 1980), 481-488.

      The relationship between teenage parenting and
      child abuse is examined. Three methodological
      problems, which must be considered in assessing
      the relationship between the two variables, are
      discussed. Four data sets are described which
      illustrate the methodological difficulties. The
      data indicate that the proportion of mothers who
      gave birth as teenagers is higher in child-
      abusing families than in the general population.

345. Lende, E., Gilmore, E. and N. Cavanaugh. "Vivamos:
      A Summer Program for Teenage Parents," Children
      Today, 9 (September-October 1980), 9-12.

      A description of a program for teenage parents.

346. Macdonnell, S. Vulnerable Mothers: Vulnerable
      Children. Halifax, Nova Scotia: Nova Scotia
      Department of Social Services, 1981.

      A follow-up study of 346 non-married mothers in
      Nova Scotia.

235

347. McKenry, P., Walters, L.H. and C. Johnson. "Adoles-
       cent Pregnancy. A Review of the Literature,"
       The Family Coordinator, 28 (January 1979), 17-28.

       A wide-ranging review of the literature related
       to adolescent pregnancy and motherhood.

348. Miller, S.H. Children as Parents: Final Report. New
       York: Child Welfare League of America, 1983.

       The final report on a study of childbearing and
       childrearing among 12-15 year olds.

349. Olson, L. "Social and Psychological Correlates of
       Pregnancy Resolution among Adolescent Women:
       A Review," American J. of Orthopsychiatry, 50
       (July 1980), 432-445.

       A review of the recent literature on pregnancy
       resolution among unmarried adolescent women
       suggests that those who seek and go through
       with an abortion do not comprise a special
       population, but are similar to their age mates
       in many of their social and psychological
       characteristics. Previous research suggests,
       however, that teenage abortion patients differ
       from their counterparts on the number of
       significant variables.

350. Presser, H.B. "Sally's Corner: Coping with Unmarried
       Motherhood," J. of Social Issues, 36 (Winter
       1980), 107-129.

       This paper examines the coping strategies of
       unmarried mothers (mostly black) for the 45
       month period since the birth of their first
       child. The study is based on a longitudinal
       survey of first-parity mothers in New York City.
       Their expansion of role responsibilities
       (employment, school, marriage, and subsequent
       childbearing) are analyzed, as well as the
       support systems they utilize (help from the
       child's father, the woman's parents, friends,
       and public assistance).

351. Resnick, M.D. "Studying Adolescent Mothers' Decision
       Making About Adoption and Parenting," Social
       Work, 29 (Jan.-Feb. 1984), 5-10.

       The Reagan Administration has demonstrated a
       strong interest in the sexual, parenting, and
       adoption behavior of adolescent mothers. With
       this interest in mind, the author examines

existing studies on adolescent's decision making about placing their babies for adoption and proposes some theoretical and methodological considerations to guide future investigations in this area.

352. Roosa, M.W. and L. Vaughan. "A Comparison of Teenage and Older Mothers With Pre-School Age Children," Family Relations, 33 (April 1984), 259-265.

A comparison of teenage and older mothers, when their oldest child was 2-4 years old, was undertaken as part of an ongoing effort to delineate differences between the groups that might contribute to developmental differences attributed to their children. Several potentially critical differences in backgrounds, knowledge and attitudes were reported, all favouring the older mothers.

353. Russell, C.S. "Unscheduled Parenthood: Transition to 'Parent' for the Teenager," J. of Social Issues, 36 (Winter 1980), 45.63.

The unscheduled transition into parenthood for the teenager is discussed from three perspectives: 1) the transition to first-time parenthood; 2) accelerated role transitions, and 3) the crisis of adding new family members. The literatures of these three areas are reviewed with special attention to variables that may be associated with progress toward personal and family goals.

354. Sacks, D., Macdonald, J.G., Schlesinger, B. and C. Lambert. The Adolescent Mother and Her Child: A Research Study. Toronto: Faculty of Social Work, University of Toronto, 1982.

This descriptive study concerns the lives of 50 adolescent mothers and their babies in Metropolitan Toronto.

355. Schlesinger, B. "The Unmarried Mother Who Keeps Her Child," In One in Ten: The Single Parent in Canada. B. Schlesinger, ed. Toronto: Guidance Centre, Faculty of Education, University of Toronto, 1979, 77-86.

The number of children born to single mothers in Canada in 1973 was 31,005 which made up 9%

of the live births in that year. Approximately
80% of these children were kept by their
natural mother. This article discusses the issues related to this population.

Historically, there has been a shift from seeing
unmarried motherhood as a moral problem to a
social one. At present, there is greater
recognition of the social, emotional and economic
problems which face this group. This shift is
reflected in the transformation of the laws.

The important decision faced by single mothers
is whether to keep the child.

356. Sung, K.T. and D. Rothrock. "An Alternate School
for Pregnant Teen-agers and Teen-age Mothers,"
Child Welfare, 59 (July-August 1980), 427-436.

A model program to meet the spcial needs of
young mothers who wish to continue their
education has been developed in Kalamazoo, MI,
and has sparked a statewide plan to provide
many services.

357. Woolner, S. "Child Mother: The Catch-22 of Being an
Adolescent Single Parent," Perception, 3
(November-December 1979), 10-13.

Until recently, much of the research on, and
services for, the adolescent mother focused on
the pregnancy. Researchers investigated the
social and psychological predeterminants to
pregnancy. Conditions affecting the adolescent's
decision to terminate the pregnancy or to carry
the child to term were studied. The focus of
social agencies providing services to adolescent mothers was on adequate health care for the
mother and child, and on decision-making with
the teenager concerning the future of the child.

However, since more adolescents are opting to
raise their children, research and services
must address the circumstances of these family
units.

Services to Non-Married Parents

358. Aries, N. "Historic Trends in the Delivery of
Services to Teenage Parents," J. of Sociology
and Social Welfare, 7 (January 1980), 137-146.

This paper examines the political, social and economic factors which underlie the transition in services from unwed mothers to teenage parents over the past 15 years. The experience of agencies in the Boston area serves as the basis for this case study. Data have been collected from open-ended interviews with key service providers who have developed and implemented policy related to adolescent parents.

359. Bedger, J.E. Teenage Pregnancy: Research Related to Clients and Services. Springfield, Illinois: Charles C. Thomas, 1980.

A report of a comprehensive day care program for pregnant teenagers in Chicago.

360. Bell, C.A., Casto, G. and D.S. Daniels. "Ameliorating the Impact of Teen-age Pregnancy on Parent and Child," Child Welfare, 62 (March-April 1983), 157-163.

The resources of a private agency and those of a university program have been combined in a program for fifteen pregnant adolescents and their at-risk preschool children. Intervention consists of weekly group sessions for mothers that focus on achieving independence, improving parenting skills, and developing vocational competence. The mothers are monitored daily by a social worker. The children participate in a home-based program that is carried out by the mothers and a weekly center-based program directed by trained educators.

361. De Anda, D. and R.M. Becerra. "Support Networks for Adolescent Mothers," Social Casework, 65 (March 1984), 172-181.

A comparative study of Hispanic and white adolescent mothers in California indicates that the persons most supportive of them were their mothers and their husbands or boy friends. It also shows differences in support networks of Hispanic mothers who speak English and those who speak Spanish.

362. Erf, L.A. "A Moratorium for Growth: Group Work with Adolescent Mothers," Clinical Social Work Journal, 9 (Spring 1981), 44-56.

An urban child welfare agency ran a group for

single, adolescent mothers based on the premise
that the young mothers needed as much nurturing
as their babies. Essential elements in the program were the provision of transportation to and
from the weekly meetings, childcare, food for
the teenagers, and a male/female co-therapy
team. The group continued for over two years,
allowing a psychosocial moratorium in which the
adolescents could continue their developmental
growth.

363. Gagan, R.J., Cupoli, N., Bell, S., Weibley, T.T. and
A.H. Watkins. "Support Networks of Single Mothers of
Premature Infants," Family Perspective, 17
(Spring 1983), 117-130.

Very little is known about the networks of single
mothers of premature infants. One purpose of
this paper is to describe the networks of
these women. A second purpose is to examine the
proposition that the quality of social networks
has an impact on premature infants' behaviour
and on parent-infant interaction.

364. Kilburn, L.H. "An Educational/Supportive Group
Model for Intervention with School-Age Parents
and Their Children," Social Work with Groups,
6 (Spring 1983), 53-63.

This discussion describes the special techniques
and resources required to successfully develop
groups for teenage pregnant women and others
with infants and toddlers. Enphasis on ways
to reach-out, develop commitment through supportive contacts, useful information and personal involvement are described.

365. Levinson, P., Hale, J., Hollier, M. and C. Tirado.
"Serving Teenage Mothers and Their High-Risk
Infants," Children Today, 7 (July-August 1978),
11-15.

About 20 percent of the total number of births
in the United States are to teenagers. While
this statistic has significant implications
for educators, social service program planners
and health care providers, it is meaningless
to the young mother confronted with the
realities of her new baby. Reality for her is
represented by constant demands to provide for
her baby. Her responses to these demands will
determine the future of both mother and baby.

366. O'Leary, K.M., Shore, M.F. and S. Wieder. "Contacting
     Pregnant Adolescents: Are We Missing Cues?",
     Social Casework, 65 (May 1984), 297-306.

     Prenatal reluctance of pregnant adolescents to
     engage in a mental health services program often
     dissipates after birth occurs if the reluctance
     is understood, outreach is sustained, and inter-
     vention is tailored to clients. Methods of
     engaging women in such a program are described.

F.   SEPARATION AND ONE-PARENT FAMILIES

367. Ambert, A.M. "Drug Use in Separated/Divorced Persons:
     Gender, Parental Status, and Socio-Economic
     Status," Social Science in Medicine (Britain),
     16 (1982), 971-976.

     The purpose of this research was to explore drug
     use in a group of 49 separated/divorced persons.
     The author differentiated between nonprescribed
     psychotropic drugs, and other prescribed drugs.
     The research technique consisted of 3-hr. in-
     depth interviews. The independent variables
     were gender, socio-economic status, and the
     subjects' own parental status. Contrary to
     earlier studies, the author found a higher
     drug use among men than women.

368. Ambert, A.M. "Separated Women and Remarriage
     Behavior: A Comparison of Financially Secure
     Women and Financially Insecure Women." J. of
     Divorce, 6 (Spring 1983), 43-54.

     It has been established that women of higher
     socio-economic status (SES) tend to remarry
     less and less rapidly after divorce than women
     who are less educated and less independent
     financially. Using an exchange theory model,
     it is assumed that higher SES women stand to
     gain less from remarriage than lower SES women.
     In-depth interviews of separated/divorced women,
     thirteen at a higher SES and thirteen at a lower
     SES, explored the hypothesis that women who
     are financially secure behave differently
     towards potential mates than do women who are
     less secure financially.

241

369. Arold, R., Wheeler, M. and F.B. Pendrith. Separation and After: A Research Report. Toronto: Ministry of Community and Social Services, 1980.

This study of post-separation adjustment interviewed 277 separated parents in the Hamilton area.

370. Baker, M. "Women Helping Women: The Transition From Separation to Divorce," Conciliation Courts Review, 22 (June 1984), 53-64.

Through structured interviews with ninety-seven separated and divorced women residing in Metropolitan Toronto, the author found that the majority relied heavily on their female kin and friends to help them through the crisis of marriage breakdown. The transition from marriage to divorce was marked by closer contact with mothers and sisters than during marriage, and stronger ties with long-term female friends. Women because especially close to other separated and divorced women.

371. Bloom, B.L., Asher, S.J. and S.W. White. "Marital Disruption as a Stressor: A Review and Analysis," Psychological Bulletin, 85 (1978), 867-894.

This article describes some of the major demographic trends in the field of marital disruption, and provides an analysis of the evidence linking separation and divorce with a wide variety of physical and emotional disorders. Separation and divorce appear to be profoundly stressful life events.

372. Bloom, B.L. and R.A. Caldwell. "Sex Differences in Adjustment During the Process of Marital Separation," J. of Marriage and the Family, 43 (August 1981), 693-702.

Four different studies are reported in which the differential adjustment of men and women during the process of marital separation was investigated. In these studies consistent sex by time period findings were obtained. Prior to separation, women reported significantly more severe psychological symptoms than did men.

373. Bloom, B.L., Hodges, W.F. and R.A. Caldwell. "Marital
      Separation: The First Eight Months," (in) E.J.
      Callaghan & K.A. McKluskey (eds.) Life-span
      Developmental Psychology: Non-Normative Events.
      New York: Academic Press, 1983, pp. 217-239.

      This paper describes the ways in which the stress-
      ful nature of marital separation manifests
      itself during the first eight months of separ-
      ation. Not only is there ample evidence of a
      generally high level of stress associated with
      marital disruption, but there is substantial
      reason to believe that this stress continues
      and in some ways increases during this period.

374. Bloom, B.L. and C. Clement. "Marital Sex Role
      Orientation and Adjustment to Separation and
      Divorce," J. of Divorce, 7 (Spring 1984), 87-
      98.

      In order to examine the relationship between
      sex role orientation and adjustment to marital
      disruption, a sample of 143 newly separated
      persons was interviewed two months after separa-
      tion, and then again 6, 18, and 30 months later.
      A measure of marital sex role orientation was
      administered at the time of the initial inter-
      view, and dependent measures of adjustment
      were obtained at each of the four interviews.

375. Callahan, B.N. Separation and Divorce. New York:
      Family Service Association of America, 1979.

      This is a manual for workshops for family life
      education on the topic of separation and
      divorce.

376. Camara, K.A., Baker, O., and C. Dayton. "Impact of
      Separation and Divorce on Youths and Families,"
      (in) P.M. Insel, ed. Environmental Variables
      and the Prevention of Mental Illness. Lexington,
      Mass.: Lexington Books, 1980, 69-136.

      The review contains three major sections: The
      Demography of Marital Dissolution; A Review of
      Research on the Effects of Family Change on
      Youths and Families, and Planning Services for
      Youths and Families. The major focus of the
      review is on (1) the incidence of and effects

of family change on the social and psychological development and behaviour of adults and
youths, and (3) strategies and program approaches
for working with youths and families.

377. Chiribogo, D.A. and M. Thurnher. "Marital Lifestyles
and Adjustment to Separation," J. of Divorce,
3 (Summer 1980), 379-390.

Two hundred and ninety-eight men and women in
the process of divorce were interviewed concerning their lifestyle prior to marital separation and their current state of happiness.
Sex differences in social independence, division of household chores, and reliance on
spouse were congruent with traditional sex
role norms.

378. Desimone-Luis, J., O'Mahoney, K. and D. Hunt.
"Children of Separation and Divorce: Factors
Influencing Adjustment," J. of Divorce, 3
(Fall 1979), 37-42.

The adjustment of children of separation and
divorce is explored here in relation to demographic factors. The means employed to
measure adjustment was a behaviour checklist
that was completed by the parents of the
twenty-five children in the study. All of
these parents were members of Parents Without
Partners, and their children ranged in age
from six to twelve years at the time of separation. The incidence of multiple maladjusted
behaviours, as reported by the parents, was
uased to define child deviancy. The profiles of
these deviant or maladjusted children were then
examined in relation to the demographic data
obtained.

379. Granvold, D.K. "Structured Separation for Marital
Treatment and Decision-Making," J. of Marital
and Family Therapy, 9 (October 1983), 403-412.

Structured marital separation is an intervention method designed to assist distressed
marital couples during their critical period
of decision-making either to divorce or maintain the marriage. This paper presents a
brief review of separation models and addresses
separation counseling including: assessment,

contracting, initial adjustment to separation, relationship enhancement and individual change. Particular attention is given to the terms of marital separation contracting and a complete sample contract is provided.

380. Granvold, D.K, and R. Tarrant. "Structured Marital Separation as a Marital Treatment Method," J. of Marital and Family Therapy, 9 (April 1983), 189-198.

This article describes therapist-structured marital separation for distressed couples during their critical period of deciding whether to divorce or remain married. Characteristics of marital distress appropriate for structured marital separation are identified and discussed; potential benefits are explicated; and the design of the separation contract is specified. Issues addressed in the structure of the separation include the duration of the separation; the frequency of contact between partners; sexual contact between partners; dating; sexual contact with others; privacy; and contact with children.

381. Halem, L.C. Separated and Divorced Women. Westport, Connecticut: Greenwood Press, 1982.

The author describes the economic and psychological vulnerability of the population of separated and divorced women. The author looks at their community to see if the needed resources are there and finds large gaps. She concludes that middle-class women who are separated or divorced may be the real victims of the social service system, falling between the cracks because they are unable to afford private services and yet are ineligible for public ones.

382. Ishwaran, K. (ed.) Marriage and Divorce in Canada. Toronto: Methuen, 1983.

Four selections deal with separation and divorce in Canada.

383. Levinger, G. and O.C. Moles (eds.) Divorce and Separation: Context, Causes and Consequences. New York: Basic Books, 1979.

Nineteen selections examine marital dissolution,
Consequences for the ex-spouse, families, and
children of divorce and separation.

384. McRae, B.C. and L.R. Fish. "Separation and Divorce:
Counselling Services in Canada. The Social
Worker, 47 (Spring 1979), 99-101.

The major questions to which this study
addresses itself are: What services and programs exist to meet the needs of the divorcing
population in Canada; and to what extent has
the effectiveness of these services been
assessed?

385. McVey, W. and B. Robinson. "Separation in Canada:
New Insights Concerning Marital Dissolution,"
Canadian J. of Sociology, 6 (Summer 1981),
353-366.

The authors of this paper question the validity
of divorce statistics as an adequate indicator
of marital disruption in Canada. To give a
more accurate analysis of the state of marital
disruption in Canada, the study utilizes Census
statistics with cross-tabulations from 1976
(which include separation status) using age
cohorts and gender differentials to illustrate
regional differences and to indicate recent
trends. The authors attempt to show that the
incidence of marital dissolution is grossly
underestimated using divorce statistics alone.
In addition, causal factors associated with
increased divorce rates are examined.

386. Rowlands, P. Saturday Parent: A Book for Separated
Families. New York: Crossroad Continuum, 1982.

A psychologist gives advice to separated
parents. The book is illustrated with
personal anecdotes.

387. Spanier, G.B. and E.A. Anderson. "The Impact of the
Legal System on Adjustment to Marital
Separation," J. of Marriage and the Family, 41
(August 1979), 605-625.

There has been a dramatic increase in the
number of divorced persons in the United
States during the last decade, resulting in a

need for close examination of the factors
associated with the adjustment to marital separation. This paper reports the effect of the
legal process in one state--Pennsylvania--on
adjustment to marital separation. Two hundred
and five individuals separated no longer than
26 months completed in-depth, face-to-face
interviews about their marriages, the failure
of their marriages, and the aftermath of
marital separation.

388. Spanier, G.H. and R.F. Castro. "Adjustment to
      Separation and Divorce: An Analysis of 50 Case
      Studies," J. of Divorce, 2 (Spring 1979), 241-
      253.

      This paper reports the findings of a study
      designed to provide an in-depth analysis of
      the postseparation period. Data from 50 open-
      ended, unstructured case study interviews were
      used to identify the critical areas of post-
      separation and postdivorce adjustment. Approx-
      imately 1,000 pages of verbatim field notes
      were collected.

389. Spanier, G.B. and P.C. Glick. "Marital Instability
      in the United States: Some Correlates and
      Recent Changes," Family Relations, 31 (July
      1981), 329-338.

      The doubling of the divorce rate between the
      mid-1960's and the mid-1970's was followed by
      a period of stability and a current slight
      rise. Despite the declining birth rate, the
      number of children involved in divorce is at an
      all-time high. Increases since 1970 in
      separation, divorce, and the postponement of
      marriage have resulted in nearly a doubling of
      the number of adults who keep up a home with-
      out a spouse. Teenage marriages are shown to
      be particularly unstable.

390. Spanier, G.B. and S. Hanson. "The Role of Extended
      Kin in the Adjustment to Marital Separation,"
      J. of Divorce, 5 (Fall/Winter 1981), 33-48.

      A nonprobability purposive sample of 205
      individuals separated 26 months or less was
      interviewed about their marital separation and
      its aftermath. Contrary to expectations based

on earlier research and current theorizing,
the findings indicate that support from and
interaction with extended kin either are unrelated or negatively related to the adjustment
to marital separation.

391. Spanier, G.B. and L. Thompson. "Relief and Distress
      After Marital Separation," J. of Divorce, 7
      (Fall 1983), 31-50.

      Relief and distress as responses to the term-
      ination of marriage are examined in a study of
      a nonprobability sample of 205 individuals in
      central Pennsylvania. Respondents were inter-
      viewed in depth soon after their final separ-
      ation. Retrospective measures were used to
      assess the rewards and costs of ending marriage
      from three sources--attractions in marriage,
      external pressures to remain married, and
      alternative attractions.

392. Storm, C.L., Sheehan, R. and D.H. Sprenkle. "The
      Structure of Separated Women's Communication
      with Their Nonprofessional and Professional
      Social Networks," J. of Marital and Family
      Therapy, 9 (October 1983), 423-429.

      This study assessed separated women's
      communication with their social network
      members--family, friends, clergy, attorneys
      and therapists. Women and their social net-
      work members were asked about the frequency and
      timing of their communication pre- and post-
      separation. Of particular interest to
      therapists is the finding that women seem to
      communicate with therapists before they begin
      to seriously think about separating and after
      they have made the decision, but not during
      the decision-making process. Implications of
      this finding are discussed.

393. Stuart, I.R. and L.E. Abt (eds.) Children of
      Separation and Divorce: Management and Treat-
      ment. New York: Van Nostrand Reinhold, 1981.

      Fifteen papers examine the legal, social and
      emotional consequences of marital breakdown.
      Many of the contributions focus on the effects
      on children of separation and divorce. The
      authors come from a multi-disciplinary back-
      ground.

394. Thompson, L. and G.B. Spanier. "The End of Marriage and Acceptance of Marital Termination," J. of Marriage and the Family, 45 (February 1983), 103-114.

The circumstances surrounding the termination of marriage are examined in relation to the aftermath of marital separation. Social exchange theory provides a framework for representing the end of marriage. Data were collected from a nonprobability sample of 205 individuals in central Pennsylvania, who were first interviewed in depth soon after their final separation.

395. Waite, M.E. "Supporting Families During the Separation Process: A Crucial Role for the Rural Helping Professional" (in) Changing Structures of Families: Adaptation and Fragmentation. Ottawa: Family Service Canada, 1983, 151-170.

The focus of this paper is on the needs of separating families and their implications for the helping professional in rural areas. Specifically, three phases of the separation process are discussed in relation to the needs of both adults and children within each phase. The role of the helping professional is developed to reflect a generalist orientation to service delivery from a person-environmental perspective.

396. Weiss, R.S. "The Impact of Marital Dissolution on Income and Consumption in Single-parent Households," J. of Marriage and the Family, 46 (February 1984), 115-128.

A synthetic cohort of separating and divorcing mothers was constructed from respondents in the University of Michigan Panel Study of Income Dynamics. Household income, income sources, and food and housing expenditures were examined for the last married year and for five years after marital dissolution. In general, it is shown that income drops precipitously after marital dissolution and remains nearly at its new low level during the period of observation.

249

G. WIDOWS AND WIDOWERS AS ONE-PARENT FAMILIES

397. Anderson, T.B. "Widowhood as a Life Transition: Its
     Impact on Kinship Ties," J. of Marriage and the
     Family, 46 (February 1984), 105-114.

     This paper explores the impact that marital status
     has upon the primary kinship ties of older women.
     Interview data obtained from 132 older women re-
     veal that there is some continuity in family life
     for women in the later stages of the life cycle
     inasumch as ties with children, which are based
     largely on obligation, are not much affected by
     widowhood. However, relationships that are based
     more on mutual interest in the other's well-being,
     such as those with siblings and extended kin, are
     affected by the death of one's spouse.

398. Balkwell, C. "Transition to Widowhood: A Review of
     the Literature," Family Relations, 30 (January
     1981), 117-127.

     Widowhood is experienced by approximately 12
     million people in the United States today. This
     paper treats the death of a spouse as an event
     which leads the individual through the transition
     from married person to widowed person--including
     the formation of a new self-identify and the
     taking-on of new social roles. Factors which
     predict greater or lesser success in accomplishing
     this task are discussed as are problems associated
     with widowhood and various intervention strategies
     which may be used in helping individuals through
     this process.

399. Bankoff, E.A. "Social Support and Adaptation to Widow-
     hood," J. of Marriage and the Family, 45 (November
     1983), 827-840.

     This study examined the effects of social support
     on the psychological well-being of 245 women who
     had been widowed for less than three years. The
     survey results indicate that the role of such
     support is important but complex. Whether social
     support is helpful, harmful, or inconsequential
     to widows' psychological well-being seems to depend
     on such factors as where the widows are in the ad-
     justment process, the type of support given, and
     its source.

400.   Camper, F.A. "Children's Reactions to the Death of A
          Parent: Maintaining the Inner World," Smith College
          Studies in Social Work, 53 (June 1983), 188-202.

       Children's reactions to the death of a parent have
       consistently been examined in the psychoanalytic
       literature within a framework derived from the
       adult model of mourning. This framework has led
       to a controversial literature on whether children
       have the capacity to mourn and whether or not
       particular reactions are indicative of mourning.
       The conceptual and clinical problems posed by this
       framework are reviewed here as a basis for ad-
       vancing a different theoretical perspective from
       which to assess children's reactions to parental
       loss.

401.   Kitson, G.C., Lopata, H.Z., Holmes, W.M. and S.M.
          Meyering. "Divorcees and Widows: Similarities and
          Differences," American J. of Orthopsychiatry, 50
          (April 1980), 291-301.

       Based on findings from age-standardized survey
       data, divorced women feel more restricted in their
       relationships with others and have less favourable
       attitudes towards their ex-spouses than do widows.
       The greater clarify of the widowed role may provide
       more social support and ease adjustment to the
       end of a marraige for the widow in ways unavail-
       able to the still somewhat stigmatized status
       of the divorcee.

402.   Lucks, H.C. "Widow/Widower Outreach Program (WWOP):
          The Social Work Role with Members of a Mutual-
          Help Program and their Families," Social Work
          Papers, 16 (Spring 1981), 82-89.

       The Widow-Widower Outreach Program, a mutual-help
       program within the San Francisco Jewish Family and
       Children's Service, functions under the supervision
       of a social worker to bring a variety of supportive
       services to the newly widowed elderly in the
       Jewish community. The program uses widowed
       volunteers who reach out to the newly widowed,
       offering them emotional support and connecting
       them to the program of discussion meetings and
       social networking through which they many expand
       their friendships while confronting the variety
       of adjustments of widowhood.

403. Schlesinger, B. "Widows and Widowers as Single Parents."
     In One in Ten: The Single Parent in Canada.
     B. Schlesinger, Ed. Toronto: Guidance Centre,
     Faculty of Education, University of Toronto, 1979,
     37-45.

     There are 213,657 widowed families in Canada.
     Forty-seven percent of these families are headed
     by a person under 55 years; 247,000 children are
     affected, 50% of them under 14 years. Past dis-
     cussion of single-parent families has often
     neglected the widowed family. Their situation is
     discussed in this article.

404. Shimazu, I. "Some Characteristics of Divorce in Japan,"
     Conciliation Courts Review, 18 (December 1980),
     31-38.

     A Japanese law professor discusses selected
     characteristics of divorce in Japan.

405. Small, R. and P. Goldhamer. "The Professional Role
     Within a Self-Help Model: A "Widow to Widow"
     Project," J. of Jewish Communal Service, 56
     (Winter 1979-1980), 176-180.

     A description of a self-help program of a widow-
     to-widow project in Montreal, Canada.

H. OTHER COUNTRIES: ONE-PARENT FAMILIES

406. Allen, P. Single Parents: Work or Welfare: Report of a
     National Workshop. Melbourne: Institute of Family
     Studies, 1983.

     A report dealing with Australia's single parent
     families and work and welfare.

407. Andrup, H.H.H. and B. Buchhofer. "The Social Functions
     of Divorce Procedures: The Danish Administrative
     and the West German Family Court Solution,"
     Conciliation Courts Review, 19 (December 1981),
     7-22.

     The authors discuss some aspects of family law in
     Denmark and the Federal Republic of Germany.

408. Bytheway, W. "Divorce, the Family Life Cycle, and its
     Empirical Deficiencies," J. of Divorce, 5 (Fall/
     Winter 1981), 19-32.

This paper presents some descriptive data which
places divorce in the general context of family
histories. It examines the occurrence of divorce:
(1) within complete marital careers; (2) with a
section of the extended family, including siblings
and cousins, as well as parents, uncles and aunts; and
(3) within the children of older persons. The data
is drawn from a unique source that records complete
family histories within the British peerage.

409. Clason, C. "The One-Parent Family: The Dutch Situation," J. of
Comparative Family Studies, 9 (Winter 1980), 3-16.

A family with only one parent is considered incomplete,
which one has to be restored to the normal stage.
Through ideological, demographic, economic and tech-
nological changes the number of one-parent families
is increasing. It has become apparent that the one-
parent family is no longer exceptional and can no
longer be only considered as a temporary or marginal
phenomenon.

The one-parent family is gaining status, and is no
longer obscure and only subject to charity.

410. Clay, M.M. and V.M.J. Robinson. Children of Parents Who
Separate. Wellington, New Zealand: New Zealand Council
for Educational Research, 1978.

A study of children whose parents had separated or
divorced. Some parents were interviewed to obtain
their reaction to their children's adjustment to
divorce and separation.

411. Coleman, M. (Chairman) Families and Social Services in
Australia (Vol. 1). Canberra: Australian Government
Publishing Service, 1978.

One-parent families in Australia are discussed in
this comprehensive report.

412. Edgar, D. and M·R. Harrison. Children's Participation in Divorce.
Melbourne: Institute of Family Studies, 1984
(Discussion Paper #10).

In Australia since 1976 a total of nearly 380,000
children have been involved in their parents' divorce.
That figure includes only children under the age of 18,
so it is an underestimate of the real total. Although
an increasing number of divorcing couples are childless
(38.4 percent childless in 1982 compared with 31.7 percent
in 1974), there is an average of two children affected in
couples with dependent children. Those with three or
more children have dropped from 19.7 percent of divorces
in 1974 to 14 percent in 1982, but that still means there
were over five thousand large families whose parents
divorced in 1980 alone. The authors make a plea to marriage
counselors to consider the children of divorce in their
work.

413. Edgar, D. and F. Headlam. <u>One-Parent Families and Educational Disadvantage</u>. Melbourne: Institute of Family Studies, 1982 (Working Paper No. 4).

This paper is based on findings of a pilot study of the possible educational problems suffered by children from Victoria's one-parent families.

414. Handelman, L.S. "Administering to War Widows in Israel: The Birth of a Social Category," <u>Social Analysis</u>, No. 9, (December 1981), 24-46.

This detailed article discusses young war widows and the services offered to them by the Israeli government.

415. Horwill, F.M. "The Outcome of Custody Cases in the Family Court of Australia," <u>Conciliation Courts Review</u>, 17 (September 1979), 31-40.

A comprehensive analysis of 430 custody cases and their outcomes.

416. Kaffman, M. and E. Elizur. "Children's Bereavement Reactions Following Death of the Father," <u>International J. of Family Therapy</u>, 1 (Fall 1979), 203-299.

The war situation compelled a reinvestigation into the characteristics, course, the outcome, and the variety of bereavement reactions in early childhood. In this study, the behaviours and changes reported by the mothers and teachers of 24 normal kibbutz children over a period of 1 to 16 months after bereavement are presented. The findings lead to one clear and central conclusion: The death of a father in war brings about a severe stress situation for the child at both the pre-school and the middle-childhood age.

417. Kaffman, M. and M. Talmon. "The Crisis of Divorce: An Opportunity for Constructive Change," <u>Int. J. of Family Therapy</u>, 4 (Winter 1982), 220-233.

In this article the authors seek a partial answer to the intriguing question of the nature of the factors which help some persons achieve healthy resolution of the divorce crisis with personal gains and successful post-divorce adjustment. A

group of 24 divorced people (all members of different Israeli kibbutzim) who fulfilled the criteria
used by the authors to identify good adjustment to
crisis and personal growth after divorce reported
on the beneficial influences which, in their
opinion, contributed to the gainful outcome.

418. Kamerman, S.B. and A.J. Kahn. "Income Transfers and
Mother-only Families in Eight Countries," Social
Science Review, 57 (September 1983), 448-464.

An eight-country study of governmental income
transfers affecting incomes of families with young
children yields systematic data on the income
levels of mother-only families and the policies
and programs through which they are attained.
Countries are ranked by their relative "generosity"
to these families and the importance of family
allowance and advance maintenance payments underscored.

419. Koch-Nielson,I."One Parent Families in Denmark," J. of
Comparative Family Studies, 9 (Winter 1980), 17-30.

In spite of a sharp increase in the number and proportion of births outside marriage as well as
divorces the number and proportion of genuine one-
parent families in Denmark does seem rather
stable. This fact is explained by the large
number of couples cohabiting without a marriage
certificate.

As expected, the social conditions of the genuine
single-parent families are not as good as those of
the two-parent families although family allowances,
rent subsidy, etc. to some extent will substitute
the lack of income.

420. Le Faucheur, N. "Single Parenthood and Illegitimacy in
France," J. of Comparative Family Studies, 9
(Winter 1980), 31-48.

The ratio of one-parent families is stable in France
(9.3%), as is the sex-ration (20/80), but the
average age of single parents is falling and widowhood and separation are declining in favour of
illegitimacy and divorce as causes of single-parent-
hood. The illegitimate birth rate is now around
8.5%.

255

421. Lloyd, J. "Marital Breakdown," (in) P.G. Koopman-Boyd,
      ed. Families in New Zealand Society. Wellington:
      Methuen, 1978, 138-158.

      This chapter attempts to describe the broad
      patterns of marital breakdown in New Zealand.

422. Lobodzinska, B. "Divorce in Poland: Its Legislation,
      Distribution and Social Context," J. of Marriage
      and the Family, 45 (November 1983), 927-942.

      Legal divorce is a relatively new phenomenon in
      Poland, having been introduced in 1946. Since
      then, divorce rates have almost tripled, especially
      in urban areas, where industrialization and urban-
      ization may contribute to the high incidence.
      However, the most frequent causes of divorce pre-
      sented in court were alcoholism and adultery.
      Several changes in family law have been introduced
      in an attempt to protect the welfare of children
      in cases of family disintegration.

423. Moskoff, W. "Divorce in the USSR," J. of Marriage and
      the Family, 45 (May 1983), 419-426.

      This study examines the major causes for the
      extraordinary increase in the Soviet divorce rate,
      which has become the second highest in the world.
      In addition, it examines the impact of Soviet law
      on the level of divorce and looks at some under-
      lying reasons for recent trends. While alcoholism,
      adultery and incompatability are the ostensible
      major causes of divorce, Soviet housing problems
      and the changed role of women also have contributed
      to the rising divorce rates. Finally, the study
      suggests some of the psychological and socio-
      economic consequences of divorce in the Soviet
      Union: the impact on children, the financial status
      of women, the remarriage rate, and the impact on
      the labour force.

424. O'Brien, M. "Lone Fathers: Transition from Married to
      Separated State," J. of Comparative Family Studies,
      9 (Winter 1980), 115-128.

      In Britain the number of male-headed single-parent
      families has increased from 70,000 in 1971 to
      90,000 in 1976. Fifty-one lone fathers, who had
      full-time care of their five to eleven year-old
      children after marital separation, were interviewed
      using a structured schedule.

425. Pierce, S. "Single Mothers and the Concept of Female Dependency in the Development of the Welfare State in Britain," J. of Comparative Family Studies, 9 (Winter 1980), 57-86.

This article argues that the economic and social deprivation experienced by single mothers can only be understood by an examination of the legal and social assumption that women are, and should be, dependent on men. That is women with children are assumed to live in a relationship of dependency and subordination to a man. This assumption of dependency can be seen in the legal provisions of the welfare state.

426. Schlesinger, B. "Widows and Widowers in New Zealand: General Information," J. of Comparative Family Studies, 9 (Winter 1980), 49-56.

There are 146,000 persons over the age of 16 years classified as widowed in New Zealand. They constitute 10.7 percent of all females, and 2.6 percent of all males in the population. The paper summarizes the available social security benefits to the widowed population, and examines the work of the New Zealand widows and widowers Association a self-help group formed in 1978.

427. Schlesinger, B. "One Parent Families in Australia," Conciliation Courts Review, 18 (December 1980), 27-29.

An overview of existing knowledge related to one-parent families in Australia.

428. Schlesinger, B. "One Parent Families in Britain: A Review," Conciliation Courts Review, 20 (December 1982), 71-80.

A review of existing British studies related to one-parent families.

429. Thornes, B. and J. Collard. Who Divorces? London: Routledge and Kegan Paul, 1979.

Two British social scientists present a study of divorce petitioners in the West Midlands area of Britain.

430.   Trost, J. "Children and Divorce in Sweden," J. of
       Comparative Family Studies, 12 (Winter 1981), 129-
       138.

       A discussion of different types of divorce and the
       factors leading to different types of custody
       decisions is presented, based on Swedish data.
       The effects of custody decisions on the child are
       briefly discussed. A classification of different
       custodial decisions and family situations follows.

431.   Trost, J. (ed.) One Parent Family. Journal of Compar-
       ative Family Studies, 11 (Winter 1980), Special
       Issue.

       Eight papers discuss one parent families on a
       cross-cultural basis.

I.   REMARRIAGE

432.   Anderson, J., Larson, J., and A. Morgan. "PPSF/Parent-
       ing Program for Stepparent Families: A New Approach
       for Strengthening Families," (in) N. Stinnett et
       al., eds. Family Strengths 3: Roots of Well Being.

       It is the purpose of this paper to outline a pro-
       gram that has been designed to aid parents and
       children in stepfamilies in adjusting to their
       new family situation. The program is based upon
       the identified needs and problems of stepparents
       and children. It includes: (1) educational group
       discussions on problems and issues faced by step-
       parents and their children, and (2) communication
       and problem-solving skills training for both
       stepparents and natural parents in stepfamilies.

433.   Cherlin, A. "Remarriage as an Incomplete Institution,"
       ＇American J. of Sociology, 84 (November 1978), 634-
       650.

       This article primarily examines the higher rate of
       divorce in remarried families. The author develops
       the hypothesis that the higher rate of divorce is
       due to the remarried families being less 'habit-
       ualized' and 'institutionalized' therefore having
       to face a greater number of choices and having a
       greater degree of role confusion and ambiguity.

258

434. Day, R.D., and W.C. Mackey. "Redivorce Following Re-Marriage: A Re-evaluation," J. of Divorce, 4 (Spring 1981), 39-47.

It is suggested in the paper that researchers, educators, and counsellors need an accurate view of the risk of remarriage following divorce, since most of those who divorce do remarry. Also, the suggestion was made that the traditional family form may not be in as much of a decline as some report. Most people stay married; of those who divorce, most (68%) have either one child or none, and most remarry.

435. Duffin, S.R. Yours, Mine and Ours. Washington, D.C.: National Institute of Mental Health, 1978.

The steps to be taken prior to entering a R.F. are discussed. Stepparents discuss their own experiences in this booklet.

436. Espinoza, R. and Y. Newman. Stepparenting. Rockville, Maryland: U.S. Department of Health, Education and Welfare, 1979.

This booklet examines primarily the nature of the roles related to stepparenting, and the demands made on these roles.

437. Felker, E. Raising Other People's Kids. Grand Rapids, Michigan: William B. Eerdman, 1981.

A frank and positive perspective on raising step-children. Growing up in an R.F. can be just as rewarding as growing up in a biological family, says the author.

438. Furstenburg, R.F. "Recycling the Family," Marriage and Family Review, 2 (Fall 1979), 12-22.

Couples remarrying in child-bearing years and remarriage in U.S.A. takes place within 3-5 years after divorce. There are more reconstituted families with young children.

This article points out the gaps in research related to remarriage.

439. Garfield, R. "The Decision to Remarry," J. of Divorce,
4 (Fall 1980), 1-10.

Remarriage is an increasingly common phenomenon
that affects millions of men, women and children.
In this paper, the author presents a general profile of remarriage and the process by which divorced
people decide to remarry. A format is described
through which clinicians can evaluate critical
issues that determine the readiness of divorced
people to remarry. These issues are presented
along with case illustrations that demonstrate
various problems that can arise and their solutions
in therapy for the divorced.

440. Goetting, A. "Former Spouse-Current Spouse Relationships," J. of Family Issues, 1 (March 1980),
58-80.

Data from a sample of 180 divorced and remarried
men and women suggest a lack of normative integration of two relationships established by
remarriage after divorce. The relationships are
the former spouse-current spouse relationships,
and constitute the following: (1) the former
wife-current wife relationships, which consists
of the two women who at different points in time
have been married to the same man; and (2) the
former husband-current husband relationship,
which consists of the two men who at different
points in time have been married to the same
woman.

441. Goetting, A. "The Six Stations of Remarriage Develop-
Mental Tasks of Remarriage After Divorce,"
Family Relations, 31 (April 1982), 213-222.

As the incidence of divorce and subsequent remarriage in the United States continues to increase, the problems associated with the developmental tasks of such remarriage become more
relevant. An analysis of causal explanations
for the increasingly common nature of remarriage
after divorce is followed by a description of six
developmental tasks which are faced by persons
approaching the status passage from divorced to
remarried.

260

442. Goldmeier, J. "Intervention in the Continuum from
      Divorce to Family Reconstitution," Social
      Casework, 61 (January 1980), 39-45.

      Theoretical perspective for practice with fam-
      ilies where divorce, single parenthood and family
      reconstitution figure in treatment planning.

443. Greif, J.B. and S.K. Simring. "Remarriage and Joint
      Custody," Conciliation Courts Review, 20 (June
      1982), 15-23.

444. Gurak, D.T. and D. Gillian. "The Remarriage Market:
      Factors Influencing the Selection of Second
      Husbands," J. of Divorce, 3 (Winter 1979), 161-
      173.

      The data included 429 white women who ended first
      marriages in divorce and remarried and 176 white
      women who ended first marriages in divorce and
      did not remarry.

      Women who end their first marriage in divorce and
      do not remarry differ systematically from those
      who do remarry with respect to children, age and
      education.

      There is a positive association between male and
      female status in remarriage. Women with higher
      education do not lower their standards in order
      to remarry.

445. Hunter, J.E. and N. Schuman. "Chronic Reconstitution
      as a Family Style," Social Work, 25 (November
      1980), 446-451.

      The processes designated as characteristic of the
      'chronically reconstituting family' entail signi-
      ficant psychological and social consequences. The
      authors suggest there is a need for a commitment
      to a particular family group as an ongoing unit
      through time in order to ensure successful outcome
      on the psychological and social levels.

446. Hutchinson, I.W. and K.R. Hutchison. "Issues and
      Conflicts in Stepfamilies," Family Perspective,
      13 (Summer 1979), 111-121.

      This paper describes some of the presently identi-
      fied areas of conflict and other issues in
      reconstituted families.

447. Jacobson, D.S. "Stepfamilies: Myths & Realities," Social Work, 24 (May 1979), 202-207.

The emotional issues are presented, as well as suggestions of enhancing the adaptation of step-family members are made.

Despite the increasing number of remarriages, little attention has been directed to the needs and problems of stepfamilies.

448. Jacobson, D.S. "Stepfamilies," Children Today, 9 (January-February 1980), 2-6.

A discussion related to the anticipation and identification of possible difficulties in step-family life. The stresses and strains in R.F. among its members are reviewed.

449. Johnson, H.C. "Working with Stepfamilies. Principles of Practice," Social Work, 25 (July 1980), 304-308.

Too little attention has been directed to socio-logical and economic origins of stepfamilies. Tendency to see family as pathological, i.e., personal inadequacies.

450. Kent, M.O. "Remarriage: A Family System Perspective," Social Casework, 61 (March 1980), 146-153.

The behaviour of reconstituted families can be understood from a systems perspective as defining and maintaining boundaries, exchanging affective energy and negotiating shared purpose.

The article says more about system concepts in general than about reconstituted families.

451. Keshet, J.K. "From Separation to Step Family. A Subsystem Analysis," J. of Family Issues, 1 (December 1980), 517-532.

The focus on this paper is on stepfamilies which have resulted from remarriage following divorce. A structural family systems approach is used. Subsystems are seen as extremely important in stepfamilies as the history of bonds of the sub-systems are in place long before the stepfamily becomes a unit. Contrast between a step and nuclear family is used.

452. Kleinman J., Rosenberg, E. and M. Whiteside. "Common
      Developmental Tasks in Forming Reconstituted
      Families," J. of Marital and Family Therapy, 5
      (April 1979), 79-85.

      There is a strong tendency for R.F. to deny and
      cover-up tasks and problems, but there is also a
      strong desire to create a new happy family. If
      one can break through the resistance, the motiv-
      ation can be strong and can provide an excellent
      basis for family therapy.

453. Knaub, R.K., Hanna, S.L. and N. Stinnett. "Strengths
      of Remarried Families," J. of Divorce, 7 (Spring
      1984), 41-56.

      This paper focuses on remarried families' per-
      ceptions of their family strengths, marital sat-
      isfaction and their adjustment to the remarried
      situation. The sample was composed of both hus-
      bands and wives in 80 remarried families where at
      least one of the marital partners had been pre-
      viously married.

454. Koo, H. and C.M. Suchindran. "Effects of Children on
      Women's Remarriage Prospects," J. of Family
      Issues, 1 (December 1980), 497-515.

      This article reports on a study done by the
      authors. They examined the effects of the number
      of children and the age of children at the time
      of divorce on the mother's remarriage probabili-
      ties and on the length of time they remain div-
      orced before remarrying.

455. Kompara, D.R. "Difficulties in the Socialization
      Process of Stepparenting," Family Relations, 29
      (January 1980), 69-73.

      This paper examines the literature on step-
      families and highlights the socialization diffi-
      culties present in the adjustment process.

      Reconstituted families need programs to help them
      in the adjustment process and social policy needs
      to be changed to make the R.F. a legitimate family
      form with a different legal definition than
      presently exists.

456.   Lewis, H.C. All About Families the Second Time Around.
       Atlanta: Peachtree, 1980.

       The "Second Time Around Family" is different from
       the first and is full of challenges. This book
       is intended for use by the while family as a
       "workbook". It discusses the feelings and expec-
       tations of people living in step-families. It is
       written in a simple manner for children. The
       author is a social worker and a step-parent.

457.   McGoldrick, M. and E.A. Carter. "Forming a Remarried
       Family," (in) The Family Life Cycle: A Framework
       for Family Therapy, edited by E.A. Carter and
       M. McGoldrick, New York: Gardner Press, 1980, 265-
       294.

       The authors develop a table for remarried family
       formation (p. 272). In their chapter they cover
       the emotional issues in remarriage, the process of
       remarriage, and the impact of remarriage at various
       phases of the family life cycle.

       Case examples are included to illustrate key
       presenting triangles in remarried families.

458.   Messinger, K. (ed.) Therapy With Remarriage Families.
       Rockville, Maryland: Aspen Publications, 1982.

       Twelve papers discuss therapy with remarried
       families.

459.   Messinger, L., Walker, K. and S. Freeman. "Preparation
       for Remarriage Following Divorce," American J. of
       Orthopsychiatry, 48 (April 1978), 263-272.

       This article is a summary of the experience of the
       authors who ran 4 weekly group meetings of a four-
       week period with 22 couples, in which at least one
       partner had children from a previous marriage. The
       experience offered (1) societal support, (2) factual
       information and (3) opportunity for emotional
       interaction.

460.   Mitchell, K. "The Price Tag of Responsibility: A
       Comparison of Divorced and Remarried Mothers,"
       J. of Divorce, 6 (Spring 1983), 33-42.

       This study compared two matched samples of divorced
       and remarried mothers. Contrary to the research
       hypothesis, remarried mothers had both a bigher
       sense of competence and well-being than divorced
       mothers, which was signficantly related to feelings

of competence and satisfaction in the areas of
love, community, and homemaking. There were no
differences in other areas, such as work or parenting.

461. Moss, S.Z. and M.S. Moss. "Remarriage: A Triadic
      Relationship," Conciliation Courts Review, 18
      (December 1980), 15-20.

      This paper examines the bonds of the first
      marriage as they persist after divorce. There is
      discussion of the way in which attachments to the
      previous spouse affect the new marital bond.

      The presence of the ex-spouse may be felt while
      the new marital pair are trying to create a solid
      lasting unity.

462. Nelson, M. and G.K. Nelson. "Problems of Equity in
      the Reconstituted Family: A Social Exchange
      Analysis," Family Relations, 31 (April 1982),
      223-231.

      Application of social exchange principles is made
      in addressing inherent difficulties of setting up
      a stepfamily. A host of factors poses obstacles
      to role adjustment and maintenance of equity among
      members. The disruption of prior interaction
      patterns, the complexity in the formation of new
      ones, and the lack of social supports place an
      additive burden on family problem solving. It is
      concluded that if the reconstituting family can
      establish a basis of trust whereby attractions are
      formed freely between persons both within and out-
      side of the immediate household, the stepfamily
      can merge as a developmental unit toward expansion
      and commitment.

463. Paris, E. Stepfamilies: Making Them Work. Toronto:
      Avon Books, 1984.

      An advice-giving book about stepfamilies.

464. Perkins, T.F. and J.P. Kahan. "An Empirical Comparison
      of Natural - Father and Stepfather Family," Family
      Process, 18 (June 1979), 175-183.

      Several dimensions in the way the two types of
      family systems differ are important for their
      implications for practice. Findings strengthen
      the need for a family therapy approach. It is

necessary to treat the sepparent family with an
awareness of the system's differences. Professionals should help the R.F. members open their
interpersonal subsystems. Their interpersonal
relationships and perceptions affect the stepparent
family system, and its ability to function adequately. The sample size was 40 volunteer natural
father and stepfather families.

465. Pill, C.J. "A Family Life Educational Group for Working
      with Stepparents," Social Casework, 62 (March
      1981), 154-166.

      Few services are available for persons who are
      struggling with the issues inherent in stepfamily
      situations. This article describes a family life
      educational approach to stepparents and describes
      the specific issues involved, outlines the goals
      for this kind of group, and provides a guide for
      group format.

466. Rosenberg, E.B. "Therapy with Siblings in Reorganizing
      Families," International Journal of Family Therapy,
      2 (Fall 1980), 139-150.

      The loss of parenting figures through death, divorce
      or others kinds of separation often leaves children
      without consistent parental support and with in-
      creased fears of abandonment. In the natural cycle,
      siblings can maintain almost lifelong relationships
      and therefore are in a position to offer each
      other a significant support system over an extended
      period of time. The author found that work with
      sibling subgroups can help children to resolve
      their individual and shared conflicts, as well as
      to remove interferences to mutually supportive
      relationships. Illustrative cases are presented
      and treatment guidelines offered.

467. Sager, C.J., Brown, H.S., Chrohn, H.M. and E. Rodstein.
      "Improving Functioning of the Remarried Family
      System," J. of Marital and Family Therapy, 7
      (January 1981), 3-13.

      This report presents salient issues for therapists
      in understanding and treating the remarried family.
      The structure of the remarried family is different
      from that of the intact family. Specific treat-
      ment goals for remarried families are elaborated
      and various treatment modalities advocated. The

need to include former spouses and to consider
the metafamily system are discussed. Common
reactions and difficulties engendered in therapists
when working with remarried systems are explicated.

468. Sager, C.J., Brown, H.S., Crohn, H., Engel, T., Rodstein,
E. and L. Walker. Treating the Remarried Family.
New York: Brunner-Mazel, 1983.

A presentation of the theory and clinical techniques
related to remarried families.

469. Sager, C.J. "Treatment of Remarried Families: Demo-
graphy and Outcome," J. of Jewish Communal Service,
60 (Spring 1984), 230-238.

This is a report on the demographic and outcome
findings of 100 remarried families treated at the
Jewish Board of Family and Children's Services of
New York City. The population was unselected,
except for their recognition that they needed
therapeutic help and that they accepted entering
a treatment program. Religion was self-designated.
No attempt was made to develop matching control
groups.

470. Schlesinger, B. Remarriage in Canada. Toronto:
University of Toronto, Faculty of Education,
Guidance Centre, 1978.

This booklet discusses remarriage in Canada and
reports on a study of 196 remarried families living
in Metropolitan Toronto.

471. Schlesinger, B. "Remarriage in America and Canada: An
Overview of the Literature, 1943-1980," Conciliation
Courts Review, 19 (June 1981), 21-32.

A review of the literature related to remarriage
during the 1943-1980 period. It covers published
Canadian and American studies.

472. Schlesinger, B. Remarriage: A Review and Annotated
Bibliography. Chicago: Council of Planning
Librarians, 1983.

A review essay and an 132-item annotated bibliography on remarriage up to July 1, 1982.

473. Visher, E. and J. Visher. Stepfamilies: A Guide to
Working with Stepparents and Stepchildren. New
York: Brunner-Mazel, 1979.

This book provides a detailed explanation of the stepfamily experience and develops a number of guidelines for the practitioner.

The authors state that the content of their book is primarily derived from the experiences of a middle-class population and clinical settings providing service to this same population. There is no mention of the exact number of persons consulted or interviewed.

474.   Visher, E. and J. Visher. How to Win As a Stepparent.
        New York: Dember, 1982.

The pioneers in the area of examining the R.F. in the 1980's, have written a comprehensive guide to living in a R.F. The authors are both mental health professionals, and living in a R.F.

475.   Wald, Esther. The Remarried Family: Challenge and
        Promise. New York: Family Service Association of
        America, 1981.

The intent of this book is to articulate a body of substantive knowledge about the remarried family system that narrows the existing information gap and provides the therapist with an objective under-standing of the factors that make it a special case of family. This knowledge base in grounded in the author's research and clinical experience with this family, and, in addition, derives from information gathered from participants in pro-fessional workshops and family life education courses on the remarried family. Although the focus is on remarried families who sought pro-fessional help, it is possible, and in fact very likely, that many of the issues and problems these families report exist in remarried families who have never sought such help.

476.   Walker, K.N. and L. Messinger. "Remarriage after
        Divorce: Dissolution and Reconstruction of Family
        Boundaries," Family Process, 18 (June 1979), 185-
        192.

The article presents a clear analysis of the tasks faced by family systems in adjusting to divorce and remarriage.

The lack of socially described parental roles in
remarried families necessitates a process of
achieving new roles and constructing more permeable
boundaries congruent with a remarried family.

477. Weingarten, H. "Remarriage and Well-Being--National
Survey Evidence of Social & Psychological Effects,"
J. of Family Issues, 1 (December 1980), 533-559.

This study explores by means of a cross-sectional
survey whether differences in family role orientation exist between first married and remarried
adults. It compares remarried and first married
adults on a wide variety of adjustment indicators.

Ninety minute structured interviews with 2,264
adults in 1976, sample contained first married and
second married adults. Data were analyzed in two
stages using "contingency table analysis."

J.   MISCELLANEOUS ITEMS (Found After Completion of Annotations)

478. Adams, J. Sex and the Single Parent. New York: Coward,
McCann and Geoghegan, 1978.

A journalist explores the little-talked-about area
of sexuality and the single parent. It gives the
reader a picture of the single parent as a sexual
person.

479. Charnas, J.F. "Joint Child Custody Counseling--Divorce
1980s Style," Social Casework, 64 (November 1983),
546-554.

Joint child custody is proposed as a viable and
constructive arrangement following divorce. Theoretical considerations and rationales supporting
this custody option are offered, and a treatment
model is presented that demonstrates its clinical
application. The goals of joint custody counseling
are to assist parents in (1) dealing with the
realitices of a unique type of parenting, (2) assessing their parenting desires, strengths, and lia-
bilities, (3) defining the demands and needs of
their new lifestyles and living arrangements as
well as those of their children, and (4) arriving
at a satisfactory and workable plan for parenting
that can optimally fulfill and reconcile their
severed roles as spouses with their continuing
roles as parents. Case examples illustrate various
patterns of joint custody.

269

480. Cutsinger, C.J. and A. Glick. "Structured Group Treatment Model for Latency-age Children of Divorce,"
School Social Work Journal, 8 (January 1983), 16-
27.

Nine elementary school students participated in a
study that evaluated an eight-week structured group
treatment model for late latency-age children whose
parents have divorced. The intervention focused
on raising the subjects' level of self-esteem,
mitigating their acting-out behaviour, and exploring the impact of divorce on the parent-child
relationship.

481. Dillard-Armstrong, P. "Developing Services for Single
Parents and Their Children in the School," Social
Work in Education, 3 (October 1980), 44-57.

The author discusses a program to aid parents and
pupils of single-parent families.

482. Dulude, L. Love, Marriage and Money: An Analysis of
Financial Relations Between the Spouses. Ottawa:
Canadian Advisory Council on the Status of Women,
1984.

An analysis of family law in Canada as it relates
to married and post-married women.

483. Family Relations. Single Parent Family. 35 (January
1986). Special Issue (In Press)

This special issue will have articles dealing
with the single-parent family.

484. Furstenberg, F.F. and G.B. Spanier. Recycling the
Family: Remarriage After Divorce. Beverly Hills,
California: Sage, 1984.

Synthesizing the results of an eight-year study,
Furstenberg and Spanier examine social, psychological, and economical aspects of adjustment
unique to the marriage-divorce-remarriage transition. Combining insightful commentary with
revealing data analysis, the researchers demonstrate how and why remarried is a fundamentally
different process from that of a first marriage.
Some key factors which redefine family life
include: difficulties in coparenting; keeping a
distance from one's former spouse; inheriting

270

stepchildren; convolution of traditional blood
and legal relationships; and built-in expectations
of marital instability.

485. Harper, P. Children in Step Families: Their Legal and
Family Status. Melbourne: Institute of Family
Studies, 1984 (Policy Background Paper #4).

With a divorce rate in Australia of around 40 percent for both first marriages and subsequent
marriages, the number of children in stepfamilies
has been rising. The rough estimate is that in
1982 alone over 30,000 children became step-
children. What this paper address is the way the
law responds to define the nature of family
relationships and the legal status of children
in stepfamilies.

486. Little, M. Family Breakup. San Francisco: Jossey-Bass,
1982.

This book studies the causes, patterns, and effects
of family breakup and analyzes how different types
of families make custody decisions.

487. Parsons, R.J.S. "Social Work with Single Parent
Families: Consumer Views," British J. of Social
Work, 13 (October 1983), 539-558.

This article describes a research project to
determine the satisfaction of single parents with
the service they were given.

488. Spanier, G.B. and L. Thompson. Parting: The Aftermath
of Separation and Divorce. Beverly Hills,
California: Sage, 1984.

For millions of Americans each year, divorce becomes
a fact of life. For some, it means liberation; for
others, depression--or frustration--or trauma.
There is no universal response to the end of a
marriage, but there are some common threads found
in the experiences of those involved. Spanier and
Thompson unravel the process of marital breakup,
presenting a vigorous and comprehensive longitudinal study of separation and divorce.

489. Yonas, S.P. "Teenage Pregnancy and Motherhood: A Review
of the Literature," American J. of Orthopsychiatry,
50 (July 1980), 403-431.

Medical and nonmedical studies are reviewed and
the state of our current knowledge is assessed.

490. Zitner, R. and S.H. Miller. Our Youngest Parents. New
      York: Child Welfare League of America, 1980.

      This countrywide study of mothers, practically
      all unmarried and aged 13 to 19 when their babies
      were born, centers on what help they used and
      what they needed. Perhaps most significant was
      the finding that the longer the mothers used
      agency help, the more likely they were to seek
      ongoing support services to stabilize their lives.

AUTHOR INDEX   ABSTRACT NUMBER

Abarbanel, A.   173
Abt, L.E.   393
Adams, J.   478
Adelberg, T.   20
Ahrons, C.   85, 145
Ahrons, C.R.   124, 143, 144, 146, 174, 175
Albrecht, S.S.   208
Alexander, S.J.   125
Allen, P.   406
Altis, R.   177
Ambert, A.M.   126, 209, 210, 367, 368
Anderson, E.A.   387
Anderson, J.   432
Anderson, T.B.   397
Andrup, H.H.H.   407
Anker, J.M.   118
Aries, N.   358
Armstrong-Dillard, P.   1
Arnn, S.   85
Arnold, R.   369
Asher, S.J.   371
Atlas, S.L.   2
Bader, L.   147
Bahr, S.J.   211
Baker, M.   370
Baker, O.   376
Bala, N.   189
Baldwin, W.   322
Balkwell, C.   398
Ballantine, C.   102
Balswick, J.O.   243
Bankoff, E.A.   399
Barrera, M.   304
Barret, R.L.   323, 324
Barsky, M.   167
Bartz, K.W.   127
Beal, E.W.   86, 212
Becerra, R.M.   361
Bedger, J.E.   359
Bell, C.A.   360
Bell, R.   281
Bell, S.   363
Benedek, E.P.   87
Benedek, R.S.   87
Bequette, S.Q.   247
Berman, W.H.   213
Berns, J.   331

Bienenfield, F.   88
Bilgé, B.   89
Billingsley, A.   12
Bishop, T.A.   252
Black, K.N.   90
Blechman, E.A.   56
Blisk, E.   162
Bloom, B.L.   238, 371, 372, 373, 374
Blythe, B.J.   319
Bolton, F.G.   305, 332
Bonkowski, S.W.   246
Boonhower, S.   247
Booth, A.   198, 214
Borowski, H.   333
Bowman, M.R.   146
Bradburg, K.   274
Branson, M.L.   128
Brendler, J.   60
Brinkerhoff, D.B.   198
Brown, B.F.   57
Brown, D.G.   168
Brown, E.M.   148
Brown, H.S.   457, 468
Brown, R.J.   296
Brown, S.V.   325
Brown-Wilson, K.   216
Buchofer, B.   407
Buchsbaum, H.K.   103
Buehler, C.   17
Buehler, C.A.   275
Bumpass, L.   91
Burden, D.S.   334
Bureau of the Census   3
Byrne, D.   306
Bytheway, W.   408
Cain, V.S.   322
Caldwell, R.A.   372, 373
Callahan, B.N.   375
Camara, K.A.   62, 63, 205, 376
Camiletti, Y.   248
Camper, R.A.   400
Cannon-Bonventre, K.   307
Cantor, D.W.   92, 93, 249
Carter, E.A.   457
Cartoff, V.G.   335
Cashiou, B.G.   276
Cassetty, J.   94
Casto, G.   360
Castro, R.F.   388
Chang, P.N.   286

AUTHOR INDEX ABSTRACT NUMBER

Charnas, J.F.	479
Chatelain, R.S.	81
Cherlin, A.	433
Cherlin, A.J.	239
Chilman, C.S.	308, 309, 310, 311
Chiriboga, D.A.	236, 377
Choldin, H.M.	281
Clarke, K.L.	189
Clason, C.	409
Clay, M.M.	410
Clement, C.	374
Clingempeell, W.G.	176
Cobb, C.	271
Coche, J.	250
Coleman, M.	411
Collard, J.	429
Colletta, N.D.	149, 199, 200
Cordier, D.C.	264
Cottle, T.J.	201
Cox, M.	101
Crandall, L.	61
Crawford, A.G.	337
Crohn, H.	468
Crohn, H.M.	467
Crosby, J.F.	202, 240
Cunningham, D.	4
Cupoli, N.	363
Cutsinger, C.J.	480
Daniels, D.S.	360
Danzinger, S.	274
Davids, L.	241
Day, R.D.	113, 434
Dayton, C.	376
De Anda, D.	361
De Frain, J.	147, 203
De Shane, M.R.	216
Deckert, P.	215, 261
Desimone-Luis, J.	378
Deutch, M.	171
Dienard, A.S.	286
Dietl, L.K.	5
Dillard-Armstrong, P.	481
Dixon, R.B.	190, 191
Dominic, K.T.	129
Drake, E.A.	93, 95
Drefus, E.A.	251
Duffin, S.R.	435

AUTHOR INDEX ABSTRACT NUMBER

Duffy, M.	150
Dulude, L.	482
Earl, L.	58
Earls, R.	326
Edgar, D.	412, 413
Edwards, D.W.	6
Effron, A.K.	96
Eirick, R.	203
Eisenstein, I.	192
Elizur, E.	416
Elkin, M.	193
Erf, L.A.	362
Ericcson, M.	130
Ernst, I.	177
Espinoza, R.	7, 436
Esses, L.	8
Everett, C.A.	131
Family Relations	483
Farber, S.S.	97, 252
Featherman, D.L.	62, 63
Felkner, E.	437
Felner, R.D.	252
Fenn, C.B.	236
Fischer, E.O.	151
Fischer, J.L.	9
Fischman, S.H.	336
Fish, L.R.	384
Fisher, T.	330
Fisher, W.A.	306
Folberg, H.J.	178
Foster, H.H.	194
Fowler, E.	10
Freed, D.J.	194
Freeman, J.	277
Freeman, R.	253
Freeman, S.	459
Fulmer, R.H.	11
Fulton, J.A.	98
Furstenburg, F.F.	312, 313, 337, 484
Furstenburg, R.F.	438
Gage, B.A.	202
Gallas, H.B.	314
Galper, M.	179
Gardner, R.A.	59
Garfield, R.	439
Gatley, R.H.	287
Gershenson, H.P.	338
Gilchrist, L.D.	315, 319, 320

AUTHOR INDEX	ABSTRACT NUMBER
Gillian, D.	444
Giovannoni, J.R.	12
Glick, A.	480
Glick, P.C.	99, 389
Glossop, B.	339
Goetting, A.	217, 440, 441
Goldhammer, P.	405
Goldman, J.	152, 250
Goldmeier, J.	254, 442
Goldsmith, J.	153
Goldstein, S.	204
Gonder, J.	13
Gongla, P.A.	278
Gonzola, P.A.	46
Gordon, S.	13
Gottlieb, S.J.	226
Graham, A.V.	257
Graham, M.	178
Graham-Cambrick, L.	60
Granvold, D.K.	379, 380
Green, D.	180
Green, R.G.	154
Grief, J.B.	181, 443
Grief, G.L.	132, 288
Grossberg, S.H.	61
Grow, L.J.	340, 341, 342
Gurak, D.T.	444
Gursky, L.	60
Gverney, L.	255
Haddad, W.	184
Hajal, F.	77
Hale, J.	365
Halem, L.C.	381
Hall, S.	218
Hancock, E.	219
Handelman, E.R.	78
Handelman, L.S.	414
Hanna, S.L.	453
Hanson, S.	133, 390
Hanson, S.M.H.	14
Harper, P.	485
Harrison, M.R.	412
Hassall, E.	256
Haynes, J.M.	169
Headlam, F.	413
Heath, J.	15
Henderson, G.H.	343
Hendricks, L.E.	327, 328
Hendrix, C.	18
Hess, R.D.	205

AUTHOR INDEX

Hetherington, E.M.	62, 63, 100, 101
Hodges, W.F.	102, 103
Hofstein, S.	16
Hogan, M.J.	17, 275
Holland, B.F.	165
Hollier, M.	365
Hollingsworth, D.R.	316
Holman, T.B.	64
Holmes, W.M.	401
Horner, C.T.	65
Horwill, F.M.	415
Houts, P.L.	66
Hunt, D.	378
Hunter, J.E.	445
Hutchinson, I.W.	446
Hutchinson, K.R.	446
Hyatt, R.	159
Ibrahim, A.I.	220
Irving, H.H.	170
Isaacs, M.B.	221
Ishwaran, K.	382
Jacobson, D.S.	67, 68, 447, 448
Jaffee, N.	171
Johnson, A.C.	222
Johnson, C.	347
Johnson, E.S.	155, 156
Johnson, H.C.	449
Jordon, E.	279
Jordon, L.	255
Jorgensen, S.R.	222
Kaffman, M.	416, 417
Kahan, J.P.	464
Kahn, A.J.	418
Kahn, J.	307
Kalish, R.A.	157
Kalter, N.	104
Kammerman, S.B.	418
Kane, S.P.	332
Kanoy, K.	105
Kaslow, R.W.	158, 159
Katz, A.	289
Kaufman, G.	89
Kelly, C.	134
Kelly, J.B.	122, 123, 237
Kent, M.O.	450
Keshet, H.F.	290, 291, 298, 299
Keshet, J.K.	451
Khleif-Anderson, S.	160
Kilburn, L.H.	364
Kinard, E.M.	344
King, L.	195
Kitson, G.C.	161, 223, 224, 225, 257, 401

AUTHOR INDEX

ABSTRACT NUMBER

Author	Abstract Number
Kleinman, J.	452
Klerman, L.V.	334, 344
Klodawsky, F.	18
Knaub, R.K.	453
Knight, B.M.	292
Koch-Nielson, I.	419
Koehler, J.M.	135
Kolevson, M.S.	226
Kompara, D.R.	455
Koo, H.	454
Koulack, D.	287
Kraus, S.	258
Kressel, K.	171, 259
Kreutner, A.K.K.	316
Kulka, R.A.	106
Kunz, P.R.	208
Kurdeck, L.A.	107, 136, 162
Lambert, C.	354
Laner, R.H.	332
Lang, J.	260
Langelier, R.	215, 261
Larson, J.	432
Le Faucheur, N.	420
Lebbos, B.W.	188
Lebowitz, M.L.	70
Leigh, G.K.	113
Lende, E.	345
Lerner, Samuel	71
Lero, D.S.	163
Leushore, B.R.	329
Levinger, G.	383
Levinson, P.	365
Levitin, T.E.	108
Lewis, H.C.	456
Lewis, K.	293
Lewis, P.H.	227
Li, Selina	19
Lindsay, J.W.	72
List, J.A.	109
Little, M.	486
Lloyd, J.	421
Lobodzinska, B.	422
Lohmann, N.	58
Lopata, H.Z.	401
Lucks, H.C.	402
Luepnitz, D.A.	110, 111, 137
Macdonald, J.G.	354
Macdonnell, S.	346
McGoldrick, M.	457

AUTHOR INDEX	ABSTRACT NUMBER
McKenry, P.	347
Mackey, W.C.	434
McKie, D.C.	196
McLahan, S.S.	280
McLanaham, S.S.	20
McRae, B.C.	384
McVey, W.	385
Madar, D.	256
Malcabe, T.	242
Mason, P.R.	161
Matthews, S.H.	164
Melichar, J.	236
Mendes, H.A.	21, 138
Messinger, K.	458
Messinger, L.	459, 476
Meyering, S.M.	401
Miller, B.C.	105
Miller, J.B.	22
Miller, S.H.	348, 490
Mitchell, A.K.	112
Mitchell, K.	460
Moen, P.	35
Moir, R.N.	161
Moles, O.C.	383
Morawetz, A.	79
Moreland, J.	120
Morgan, A.	432
Morgenbesser, M.	182
Moses, B.	38
Moskoff, W.	423
Moss, M.S.	461
Moss, S.Z.	461
Mott Foundation	317
Murdock, C.V.	23
Musetto, A.P.	139, 264
Naron, N.	7
Nehls, N.	182
Nelson, G.	206
Nelson, G.K.	462
Nelson, M.	462
Nett, M.J.	5
Newman, Y.	436
Nieto, D.S.	294
Norton, A.J.	229
Oakland, T.	295
O'Brien, M.	424
O'Leary, K.M.	366
O'Mahoney, K.	378
Olson, L.	349

AUTHOR INDEX | ABSTRACT NUMBER

Orthner, D.K.   24, 296, 297
Ostresh, L.M.   245
Palley, H.A.   336
Paris, E.   463
Parke, R.D.   330
Parkhurst, A.   147
Parks, A.P.   80
Parsons, R.J.S.   487
Payton, I.S.   25
Pearson, J.   172
Pendrith, F.B.   369
Perkins, T.F.   464
Perlman, J.L.   230
Peters, J.F.   231
Peterson, G.W.   113
Pierce, S.   425
Pill, C.J.   465
Porter, B.R.   81
Power, T.G.   330
Prentice, B.   196
Presser, H.B.   350
Price-Bonham, S.   197, 243
Primavera, J.   97, 252
Quant, V.   248
Rachlis, R.   8
Raschke, Helen J.   73
Raschke, Vernon J.   73
Raseke, H.J.   224
Raymond, M.C.   202
Reed, P.   196
Reinhardt, H.   285
Rembar, J.   104
Reppucci, N.D.   176
Resnick, M.D.   351
Reynolds, R.R.   245
Ricci, I.   183
Riechers, M.   140
Riley, B.   26
Rindfuss, R.R.   91
Robinson, B.   17, 385
Robinson, B.E.   323, 324
Robinson, V.M.J.   410
Robson, B.   114
Rodstein, E.   467, 468
Rofes, E.   115
Roman, M.   184
Roncek, D.W.   281
Roosa, M.W.   352

AUTHOR INDEX   ABSTRACT NUMBER

Rosen, R.   116, 117
Rosenberg, E.   452
Rosenberg, E.B.   77, 466
Rosenthal, K.M.   290, 291, 298, 299
Rosenthal, P.A.   262
Ross, A.   318
Rothrock, D.   356
Rowe, G.K.   244
Rowlands, P.   386
Russell, C.S.   353
Sacks, D.   354
Sager, C.J.   467, 468, 469
Salts, C.J.   263
Santrock, J.W.   141
Saul, S.C.   232
Saunders, B.   233
Scheiner, L.S.   264
Scherman, A.   232
Schinke, S.P.   315, 319, 320
Schmidt, D.D.   257
Schlesinger, B.   27, 28, 29, 30, 31, 32, 33,
                                  34, 74, 75, 82, 129, 300,
                                  354, 355, 403, 426, 427,
                                  428, 470, 471, 472

Schorr, A.   35
Schreiber, R.F.   186
Schuman, J.E.   445
Schwebel, A.I.   120
Sell, K.D.   234
Seward-Patten, P.   265
Sheehan, R.   392
Shimazu, I.   404
Shore, M.F.   366
Siegel, B.   326
Siesky, A.E.   107, 136
Simring, S.K.   443
Slesinger, D.P.   282
Small, R.   405
Small, R.W.   320
Smith, C.W.   301
Smith, M.J.   36, 37, 38
Smith, R.H.M.   76
Smith, R.M.   301
Smolensky, E.   274
Smolensky, P.   274
Smyer, M.A.   165
Snyder, L.M.   39
Social Planning Council of
  Metropolitan Toronto   40, 41, 42

282

AUTHOR INDEX   ABSTRACT NUMBER

Soper, M.   43
Spanier, G.B.   387, 388, 389, 390, 391,
                                     394, 484, 488
Spector, A.N.   18
Spira, L.   266
Sporakowski, M.J.   154
Sprenkle, D.H.   267, 269, 392
Sprey, J.   164
Srong, J.   84
Stack, S.   268
Stark, R.   83
Statistics Canada   44
Steele, M.   45
Steinman, S.   187
Stern, E.A.   283
Stinnett, N.   453
Stolberg, A.L.   118
Storm, C.L.   267, 269, 392
Stuart, I.R.   321, 393
Suchindran, C.M.   454
Sung, K.T.   356
Sussman, M.B.   225
Talmon, M.   417
Tarrant, R.   380
Tcheng-Laroche, F.   235, 284
Tessman, L.H.   270
Thompson, E.H.   46
Thompson, J.G.   245
Thompson, L.   391, 394, 488
Thornes, B.   429
Thurnher, M.   236, 377
Tierney, C.W.   103
Tirado, C.   365
Titkin, E.A.   271
Todres, R.   47, 82, 302, 303
Trilling, J.A.   14
Trombetta, D.   188
Trost, J.   48, 430, 431
Troyer, W.   119
Tuchman, B.   171
Turk, D.C.   213
Turner, P.H.   76
Turow, R.   49
Vanderkooi, L.   172
Vaughan, L.   352
Vess, J.D.   120
Vinick, B.H.   156

AUTHOR INDEX	ABSTRACT NUMBER
Visher, E.	157, 473, 474
Visher, J.	473, 474
Volgy, S.S.	131
Waite, M.E.	395
Wald, Esther	475
Walker, G.	79
Walker, K.	459
Walker, K.N.	476
Wallerstein, J.	121
Wallerstein, J.S.	122, 123, 237
Walters, L.H.	347
Wargon, S.	50
Warshak, R.A.	141
Watkins, A.H.	363
Watson, C.	171
Watson, M.A.	142
Wattenberg, E.	285
Waxman, C.I.	51
Wechler, R.C.	102
Wedemeyer, N.V.	20
Weibley, T.T.	363
Weingarten, H.	106, 477
Weiss, R.	52
Weiss, R.S.	53, 54, 396
Weitzman, L.J.	190, 191
Welch, C.E.	197
Wells, C.F.	321
Weltner, J.S.	55
Wheeler, M.	369
White, L.	214
White, L.K.	198
White, S.W.	238, 371
Whiteside, M.	452
Wilkinson, K.P.	245
Willison, M.M.	166
Wirder, S.	366
Witcher, W.C.	127
Woody, J.D.	272
Woolner, S.	357
Wylder, J.	273
Yonas, S.P.	489
Zitner, R.	490
Zongker, C.E.	263